WITH THE COSSACKS

BEING THE STORY OF AN IRISHMAN
WHO RODE WITH THE COSSACKS
THROUGHOUT

THE RUSSO-JAPANESE WAR

BY
FRANCIS McCULLAGH

The Naval & Military Press Ltd

Reproduced by kind permission of the Central Library,
Royal Military Academy, Sandhurst

Published by
The Naval & Military Press Ltd
Unit 10, Ridgewood Industrial Park,
Uckfield, East Sussex,
TN22 5QE England
Tel: +44 (0) 1825 749494
Fax: +44 (0) 1825 765701
www.naval-military-press.com

© The Naval & Military Press Ltd 2004

In reprinting in facsimile from the original, any imperfections are inevitably reproduced and the quality may fall short of modern type and cartographic standards.

MISHCHENKO AND HIS COSSACKS
SNAPSHOT TAKEN DURING THE ATTEMPT TO CUT OFF KUROKI,
EAST OF LIAOYANG, SEPT. 1, 1904

" Oh! why art thou so troubled?" asked the Cossack of the Don,
" Oh! why, in muddy eddies, does thy turbid stream flow on?
Oh! quiet Don Ivanovitch!   Oh! famous, quiet Don!
Our bátyushka!* Our Nourisher! why is thy brightness gone?"

And glorious Don Ivanovitch he answered and he said:
" No wonder that my banks are broke and muddy is my bed,
For the Cossacks are my bulwarks, the Cossacks are my stay,
How can I flow on gently when my Cossacks are away?"

BALLAD OF THE DON COSSACKS.

* Grandfather.

DEDICATED TO
THE MEMORY OF MY FRIEND
FERDINAND BURTIN,
LIEUTENANT IN THE *TIRAILLEURS
ALGÉRIENS* AND *SOTNIK* IN THE
COSSACKS OF VERKHNYUDINSK:
KILLED NEAR YINKOW DURING
MISHCHENKO'S FAMOUS RAID,
JANUARY 10, 1905

PREFACE

THE letters which form the basis of the following chapters are reprinted from the *New York Herald*, by whose kind permission they are here reproduced; and the writer of them takes this opportunity of thanking Mr. James Gordon Bennett, the proprietor of that paper, for placing him, in the first instance, in a position to write these articles at all.

The author originally intended to give a full description of his experiences in Port Arthur, and of all the battles in the late war at which he was present—*i.e.*, of every battle save the comparatively unimportant battles of the Yalu and Vafangow, but, as he found that in that case he would have to produce three large volumes, instead of one small volume, he reluctantly abandoned the idea.

Moscow, *January* 20, 1906.

CONTENTS

PART I
IN PORT ARTHUR

CHAP.		PAGE
I.	FROM TOKIO TO PORT ARTHUR	3
II.	LIFE IN PORT ARTHUR	14
III.	THE GATHERING CLOUDS	24
IV.	ON BOARD THE "COLUMBIA"	38
V.	INSIDE PORT ARTHUR	80

PART II
WITH THE ARMY

I.	I JOIN MISHCHENKO	95
II.	BEFORE MISHCHENKO'S RAID	116
III.	A CHRISTMAS WITH THE COSSACKS	130
IV.	MISHCHENKO'S RAID	160
V.	HOW I LEFT MISHCHENKO	185
VI.	THE BATTLE OF SANDYPU	201
VII.	MUKDEN BEFORE THE BATTLE	201
VIII.	THE BATTLE OF MUKDEN	221
IX.	MARCH 1 AND MARCH 2	228
X.	A VAST VODKA DEBAUCH	245

CONTENTS

CHAP.		PAGE
XI.	GENERAL KUROPATKIN'S TRAIN	255
XII.	MARCH 5, 6 AND 7	269
XIII.	THE RETREAT FROM MUKDEN	280
XIV.	OUR CAPTURE	313
XV.	FACE TO FACE WITH KUROKI	329
XVI.	BACK TO LIAOYANG	341
XVII.	FROM LIAOYANG TO DALNY	356
XVIII.	FROM DALNY TO JAPAN AS A PRISONER OF WAR	372

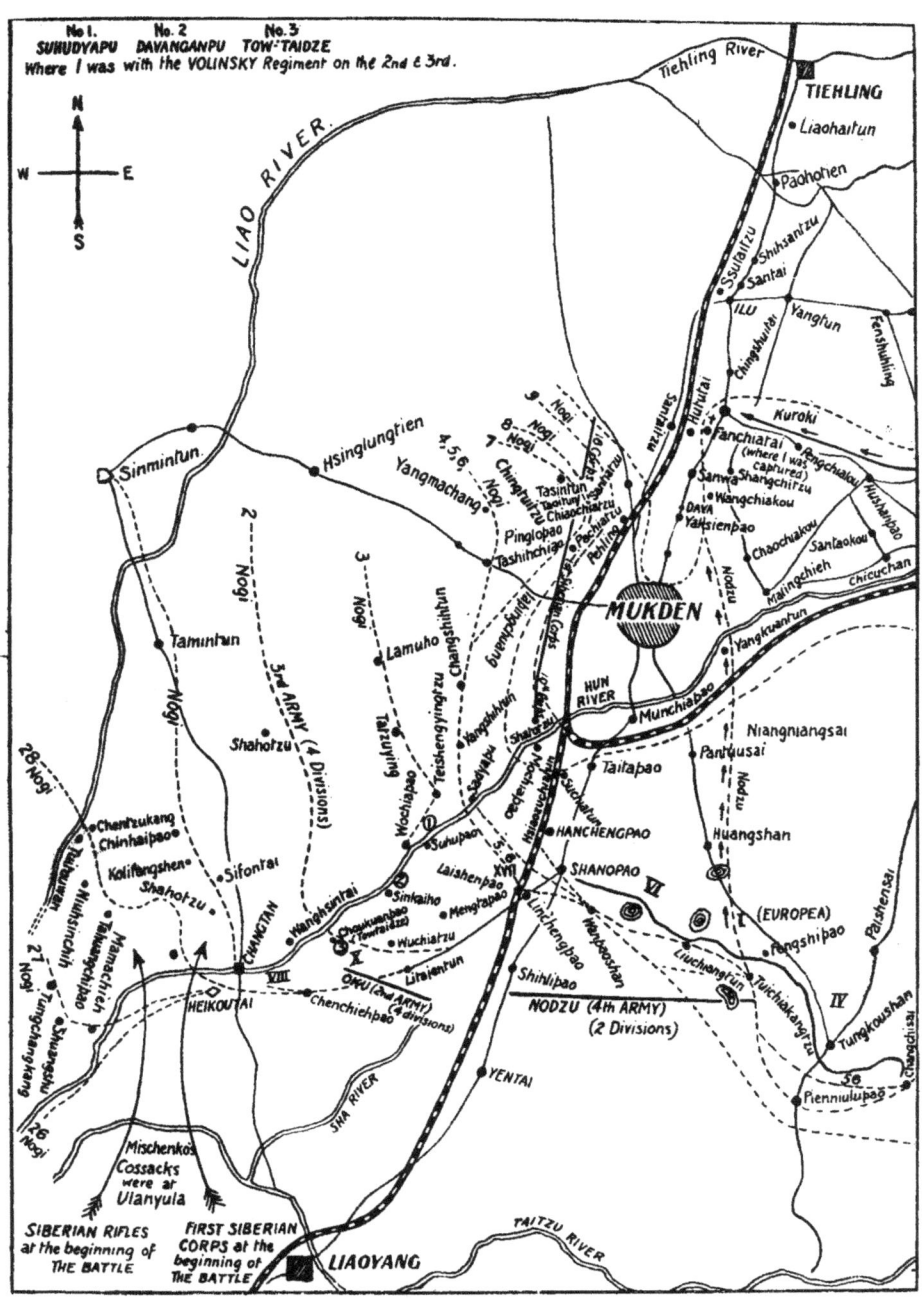

ILLUSTRATIONS

	Facing page
Mischenkos and his Cossacks . . . . *Frontispiece*	
Dragoons Drinking at a Wayside Well	34
Francis McCullagh and his Cossack, Philipoff . . .	112
Mischenko's Raid	162
A Japanese Prisoner	204
The South Gate of Mukden	212
The Retreat from Mukden	282
Russian Priests Blessing Rennenkampf's Cossacks before the Russian Advance on Pen-shi-Hu, October 1904 . .	320

PART I
PORT ARTHUR

CHAPTER I

FROM TOKIO TO PORT ARTHUR

WHEN the Russo-Japanese War broke out I was on the staff of the *Novi Kraï*[*] newspaper of Port Arthur. To explain how I, a British subject, came to find myself in that singular position I shall go back a little in point of time. In 1903 I was employed on the staff of a Japanese paper, and having previously been editor of a French paper in Siam, I thought that it would not be a bad idea to complete my education in Far Eastern politics by going over to the Russian side.

Accordingly I began to take lessons in the Russian language with Father Sergius Gleboff, Chaplain of the Russian Legation in Tokio, and in August 1903 I resigned my position on the *Japan Times* of Tokio in order to go to Port Arthur, where we should, I expected, have war within about a month, that is on October 8, by which time the Russians had promised to evacuate Manchuria.

I must say that I found it hard to tear myself away from Japan, not only because I liked the country and its people, but also because to go to Port Arthur was to take a leap in the dark, for I did not know if I could get employment there.

True, I had arranged to send a circular letter several

[*] " Novi Kraï " is the Russian for " New Land."

times a week to a number of Far Eastern papers, but it turned out that the money I got at irregular intervals from this source was not quite sufficient to pay for my washing. Luckily I had not been long in Port Arthur before I joined the *Novi Krai* and was appointed correspondent of the *New York Herald*, a paper which I had represented in Siam some five or six years earlier.

I went to Port Arthur in a Japanese vessel, the *Tairen Maru*, and Dalny was the first Russian port we touched at. I got my first view of Dalny early one morning, when, on getting up, I found that we were approaching a quay of solid masonry, provided with all modern appliances for loading and unloading cargo, and with railway trains waiting close by to carry off that cargo, not only to Siberia, but to Europe. The length and amplitude of the quays, and the magnificent blocks of concrete used in their construction, impressed me profoundly when I went ashore. The men who were responsible for that work had evidently built, not for an age, but for all time. There was no necessity for making the quays so large and elaborate, but there was something Roman, something characteristic of the empire-builder, about this lavish waste of money; and, in view of the threatening attitude of the Japanese, the serene confidence which this vast expenditure indicated was particularly impressive. If somebody had prophesied to me at that moment that inside of eighteen months I should be a prisoner of the Japanese in a conquered Dalny, I should have been little disposed to believe him.

Dalny itself was a brand-new European town, with nothing Chinese about it save a few streets of Chinese hovels, which were only to remain temporarily; for the Australians themselves are not more resolved now to keep the Yellow Race out of Australia than the Russians then were to keep the Yellow Race out of Dalny.

Considered as a great port, Dalny's one defect was that it had practically no inhabitants. It was like a city of the dead.

The only people one met were soldiers or functionaries. A stonemason would walk slowly down the street, and the echo of his footsteps would have died away in the distance before any one else would come along. Then a Cossack would gallop past on a hairy, unkempt Chinese pony.

Sometimes an "izvoshcheek" (carriage), with an officer in it, would tear past at a great rate. Then silence would again prevail.

Can the reader picture to himself a suburb of some European or American town which has been suddenly run up during the prevalence of a building craze, and which has almost, but not quite, left the hands of the builder? Many families are living in rows of unplastered houses, with blinds on the windows and glaringly new tiles on the roof. Other houses are completed, but are still unoccupied, and the floors are encumbered with mortar, nails and pieces of brick. Still other houses are surrounded by scaffolding, and only half completed; and, in their vicinity, planks, heaps of mortar, piles of brick, stone and slates are lying about in all directions. Imagine what such a suburb looks like at some unearthly hour in the morning, say at 4 A.M., in the summer-time, and you have a good idea of what Dalny looked like when I visited it at noon one day in September 1903. I must admit, however, that the day in question happened to be a Russian holiday, and that work had, in consequence, been suspended. Everybody was in the little brand-new church, which I entered and found crowded to suffocation with people—mostly soldiers—who were all standing up and all crossing themselves at frequent intervals, while black-bearded Russian priests, perspiring in gorgeous vestments, celebrated the Mass. The only busy place in the town was the railway station, from which a company of soldiers marched singing.

Dalny's only place of amusement seemed to be a public garden situated at a distance of some versts from the town, and planted with trees that were all very young and did not look as if they would ever get much older. The greatest attraction in this garden was a small zoological section which contained deer, monkeys, and two bears. On the occasion of my visit two tall Russians were apparently deriving great amusement from the work of giving these bears lumps of sugar, and two very small Japanese in faded European dress were looking on with simulated interest from a respectful distance and cackling obsequiously.

With regard to scenery, I found Dalny to be about the bleakest place I had ever set eyes on. High, bare, quartzite hills, yellowish in colour and with hardly a blade of grass to hide their repulsive nakedness, lay at the back of the town and stretched away towards Port Arthur.

The appearance of these hills was not improved by the fact that the Russians had evidently begun quarrying for stones on almost every one of them, and had abandoned nine out of every ten of the quarries, after having made ugly yellow gashes on the flanks of the mountains and strewn the hill-sides with clay and with unsightly blocks of quartzite. At Port Arthur the case was exactly the same.

We left Dalny for Port Arthur at about three o'clock in the morning, and I got up at daybreak and remained on deck until we had reached our destination, for I had a presentiment that this coast would become famous. The rocky shore was to the last degree bleak and inhospitable, the only signs of life I saw being the poles of a military telegraph wire which here and there stood out against the sky; and, in one place, a Chinese fishing village at the foot of the cliffs.

Long before we had reached Port Arthur we saw in the heavens a striking object which indicated that we were in the vicinity of Russia's "inaccessible stronghold" and of the fleet which Admiral Alexeieff had been gradually concentrating there for years past. That object as a colossal pillar of black smoke, ending at the top in a mushroom-shaped cloud, which could be seen towering over the mountain tops in the remote distance. It rose from the Russian battleships assembled at Port Arthur. There the King of the North had his chariots and his horsemen and his many ships.

Skirting the huge bulk of Liao-Tau-Shan, which rose, black, bleak and menacing, fifteen hundred feet above the sea, we cast anchor at about eleven o'clock in the morning opposite the entrance to the inner harbour.

Above us towered Golden Hill, with its summit all cut away in order to make room for the huge guns, of which six or seven were clearly visible to the naked eye. On the left-hand side of the summit was a flagstaff for signalling purposes. Behind the flagstaff was a low stone house, and in front of it was a platform of cement, on which, on February 9 of the following year, I was to see Admiral Alexeieff and his staff watching the naval battle raging below.

From their unmistakable, pared-away tops it could be seen, even by the most unpractised eye, that most of the other hills in sight were also fortified. Towering over Tiger's Tail Peninsula, I could see the masts and the sinister fighting tops of the Russian warships in the inner harbour; and, inside the entrance on the left-hand side, was the torpedo-boat shed, the sea-front around which looked as if it had been covered thick with the stumps of trees. These were the short masts of a swarm of new torpedo-boats.

"These boats come by rail, in sections, from St. Petersburg," said a Russian passenger to me, " and we put them together here at the rate of two every month, so that every month Japan waits she'll have two additional torpedo-boats to reckon with."

Beside us in the outer roads, lay the *Rurik*, in comparison with which we looked very humble indeed. Little think'st thou, O Imperial *Rurik!* awesome in all thy warlike panoply, that, a twelvemonth hence, that Sunrise flag shall send thee flaming to the bottom of the Japan Sea!

My first impressions of Port Arthur city were not favourable. The sea-front was covered with hillocks of coal flanked by enormous piles of vodka casks; the day was hot, the air was full of dust, and the reflection of the sun from the buildings and the bare stony hills

FROM TOKIO TO PORT ARTHUR 9

made walking very disagreeable. The streets were crowded, principally with soldiers and sailors, most of whom wore enough medals to drown them in case they fell into the water; and the izvoshcheeks that tore past every moment made it sometimes risky to cross them. I was surprised to find this love of rapid motion in a half Oriental people like the Russians, although Gogol might have prepared me for it.

After having rescued my luggage from an onrush of jabbering coolies, I tried to find a room in one of the hotels, or "nomeras" as they are called, but it was difficult work.

These "nomeras," I should explain, were merely Chinese houses, whitewashed and with glass windows let into each of the very small, stuffy and dirty rooms into which the interior was divided. The windows were never opened, and, though they never seemed to admit air, they certainly admitted large quantities of fine dust, so that no matter how often a room was cleaned, it always remained dirty. I went from one of these hotels to another, wearily looking for a room, but in the first three I met with such an indignant "nyet" that I wondered what on earth I had done.

It could not be that there was anything wrong with my manner of asking, as my interpreter was a Russian who had long been resident in Port Arthur, so I simply put it down to ill-breeding.

In the last available "hotel"—a place called "the Efeemoff," from the name of its proprietor—I found a small, dirty, ill-ventilated chamber, for which I paid three and a half roubles a day. This did not include lighting, water, towels, soap, bedclothes, etc. etc., so that I paid as much per day for this wretched hole as I would have paid for a room in the Carlton. The chamber was so small that there was hardly space for the bed in it, and the door was secured on the outside by a padlock and hasp, which completed its resemblance to a stable. Most of the other rooms seemed to be occupied by young Jewesses, who were beautiful but had no visible means of support. Their frequent cries of "*boyka! boyka!*" indicated that a Chinese "boy" was supposed to attend on us, but though on several occasions I listened to his voice, his celestial features I never had the honour of gazing on during all the time of my stay in the " Efeemoff."

I had to go outside for my food, as there was none to be had on the premises, and, as no " samovar " in Port Arthur was heated before ten or eleven o'clock in the morning, I quickly contracted the pernicious habit of late rising.

All the Port Arthur hotels, save one, were kept by Armenians, and all of them sheltered young damsels of the same type as those in the " Efeemoff." Whenever I mildly hinted to Russians that in England it would not be considered respectable for *all* the hotels in a town to contain such guests, they would jump with amazement at my Puritanism. "Why, you should have seen the place six months ago!" they would invariably cry. "It's a monastery now, compared with what it was then!"

It was just the usual luck of the Russians, I suppose, that two fine new hotels were completed in New Town just in time to serve as targets for the Japanese.

The reader already knows that there were an old Port Arthur and a new Port Arthur. The old Port Arthur was simply the Chinese village which existed

FROM TOKIO TO PORT ARTHUR

when the fortress was garrisoned by Celestial troops. Nearly all the Chinese houses remained, but their interiors had, like the "nomeras," been altered so as to make them serve as shops and European residences.

The shape of the town was, roughly, that of a triangle—the base, which fronted the bay, being about two hundred yards long, and consisting mostly of small houses built in the European style, and the sides meeting a few hundred yards inland. A continuation of one of these sides contained the most important shops and commercial offices in the town, and led eventually to the new Chinese town, several miles distant.

The new Russian town was situated along the bay to the west, and was reached by a road running along the shore of the bay from Old Town. The two towns were about a mile or so apart, and the road between them was always, except in winter, either so dusty or so muddy as to be well nigh impassable.

Towards nightfall Port Arthur was at its worst. It was not lighted at all, and the narrow wooden footway that ran along the streets and raised one above the roadway, on which in summer time the mud was ankle deep, was full of treacherous holes. Some planks were all right as long as somebody was walking on the other end of them. When this was not the case—well, then they were not all right, as I several times learned to my cost.

The shops in Port Arthur generally sold liquor, tinned meats, lamps and other such necessaries of life. Thrifty people bought their goods in Chinese stores, while officers and their wives were always to be found in the large stores such as Kunst and Albers, Sietas

Block, etc., where they were always attended to before a civilian. Business was always very brisk.

The only bank in the city was the Russo-Chinese Bank, which was small and always crowded like an important but inadequate railway station, with officers, soldiers, and shaggy business men. Unless one was a lady or a military officer, he had as a rule to wait there in a fœtid atmosphere for at least four hours before being attended to. At the Post-office things were nearly as bad.

The new town of Port Arthur was built in a good position, commanding as it did the bay, and being at the same time well sheltered by high hills from the piercingly cold northern wind that blows well-nigh all the winter. No Chinese were allowed to reside in it, and all the houses had to be built in European style. Quite a considerable number of houses had been built at the time the war broke out, but from an architectural point of view the whole effect was not exactly good. Many houses were built in weak imitation of the German style, that is, with little turrets and odd gables and chimneys. The quarters of the General Staff consisted of a massive block, two storeys high, near which an Officers' Club was being constructed, at an estimated outlay of about £20,000. The naval barracks at the far end of the bay were completed at the time the war broke out, and were the best buildings of their kind in all the Far East, with the exception perhaps of some of the barracks in India. They are three storeys high, above three hundred feet long, and capable of accommodating very comfortably one thousand sailors. Opposite them, on Tiger's Tail Peninsula, were other barracks much on the same plan and capable of housing about the same number of men. In these barracks the men's food was prepared, and in winter the whole place was heated by steam.

New Town resembled Dalny inasmuch as it contained a great number of half-completed buildings, and was at all times as deserted as a graveyard. The two or three shops that were opened there looked painfully new, and as no customer ever by any chance strayed into them, the shop assistants were generally to be found dozing in a back room. In July 1904 Old Town was to be abandoned and afterwards razed to the ground, but, in spite of this, few of the merchants took any steps to provide themselves with premises elsewhere. Perhaps they had a presentiment that New Town would never receive them.

The most remarkable public work that was going on in Port Arthur at the time the war began was the Sobor or Russian Cathedral. The top of the hill between New Town and Old Town and overlooking the harbour had been sliced off at enormous expense in order to make room for the massive foundations which, looking like the stump of some gigantic feudal castle, formed a striking feature in the landscape. This unfinished work was the first thing my eyes used to fall on in the morning after I had left my house in New Town to walk to the *Novi Kraï* office, and I can still remember it covered with pigmy figures of stonemasons and Chinese labourers going to and fro. The broad roadway that wound gracefully up to it was the only good road in Port Arthur, I suppose because it was the one road that was never used.

When completed, this Cathedral was to have been

as high as St. Paul's, and, if one can judge from the designs, of great architectural beauty. In fact there would have been in the Far East no Christian church, save perhaps the Russian Cathedral at Tokio, to compare with it; and the Russians often told me that the powerful electric light which would be placed on the cross at its summit would be visible to mariners far off at sea. Alas! that light will never shine!

CHAPTER II

LIFE IN PORT ARTHUR

ON the second day after my arrival in Port Arthur I went to see Colonel Artemieff, the editor of the *Novi Krai*, a Russian tri-weekly paper supposed to be the organ of Admiral Alexeieff, and well known at that time on account of its periodical outbursts against Japan. I found that the colonel had been informed of my arrival, and had published a flattering notice of me in his paper. He told me that he was going to start an English edition of the *Novi Krai* in a month or so, and that he would like me to edit it. In the meantime he would pay me a retaining fee. As this was a straightforward business offer which left me free to write as I liked about the Russians, I at once accepted it ; and, a few days after, the colonel got me a little sanctum of my own at the office in Pushkin Street, and asked me to come there every day to get practice in Russian by conversing with the members of his staff, to whom he ceremoniously presented me as " our new English editor." The publication of the English paper was, I may remark, the idea of the Viceroy, who was pro-English, and very anxious to come to some arrangement with England instead of with Japan, which he regarded as an upstart Asiatic Power.

The *Novi Krai* office was somewhat different to the

newspaper offices to which I had been accustomed, inasmuch as nearly everybody in it was either an officer or a soldier. The colonel seemed incapable of writing an editorial unless he were in full uniform, with his sword hanging by his side. The printer's devil was a soldier who saluted and stood to attention when he brought the proofs, and the office was filled all day long with Siberian Fusiliers carrying messages from their chiefs, and also carrying rifles and fixed bayonets. One would have thought that the serpent of treason would never enter such a military Eden as this, but, some time after my arrival, our manager was discovered to belong to a revolutionary body, and was accordingly lodged in the "arrestny dom," or house of detention. Another of our men was a student who had for political reasons been exiled from St. Petersburg, a third was the son of a political exile, and a fourth was a young man called Trotsky, who had a somewhat remarkable history. The son of a prefectural Governor in European Russia, he was cursed by a bad temper, which had led him just before my arrival to assault a superior officer, for which offence he was court-martialled and reduced to the ranks. When, in the middle of 1904, I joined General Mishchenko, I met Trotsky in that commander's *état-major*, still a private soldier but attached in some way to the staff. He took part in all the fighting, always displaying great bravery, and, just before the battle of the Shaho, he made, with three or four Cossacks, an important reconnaissance, which necessitated his lying hidden for days in the "Kiaoliang" fields, with the result that his health was seriously impaired. He was promised a commission,

LIFE IN PORT ARTHUR

however; but, while celebrating the occasion in a Mukden tavern, he assaulted a colonel, for which offence he was court-martialled and shot.

At first I felt a great repulsion for the Russians and an intense dislike for Port Arthur. This was primarily due to a feeling of acute mental distress, *une inquiétude de deraciné*, which I suffer from every time I change my country, but it was also due to home-sickness for Japan, whose loveliness now seemed by contrast to be something heavenly. This feeling gradually wore off, however, as my circle of friends widened, and I soon began to take a lively interest in the Russians and in their great fortress over which the shadow of war then lay deep.

What contributed a good deal to dissipate my gloom was the fact that I soon got comfortable quarters in the house of Captain Yanchivetsky, an officer of the Fortress Artillery, who lived in New Town. Yanchivetsky, who was a good sculptor in wood and an enthusiastic gardener, spent all his spare time with his wife and little children, and led, in short, the happy domestic life that the average Russian officer leads. I generally walked to Old Town every day, dining there in the evening at the "Saratoff," a small bungalow-shaped building which faced the harbour and which was regarded as the Café Royal of the city. The "Saratoff" was almost always crowded with officers drinking amber-coloured tea out of beer glasses, and speaking loudly, and occasionally it was difficult for a mere civilian to get served at all. Sometimes I used to wait hours there, the Russian waiter peevishly shouting, "Sichas!· Sichas!" (Immediately! Immediately!) every time I called "Tchelovek!"

and then going off and forgetting all about me. I never before saw such dirty table-linen as that of which the "Saratoff" boasted, and its *clientèle* was on a par with its table-linen, for most of the people I met there—and they included some of the leading business men of the place—looked as if they made it a habit of sleeping in their clothes.

As a rule there was more noise than drunkenness in the "Saratoff," but occasionally, owing to some trifling circumstance, such as an air that recalled the Don or the Volga or the singing of the Tsiganes at the "Tachkent" or "Samarcande" in St. Petersburg, from the broken-down string band which performed in the verandah, a wave of intoxication would sweep over the place, and those overwhelmed by it would wake up next day in the Amerikansky Dom or the Yaponsky Dom, or perhaps in the middle of the street.

There were few outdoor amusements in Port Arthur. Sometimes I went with some Russian friends on a picnic to Pigeon Bay or Louisa Bay or the Waterworks, in which latter place a few stunted trees and several blades of grass made the scene look almost home-like.

Sometimes we hired a "sampan" (Chinese boat) and, passing down the formidable lane of battle-ships, had a swim and an *al fresco* lunch somewhere along the rocky coast. Horse-races were held once or twice a year on the parade-ground, and at these races a good rider named Collins won many prizes, and became in consequence a great favourite with the Russian officers. Collins, who is half English and half Japanese, is now serving a sentence of penal servitude

LIFE IN PORT ARTHUR

in Japan, where he was arrested soon after the war broke out on a charge of espionage.

Port Arthur was a strange cross between Waldersee's Lager and a mining camp in the Wild West with a strain of the St. Petersburg *salon*. If it had been garrisoned by English troops it would have been clean, respectable, and deadly dull. Under the Russian *régime* it was very dirty and very gay. The Viceroy, the generals, the admiral and the higher civil, military and naval officers were continually giving dinners, but the two great social fixtures of each week were the balls at the Morsky and Garizonye Sobranie (Naval and Military Clubs).

The Naval Club was installed in an old Chinese temple near Admiral Alexeieff's house, and, on special occasions, the balls there were attended by the Viceroy, who never danced however, but generally sat at the head of the hall, talking to Madame Starck in German, for, like her husband the admiral, Madame Starck did not speak Russian very fluently,

After the Saturday night ball at the Military Club there was always a theatrical performance given by amateurs, and at every one of these performances Madame Stoessel insisted on playing the leading female part. Luckily she played well. Scenes from the Russian dramatists, generally Ozerov, Tolstoi, Tchekoff, Griboïédof, Tchirikov, Andreeiv, and Gogol, and from English, French and German dramatists, were usually selected. In January there was a fine exhibition of Russian and French oil paintings which the Viceroy had persuaded somebody, by the offer of a subsidy, to bring all the way from Irkutsk.

The balls were very enjoyable functions, and, owing

to the overwhelming preponderance of the military element, very picturesque. The sight of the officers dancing the Mazurka in their variegated uniforms and with jingling spurs, while, outside, the clouds gathered thick on the political horizon, made me frequently repeat to myself that well-worn quotation from Byron in which the lamps shine o'er fair women and brave men. What added, in a way that I cannot quite explain, to the eerie feeling of impending disaster that sometimes took possession of us was the whisper which one heard repeated everywhere among the Russians, that the Viceroy who ruled this turbulent, doomed city owed his position to the fact that he was a natural son of the Tsar Alexander II. by a Roumanian woman, and the admiral's personal appearance lent some support to this theory.

As is generally the case in Russia, the dancing was the best in the world, and the music was such as is seldom heard in the Far East; but, unfortunately, the tragic events which followed so rapidly make this gay music, when I hear it now, sound in my ears like a funeral march. To quote the Russian poet Vaesemsky:

> That ballad !—'tis now a funeral dirge,
> That dance !—the memories of it chill me,
> Like the sheeted ghosts of the dead.

Over a dozen dear friends whose acquaintance I made at these functions are now at the bottom of the Yellow Sea. Two of them went down in the *Petropavlovsk*.

Most of the Russian naval officers I found to be much superior in manners and in education to the average military officer. The only fault I could find with them—and it was not a serious one from a sailor's

LIFE IN PORT ARTHUR

point of view—was that some of the younger men were too ostentatiously immoral. As for the bluejackets, they all looked like farm-hands that had never been aboard ship in their lives; and at Christmas, Easter and other solemn holidays of the Church, they got drunk with a unanimity and a completeness that has never, perhaps, been surpassed in any navy, even in Nelson's.

Happening to call on some friends at the " Morsky Lazarette" (Naval Hospital) on New Year's Day, 1904, I found such a stream of wounded men being carried into the building that I came to the conclusion that a battle was being fought somewhere in the neighbourhood. The explanation was that the men had all got so dead drunk that they were being constantly run over by "izvoshcheeks," falling down staircases, and getting into all sorts of scrapes.

Another place of amusement was the subsidised theatre, the Tifontaï Theatre as it was called after its proprietor, a Chinese millionaire, who owned an enormous amount of property in Port Arthur, Dalny, Liaoyang and Mukden, and was a great favourite with the Russians. Some fairly good Russian companies performed in this theatre during the winter I spent in Port Arthur, the plays of Tchekoff and Gogol being the favourites. Gogol's "Vü" was a great success in January; and just before the war broke out, Jerome K. Jerome's play, *Miss Hobbs* (or as the Russians spelt the name, owing to the deficiencies of their alphabet, Gobbs), was being played; but the great attractions at that time were a circus, Barowfski's Circus, in which there were some good performing horses, and a new *café chantant* in "Novi Gorod" (New Town), both of which places were well attended, even on the night of Togo's attack. At that time the new *café chantant* was still respectable enough for married people to go to, but a few days more and it would have gone the way of its predecessor the Palermo, in " Staré Gorod " (Old Town) which had to be closed on account of the orgies which officers used to indulge in there.

The Russian officer is, as a rule, a sober, well-behaved man, with a good knowledge of the beautiful literature of his own country ; but in every regiment there are a few Russian officers who take their pleasures, not sadly, but madly, rushing on the stage to embrace actresses, firing their revolvers, hacking at chairs and tables with their swords and behaving generally like gay young seigneurs at the Strelna or Mauritania in Moscow. Unfortunately these men have given a bad reputation to the whole army.

As for the soldiers, the only specimen who came directly under my observation at this time was a young Pole, one of Captain Yanchivetsky's orderlies, who tidied up my room every morning. He used to enter cautiously in high boots, great coat and busby, looking like some large winter animal that has lived all its life in the outer cold and consequently feels uneasy inside of four walls. The other soldiers in the garrison seemed to spend most of their time carrying huge ikons for the regimental church or the pots and pans and furniture of their officers. Sometimes Russian officers went in too systematically for making money out of their men, with the result that the higher authorities had to interfere. I remember that one wretched, weedy-looking private used to come around

LIFE IN PORT ARTHUR 23

to my house every morning in order to sell me milk and cheese on the part of his captain's wife.

The Jews had a remarkable hold in Port Arthur. All the leading merchants seemed to be Jews, and almost all the people who made money out of Russia along the China coast throughout the war were Jewish capitalists. One rich Russian Jew in Shanghai made enormous profits out of the repatriation of the wounded and paroled soldiers and officers from Port Arthur; and another, the well-known Baron Ginsberg, probably trebled his vast wealth by supplying stores to Rodjestvensky's fleet. I met Ginsberg's brother supervising this work in Saïgon, and I regret to say that a lot of the stores he supplied were refused by the captains of the German transports which accompanied the Fleet. Some of these captains curtly declared that the stores were rotten, but I do not know if this was really the case.

CHAPTER III

THE GATHERING CLOUDS

IT was an important day for me who had spent so much of my life in the torrid zone, when I saw my Polish soldier double the windows in my room and light a fire in the tall Russian stove, for I knew that I was going to see for the first time what a northern winter was like.

Stern winter was kind as a mother to Port Arthur. She covered his scars and wrinkles with a mantle of snow, so that sometimes he became marvellously beautiful. This was especially the case in the early morning when the red sun rose behind Golden Hill, throwing a long bridge of light across the blue-green sea, when 203-Mètre Hill wore a spotless robe of white, and Liao-Tau-Shan's scarred summit, crowned with a diadem of snow, stood out clear-cut against a cloudless sky. Towards Christmas the water along the sea shore was frozen hard, a cutting wind had set in from the north, and nobody ventured out without a great-coat. The days became gloomy, but not so gloomy as the political horizon, which was now as black as Erebus. In fact, from the day I landed in Port Arthur, the clouds, which afterwards burst in such a terrific tempest, slowly began to gather; but, in some manner that I cannot quite explain, we were all blinded to the logical outcome of the situation, and believed till the very last that there would be no war. The fatal October 8 came, and Alexeieff celebrated it by combined naval and military manœuvres, whose meaning was emphasised by an editorial which he caused to be written in the *Novi Kraï*. In this editorial Artemieff —or rather Alexeieff—declared that the Russians would never leave Manchuria, and made use in this connection of MacMahon's famous phrase, *J'y suis ; j'y reste*.

The manœuvres were followed by a naval review off Talienwan, after which Alexeieff went on board each ship and made an appropriate speech to the officers and men.

On the *Sevastopol*, for instance, he spoke of the brave defence which the city of Sevastopol had made against the English and French, and declared that, if necessary, the Russians of to-day would fight as well as their fathers had done.

On Sunday, October 11, there was a great review in the Suwarov Parade-ground, on which occasion Alexeieff, addressing the officers, hinted that they might soon be called upon to prove their devotion to the Tsar and to Russia. The Russians told me that there were about 40,000 men at that review, and I accordingly said so in my wire to the *Herald*, but I afterwards discovered that 15,000 or 20,000 was nearer the mark. Mr. Davidson, an American Consul, who was present, was told that the number was 75,000, and I understand that he believed it, and wired the American Government accordingly.

The *Novi Kraï* came out next day with a most enthusiastic account of this function and of the appearance of the troops, and inveighed at the same time against Japanese spies, who were, it declared, getting infromation of every military movement that was taking place in Manchuria. This was, I think, on account of the presence at the review of a number of Japanese, who seemed too absorbed in the enumeration of the forces and the examination of the soldiers' shoulder-straps to pay any attention to the indignant glances that were levelled at them by the Russians. As a result of this incident, perhaps, all the Japanese workmen employed at the new naval dock were discharged on October 16.

About this time (October 19), the *Novi Kraï* scolded America for insisting on Mukden being opened to international commerce; and on October 19 I saw Alexeieff in his house, and, among other things, asked him about this Mukden business. But he responded airily, with the observation:

"We shall settle that matter easily, without impairing our old friendship with America. International commerce must have its way."

When I told him what the Japanese and English papers were saying about Yongampho, he said: "These stories are all fabricated with the object of causing a sensation. There's no fort, no cannon, not a single Russian bayonet at Yongampho."

He spoke about the trouble he had with the bandits in Manchuria. "Outside the railway zone," said he, "and especially in the east of Manchuria between Harbin and Vladivostock, we have trouble with them all the time. Manchuria is a robber-ridden country. I often receive petitions from the Chinese begging me to retain my troops in the country, and I should

THE GATHERING CLOUDS

receive many more such petitions were it not that the people are terrorised by the Mandarins."

In November there was a lull, but in December the clouds began to thicken, and the air was filled with rumours of war. On December 20 we heard of an assembly of military transports in Hiroshima. A few days after we learned that 2000 picked recruits had passed the Dardanelles in the *Kazan*.

In common with most other Russian papers in Europe and Siberia, the *Novi Kraï* began at this time to get very anxious about the future of the White Race owing to the Yellow Peril, and came to the conclusion that it would be necessary to oppose a pan-European alliance to the pan-Asiatic alliance which Japan was forming. For a short sime I was impressed by this cry, for I thought it possible that the Russians had an instinctive dread of again coming under the heel of the Yellow conqueror, who had trampled on them for centuries; but I finally came to the conclusion that all their fears of the Yellow races over-running Europe were simulated.

The English edition of the *Novi Kraï* was to come out on January 1, but, when questioned about it, Alexeieff, whose nerves were at this time beginning to give way under the strain of the negotiations with Japan, exclaimed with a dramatic gesture: "How can you expect me to think about a newspaper at such a time as this, when the clouds are becoming blacker and blacker?"

Early in January, the *Novi Kraï*, which was now a daily paper, came out with a very violent utterance on the Manchurian question.

"Manchuria," it said, "is henceforth Russian and

will never be surrendered. At present the Russo-Japanese negotiations deal only with Korea, and these negotiations will terminate most favourably for Russia if she keeps a powerful fleet at Port Arthur, and 300,000 bayonets in Manchuria. Russia is not afraid of war but she does not want it, and is therefore trying to make it impossible."

The Japanese Foreign Office seems to have called the attention of the Russians to this statement in the *Novi Kraï*, for that paper now placed in a prominent position on its front page a standing notice to the effect that it was *not* semi-official.

On January 6, a month before diplomatic relations were broken off by Japan, the Russian warships, then lying in the inner harbour, began to put on their war-paint, and, singularly enough, quite a number of young naval officers, nearly all of them belonging to the *Petropavlovsk*, began about the same time to get married!

My first glance as soon as I left my house every morning was now directed towards these ominous black battleships as they lay in the inner harbour, for I felt that as soon as they went to sea, it was war. My excitement was great therefore when on the morning of January 7 I found that four warships were missing. At the *Novi Kraï* office they told me that these four had gone outside with sealed orders, but that their object was probably to reinforce the Russian cruisers already at sea, by which I suppose the Vladivostock and Chemulpo vessels were meant, and in combination with these to attack a Japanese squadron of four ironclads that were approaching the Korean coast.

THE GATHERING CLOUDS

Three days after, we heard that the Vladivostock warships started to come south, but that, after having gone a certain distance, they had returned to port. The object of these mysterious movements was to bring about a junction of the Vladivostock and Port Arthur squadrons; but the Russians saw that, sooner than allow this junction to take place, the Japanese would make war at once, and they therefore fell back on their old policy of waiting.

On January 12 we got a wire saying that the elder statesmen of Japan had been assembled by the Mikado, and, while we were wondering what this might mean, the Japanese shopkeepers in Port Arthur and Dalny began with one accord to sell out. Great crowds of Russians, especially officers' wives, attended these sales, and I took advantage of the opportunity to buy some expensive furniture for my room in Novi Gorod. The Japanese shopkeepers indignantly denied that anybody had told them to clear out. They said that they were going away of their own accord, because they were afraid that there would be war. As is generally the case in a clearance sale, they all got very good prices for their goods.

Then arose a crop of rumours, in the midst of which came, silently, one disquieting fact. The sailing of all the Nippon Yusen Kaisha steamers had been cancelled; the lines to America, Australia, Bombay and Europe had been suspended; and eighty fine passenger steamers were now at the disposal of the Japanese Government. From this date the Japanese flag was seen no more in Port Arthur until it came to stay.

The Russians, who had up to this believed that the Japanese were only "bluffing," now began to look serious, for on January 18 a meeting of generals was held to make arrangements for mobilisation.

On January 20, and during the succeeding few days, 7000 troops belonging to the 3rd Brigade of the East Siberian Rifles left Port Arthur by train for the Yalu. They were accompanied by several batteries and several sotnia of Cossacks, and were carefully watched by three Japanese, whom I can scarcely call secret agents, for their mission was plain.

One day, while this ominous exodus of troops was taking place, and while I was reading Turgieneff in my over-heated Russian room, a seedy-looking man came to see me. He at once told me that he was a military officer of a certain great Power—in fact, I may as well say that he was Colonel Ducat, the British military *attaché* at Peking—and had come to Port Arthur *incognito*, in order to see for himself how things stood there. He questioned me very closely about the garrison, and finally suggested, in an affable, offhand way, that I should procure for him any military lists, regulations, etc., that were being printed at the *Novi Kraï* office. Now, as a matter of fact, the *Novi Kraï* was very busy at this time printing such documents, but of course I could not betray my Russian employers in this way.

On the 20th we got word that the *Aurora*, *Orel*, and nine torpedo-boats, had entered the canal, and that the *Kasuga* had left Aden and the *Nisshin* had left Perim. The race was getting exciting.

On January 24 all the flour in Port Arthur was bought up. On January 25 all the horses belonging to residents were examined by the military authorities,

THE GATHERING CLOUDS

who said that, if necessary, they would impress such as proved suitable for military purposes.

On January 28 Alexeieff had a wire from the Russian military *attaché* at Tokio, respecting the mobilisation of the Japanese army.

On February 1 the *Kassuga* and *Nisshin* were at Singapore. On February 2 the *Retvizan*, *Peresviet*, *Tsarevitch*, and *Sevastopol*, which had, up to this time, been in the inner harbour, joined the outside fleet, which consisted of the battle-ships *Pobieda*, *Petropavlovsk*, *Poltava*, and the cruisers *Diana*, *Pallada*, *Askold*, *Bayan* and *Boyarin*, and on February 2 all the vessels were in battle array in the outer harbour. Just before this junction was effected a British merchant steamer collided with another steamer in the inner harbour, and ran down a steam-launch on its way out; and this led the Russians to say that the Japanese had offered the captain 50,000 roubles if he would sink his ship or some other ship in the narrow entrance, and thus prevent the two sections of the Russian fleet from joining for a day or two. The story is not incredible; anyhow it scared the Russians very much; and on the pretence that several cases of cholera had been discovered in Chefoo, they now imposed forty-eight hours' quarantine on all foreign steamers, and, when that period was expired, insisted on a Government tug-boat tugging them into Port Arthur. In this way they could not accidentally sink themselves, and could not run on mines. On the 5th the quarantine was lifted for about ten minutes and then reimposed again.

Things were now getting exciting, so I went to see M. Plançon, the chief of Alexeieff's Diplomatic Bureau, and found him exceedingly wroth with the Japanese.

"They're mad! The Japanese are mad!" he cried. "They're now making naval demonstrations along the Korean coast. There are even transports with their fleet. Now, they expect us to go out and sink those transports and thus begin the war."

"And will you?" I asked breathlessly.

"Well, I can't say what we'll do," said M. Plançon, "but I *can* tell you that if this sort of thing goes on much longer Russia will strike, and will strike hard."

"Well now, between ourselves, M. Plançon," said I, "what do you think it all means?"

"I think," said he, "that it means this. Japan is now awaiting our answer to her last proposal, and she thinks by these demonstrations, which really mean nothing at all, to make us yield as much as possible. But she'll find that she's mistaken. We shall just make the same proposals as we should have made had there been no demonstrations at all."

I wired to the *Herald*, through Chefoo, a *resumé* of this conversation, but I don't think it ever reached the *Herald*. It reached the Japanese Consulate in Chefoo, however; for, a few days after, Mr. Midzuno startled me by accidentally bringing into the conversation some of M. Plançon's phrases, and by adding bitterly, "Yes, Mr. Plançon will soon see if the Japanese are mad."

On January 30 the order to mobilise was received in Port Arthur. I happened to be in the naval quarters at the time, and everybody seemed to think that there was no longer any hope. The doctors had received orders to prepare to receive wounded, and vast quantities of lint and bandages were on their way from Europe.

THE GATHERING CLOUDS

I now watched the Russian fleet in the outer harbour with the same attention as I had watched it when it was in the inner harbour; but on looking for it one morning—February 3—I found it had vanished.

I at once hurried into town, where they told me that the fleet had left at dawn "with sealed papers." There was a good deal of excitement at this time on account of the British Mission to Thibet, and it rather looked as if a universal war were brewing.

The excitement was considerably allayed, however, by the return of the Russian fleet at four o'clock on February 4, but was fanned again by the report that sixty Japanese vessels were off Wei-hai-wei—a report which led to new tirades against the English.

On the 5th many Japanese left Port Arthur, and we got a telegram to the effect that the *Nisshin* and *Kasuga* had left Singapore. But, hurrah! Admiral Wirenius has left Suez. The day after he left Suez Japan broke off diplomatic relations.

There had been so many false alarms, however, that there was not much excitement in town. Twenty Norwegian steamers full of coal were lying in the inner harbour, and on the jetty a number of Chinese coolies, under the direction of a soldier, were working on a submarine mine!

Before this time there had come overland from Europe a large number of bluejackets, among whom were the best gunners and mechanicians of the Baltic and Black Sea squadrons. I wonder what kind of a showing the Russian fleet would have made if these men had not come!

The last time I saw the Viceroy before war broke out was early in February, at a belated celebration of the Russian New Year, in the Realny Uchilishtché, a fine Russian Government school in New Town. It was a function which did not tend to give any of those present the impression that the city would be bombarded in a few days. The class-rooms were richly decorated; there was a band in attendance; there were plenty of refreshments; the Viceroy was surrounded by his brilliant staff; the guests were numerous, and there was a surprisingly large number of clean, fair-haired boys and girls, who, after the Russian custom on such occasions, danced sedately together for hours. Among these children were about a score of fine Chinese lads, whose rich silk gowns and caps added a picturesque foreign touch to the scene. Every child seemed to get a prize of some kind, and, at the end of the distribution, the Viceroy went around among the children cracking jokes with them. After talking for some time in Russian to the Chinese boys, he turned to the Russian boys and told them that they should be ashamed of themselves for not being able to talk Chinese as well as these Chinese talked Russian.

As a matter of fact, the Viceroy was very keen on the subject of bringing the Chinese and the Russians together; and with that object in view he had, a few days before, induced the head master of this school to engage a Chinese-speaking Russian, probably the only one in Port Arthur, to teach Chinese to as many of the Russian boys as cared to study it.

He had also persuaded, or perhaps ordered, Colonel Artemieff, the proprietor of the *Novi Kraï*, to make

DRAGOONS DRINKING AT WAYSIDE WELL.

arrangements for getting out a Chinese paper at the same time as the new English paper; and a very intelligent Chinese, who spoke Russian perfectly, was engaged in advance as editor.

While visiting English steamers which touched at Port Arthur I discovered about this time that nobody was now allowed to leave or enter the port without a special permit; and that Japanese were continually travelling to and fro between Port Arthur and Chefoo. To put a stop to this latter practice, a military officer was told off to visit each ship before it left, but as he had a number of whiskeys and soda on board every vessel he visited, he was not always able at the end of his tour to distinguish a Japanese from a ship's binnacle, though I must say that he invariably began with the best intentions.

One or two Russian deserters, generally German-speaking Jews, now left by every steamer, generally bribing the Chinese crew to conceal them, for the English captains would not take them if they could not show their passports. It reminded me of rats deserting a sinking ship, although in this case the rats were deserting "the most impregnable of all first-class fortresses" for the unstable sea; and the event proved their wisdom. Was it instinct that made these intensely ignorant men fly from the doomed fortress, or had some sort of warning been circulated among the Jews?

The steamer on which I felt most at home was the *Columbia*, a little British vessel built originally for river traffic in South China, but at this time running between Chefoo and Port Arthur.

On the evening of February 6 I was sitting in

the cosy dining saloon of this vessel, telling Mr. Wright, the chief officer, how I had to go some time or other to Chefoo in order to charter a steamer for the *New York Herald*. That day I had tried to charter a launch from Baron Ginsberg, the great Jewish capitalist, whose timber concessions on the Yalu had been the last straw on the back of Japan's patience, and the Baron had tried to sell me a launch which would be pretty sure to sink beneath me before it had got half way across. I therefore said that I had better go to Chefoo, whereupon Mr. Wright said, " Why not come with us to-night? We're sailing at eleven, and there are no other passengers. Besides, there's no quarantine now, so that you'll have no trouble getting back." Finding that I had an hour to spare, I went to my lodgings, put a few shirts into a little carpet-bag, and bade a hasty good-bye to Captain Yanchivetsky and his wife, telling them that I would be back on the morning of the 8th. Little did I think that at that moment diplomatic relations between Russia and Japan had been severed, that Kurino had left St. Petersburg, and that Togo had left Saseho.

As we passed through the fleet, which was now anchored in the outer harbour, the officers told me how annoyed they had been on a previous trip by the searchlights of the battle-ships which almost blinded them, and, on this night, a searchlight shone on us until we dipped below the horizon. Wrapped in my great-coat I watched the receding fleet, until the lights on the mast-head of the *Angora* had disappeared, and then, being almost paralysed by the intense cold, which instantly froze the spray that fell at our feet, I went down to my cabin or rather tc

THE GATHERING CLOUDS

the captain's cabin, which had been kindly placed at my disposal, and got into bed.

At Chefoo next day I found that my mission was vain, owing to the impossible terms asked by the shipowners there. Not only did they expect me to pay exorbitant charter-money, but they insisted that if the captain saw on the horizon any of the rival fleets, or even specks which he took to be battle-ships, he was at liberty to return at full speed to Chefoo. This being the case I went back to Port Arthur the same evening by the *Columbia*. Arriving in the outer harbour on the morning of the 8th, I was delighted to see that the fleet was still there and that no naval action had taken place in my absence.

CHAPTER IV

ON BOARD THE *COLUMBIA*

BEFORE I had left Port Arthur on board the *Columbia* I had ascertained that the quarantine on vessels coming from Chefoo had been raised, so that my disappointment was great when, on my return, I found that we had to go into quarantine for the space of twenty-four hours. To be thus compelled to remain inactive on board a wretched little steamer in sight of Port Arthur, where great events were likely to take place at any moment, almost drove me mad. We had been told to anchor in the outer roads, nearly opposite the entrance to the inner harbour and within a stone's throw of the *Novik*, so that with the ship's telescope I could distinctly see the people passing to and fro in the town, and the "izvoshcheeks" driving about at their usual speed. I suffered the tortures of Tantalus, for though I could see Port Arthur I could not get any news of what was going on there. Noticing my agitation, the Russian soldier who had been placed on board as a guard, watched me carefully; but I managed to elude him for a moment, and to throw a letter into a Government launch of some kind that was passing very close to us on its way from some of the battle-ships to the shore. This letter I had addressed in Russian to an intimate friend of mine who was at the head of the quarantine service, and who would at once have brought about my release if he had known that I was on board. But the only result of this attempt was that the launch stopped for a moment at our gangway and that a soldier brought me back my letter, unopened, and then remained on board. Thus we had now two guards patrolling the deck with rifles and fixed bayonets. We made frantic attempts to get the Chinese " sampan " men, who were paddling around, to come close enough to take letters to another British steamer which was lying a short way off, also in quarantine ; but our guards pointed their rifles at these Chinamen and refused to allow them to approach. Captain Anderson was determined, however, to communicate with his brother captain, so he got the Chinese " boys " on board the vessel to coax the two Russians below, on the shallow pretence of giving them breakfast—" shallow," I say, for breakfast time had long passed—whereupon he managed to throw a letter and a few coins, contained in an empty cigar-box, to an enterprising "sampan" man, who at once conveyed the message to its destination, and afterwards brought back a note saying that there was nothing new except that the Japanese Consul at Chefoo was at that moment in Port Arthur, his mission being to take away all the Japanese residents of that port in a British merchant steamer which he had chartered for that purpose at Chefoo. This news made me feel still more discontented at my detention, for it plainly indicated that, although nothing seemed to have changed, things must really have taken a serious turn. As a matter of history, they *had* taken a serious turn, for on the previous evening Togo had left the Korean coast with a fleet of fifty ships, and sailed towards the Elliott Islands.

I remember that on this day the weather was particularly fine, the sun shining brightly, and the air being sufficiently warm to admit of my strolling at intervals along the deck without an overcoat. Sometimes I went inside and worked in a leisurely manner at a newspaper article, in which I clearly demonstrated that, even if war did come, the Japanese would never dare to attack Port Arthur. This article I need not, I suppose, reproduce here.

Sometimes I watched one of the war vessels engaged in target practice, the target being a miniature man-o'-war which was towed by a steam launch, and, although the shooting was not good, it was not quite so bad as I had previously been led to believe. At mid-day a band played magnificently on board one of the battle-ships. "What a pity," thought I, "if a nation of musicians like that should ever be crushed by a people who have no music in their souls!"

Of course I again and again scrutinised closely, through the ship's telescope, the imposing array of battle-ships and cruisers by which I was surrounded. The little training-ship *Gilyak* afforded us some amusement by the clumsy attempts of the boys on board to furl the sails, attempts which were so unnautical as to make our skipper curse dreadfully, and further to sour his temper, already badly affected not so much by the quarantine as by the favouritism shown to a steamer belonging to a rival company. This steamer had come at the same time as we, but owing to the fact that she had cattle on board, no quarantine was imposed, and after discharging her cargo she left the same evening. Besides the cattle she had also on board two rival correspondents from Chefoo,

ON BOARD THE *COLUMBIA* 41

and as I watched them going into the inner harbour and afterwards leaving for the south and a free wire, no doubt with a big budget of news in their note-books, I was strongly tempted to follow Captain Anderson's example and use profane language.

I noticed that the battle-ships had all partially cleared for action and, in some cases, sent ashore their boats. But as the day wore on and nothing more happened, we gradually ceased thinking of what these ominous signs portended, and confined ourselves to wondering if we would get out of quarantine next morning or get an additional dose of twenty-four hours.

In the afternoon the tide swung us so close to the *Novik* that we could read her name, in Old Slavonic letters, on the bow. Towards dusk the three torpedo-boats that had been in the habit of patrolling outside the fleet every night swirled past us with a great splashing and pounding, leaving a stream of foam-flecked, broken water in their wake.

On the whole there was a good deal of traffic all day between the fleet and the shore, steam-launches, either hooded naval launches or open launches belonging to trading companies, passing continually to and fro. Some of these launches carried coal, to make up for that burned by the warships during the day ; one carried some ladies, who probably went to dine on board one of the vessels, and another carried a ship's band that had doubtless been performing at some function ashore.

Alongside the *Novik* we noticed a small boat with a red flag. We thought at first that this boat carried powder, but the extraordinary length of time it remained alongside the cruiser, the fact that no powder seemed to be passed into the vessel, and the movements of the men in the boat, led us to conclude afterwards that below the boat was a diver who was searching for some leak or other defect in the *Novik*.

At this moment Togo was anchored off the Elliott Islands, only sixty-five miles east of Port Arthur. The tragedy was deepening. The crouching lion was about to spring.

I watched the sun disappear that evening. It was a sea sunset—orange shot with red. And in its glory there was no hint of tragedy.

About eight o'clock, just after we had finished dinner on board the *Columbia*, a sound of singing reached our ears, and, on going outside, I heard the Russian sailors chanting their night prayers, which consist of the "Pater Noster" in old Russian, the "Ave Maria," or a prayer corresponding to that favourite invocation of the Latin Church, and finally a short prayer for the Tsar and two stanzas of the Russian National Anthem, saddest and most melodious of national hymns, brimful of the music and the melancholy of the Slav. The Russians are generally good singers, and the hymns of the Greek Church have a weird and unearthly beauty, which, on ordinary occasions, is very impressive, but which at this solemn moment affected me as I have never been affected by the most sublime oratorio.

Softened by distance, the chants from the adjoining vessels rolled solemnly over the bay, blending together harmoniously, and it was difficult indeed to believe that this music was produced by common sailors. Even the singing on the *Novik*, which vessel was nearest to us, sounded singularly soft and sweet, while the hymns from the more distant battle-ships were naught but a faint melodious whisper. Had it not been for the unfathomable sadness of the melody, we might have imagined that we had been privileged to hear the orbs of heaven " choiring to the young-ey'd cherubim."

No doubt my singular position there, in the outer roads of Port Arthur, contributed to create this feeling. The night was dark, for the moon was in her last quarter and would not appear before daylight. The only seaward lights twinkled on board the widely scattered battle-ships. Against the black sky on either side stood out a blacker blotch of land, land that looked dark and lonely enough, at that time of night, to be the abode of lost souls.

Perhaps the spirits of dead Japanese, of the sons of *daïmyo* and *ronin* and *samuraï* who have perished on these bleak hill-sides, are watching there till their brethren come back. Be still, O restless spirits of the mighty dead! your ten years' vigil will soon be ended. You have not long to wait. Behold! the hour of your deliverance is at hand! Ere midnight your countrymen will be in the outer roads!

Behind me, the great black bulk of Golden Hill showed more clearly against the sky, and a few of the lights in the town were clearly visible, the rest being cut off by the intervening peninsula of Tiger's Tail. The glow of the city, faintly reflected in the sky overhead, looked as hospitable as the glow of a household fire, but my present banishment from that familiar hearth made me feel like an outcast. Moving backwards and forwards along the narrow space of town which our position commanded, were the lights of "izvoshcheeks."

When the singing had ceased, a sense of infinite sadness came over me, for what I had heard was not the triumphal crash of a conqueror's chorus, it sounded more like a Litany for the Dying. And such, indeed, it was. It was a Litany for a great Navy, whose long death-agony was to begin that night, for an historic flag which was soon to pass away for ever from the Pacific.

And all this time, Togo's relentless destroyers are coming nearer. THREE-QUARTER-SPEED! On his conning-tower, in oilskins and sea-boots stiff with ice, stands the lieutenant, peering into the gloom profound. At the wheel stands the coxswain, silent and dripping. At last they can make out the massive silhouette of Golden Hill.

In the sky overhead they can see the faint reflection of Port Arthur and city. At a distance that seems infinite, our lights show up before their starboard beam. SILENCE! LIGHTS OUT! As you value your lives, no flaming from the funnels! Nearer still, they can see the long, ghostly arms of our search-lights groping for them in the dark like the arms of some silent, blind, gigantic octopus. The white wash boiling away astern fills them with apprehension. The churning of the screw, the rhythmic throbbing of the engines, sound like thunder in their ears.

I then returned to the saloon and sat down to finish the newspaper article of which I have already spoken, and in which I had laid it down as a fundamental proposition that the Japanese would never attack Port Arthur.

What increased my feeling of confidence, though it ought not to have done so, was the fact that the

ON BOARD THE *COLUMBIA*

Russians seemed to think it unnecessary to make any considerable use of their searchlights. Previously they used to annoy the officers of merchant steamers by the way in which they blinded them with their flashlights, either until they were out of sight on the way to Chefoo or until they had entered the inner harbour of Port Arthur.

On leaving Port Arthur for Chefoo the previous Friday I had seen for myself that a light was kept flashing on us till we were out of sight; but on our return we were not, I was told, subjected to such a long-continued scrutiny, and on Monday night no light had been flashed on us at all up to the time I have now reached.

When it was nearly half-past eleven a feeling of drowsiness, partly due to *ennui*, partly to a heavy supper, came over me ; and, as everybody else save the officer on watch had retired for the night, I decided to follow their example.

The Chinese " boy " who had sat up with me to turn out the lights was asleep on a chair, and, without waking him, I passed noiselessly from the saloon into the outer air, for my cabin was an outside one.

Before entering my room I took a last glance at the inky shore. A profound trance seemed to hold sea and land. A sharp northerly wind was blowing outside, but here, in the shelter of the mountain, there was not even the wash of a wave. Now and then a moving light in the distant town showed me that stray " izvoshcheeks " were still passing through the streets of Port Arthur, but otherwise the fortress-city was dark as the mouth of a sepulchre.

Far out at sea a solitary searchlight on the *Angora*

swung lazily backwards and forwards, as if worked by a man who was half asleep.

But everybody was not half asleep that night. At this moment, only twelve miles off the land, Togo's darkened messengers of death are sweeping round as in a big semicircle, like a hawk circling above its prey before making the ultimate, downward swoop. They are bracing themselves up for the final rush. The lieutenant's hand is on the "telegraph" ready to jam it down. The torpedo gunners stand by, ready to press the fatal button. FULL-SPEED! Dead for our betraying lights come the torpedo-boats of Togo.

At exactly 11.30 I was undressing in my cabin when I heard three muffled explosions, which made the ship rock, and which were followed almost immediately by the discharge of small guns.

The transition was so abrupt, the silence of the night was torn so rudely, that for a second I was startled, and the wild thought, "The Japanese are on us!" rushed through my brain.

O brassy-throated bugle and hoarse words of command, how ye stir my blood! O faint, distant, throbbing drum, almost thou persuadest me that this is not mere mimic war!

But in another instant I regained myself and laughed, laughed in this the most solemn moment of my life, because from amid the blankets in an adjoining room I heard the bitterly ironical voice of Captain Anderson say, "War's declared!"

If the captain had cursed the Russians for half an hour for disturbing him in his first sleep by their practice-firing he could not have conveyed a deeper impression of disgust.

Once I had got over my first start, I thought it a nuisance myself that the fleet should begin practising at such an unearthly hour of the night, especially as the air was now so cold for sight-seers; but, as I could not afford to miss even a merely spectacular display, I hastily pulled on my boots and overcoat and went on deck. There I saw an extraordinary sight.

A transformation had come over the scene, like that which takes place in a darkened theatre when the curtain is lifted; and, as a matter of fact, though then I knew it not, the vast curtain of night *had* risen on one of the mightiest dramas that the world has seen since Troy town fell. It was a tragedy to whose gloomy grandeur only Æschylus could do justice. All the Russian vessels were now using their searchlights, so that the sea around them shone like a sheet of silver, and the air was traversed by long, oscillating, windmill arms of light, resembling gigantic shafts of sunshine shining through a chink in the shutter of a darkened room. One or two searchlights carefully swept the beach backwards and forwards, and especially the entrance to the inner harbour. Several searched again and again every cranny of the mountains and the rocky shore. One blazing eye glared at the *Columbia* for fully five minutes, making us all feel slightly uncomfortable, as if a policeman's bull's-eye had been suddenly flashed in our faces. Strong, however, in the conviction of innocence, the little group on deck bore that blinding stare unflinchingly, making at the same time sundry uncomplimentary remarks about the owner of that particular search light. We might not have stood the ordeal quite so well if we had known what was happening, and how many times during the next few days panic-stricken Russian officers would fire on harmless British merchantmen.

Meanwhile we did not hear the faintest swish of a distant torpedo-boat: there was absolutely nothing to suggest that the Japanese were prowling about, and not one of us ventured to entertain such an extravagant idea. It would have been hysterical, un-English to do so. A humorous, scoffing scepticism was the correct attitude. On the China coast it is bad form to take anything seriously.

We did not realise that, having done their deadly work, the Japanese destroyers were now rushing seawards at thirty knots, with Russian shot ploughing up the water all around them.

Dazzling bright lights now signalled like ejaculations on the mast-heads of the Russian ships—dash! dot! dash! dot! dash!—and I looked on vaguely interested, not realising in the least the nature of the thrilling drama that was now being played before me.

I noticed that some searchlights were directed upwards at an angle of about forty-five degrees, and did not seem to be brought into requisition at all. I also noticed that the lighthouse lamp burned brightly, and that the guiding lights at the entrance of the harbour had not been extinguished.

Some war-ships were, however, in complete darkness, and if I did not know that it was all make-believe I should have considered their appearance as awe-inspiring. They had ceased to be ships and become dreadful black blotches on the water, still as death, but liable to burst at any moment into manifestations of hellish energy.

Meanwhile the firing of light guns—six-pounders, I should say—continued every two or three minutes, but the noise was nothing to what I had heard on other occasions of practice-firing and the like, and I began to feel that the sight was not worth the inconvenience it caused me. I therefore returned to the saloon, where the captain asked me and the mate to join him in a whiskey and soda he was having.

"Let's drink to the war just begun," quoth the captain in his most ironical tone, and, laughing at the skipper's sally, we all clinked glasses and drank to "the war just begun."

"Well, they're in desperate earnest to-night, anyhow," remarked the mate in a serious voice as he turned to go. "You must have noticed that these first three explosions were submarine. Didn't you remark how the boat trembled? Quite a different thing, a submarine explosion, to an explosion that takes place above water."

"Yes," said the skipper, "they were submarine explosions right enough, those first three. Should say that one of their mines exploded."

The excitement of the Chinese crew caused us great amusement, and when the skipper discovered that one of them had lighted the compass and engine-room telegraphs—which are, of course, only lighted when a vessel is going to sea—and had taken up his position at the wheel as if we were going off immediately, he and the ship's officers laughed loudly.

I also laughed myself when the joke was explained to me, and on going forward and seeing the lamp that showed the compass throwing its pale light on the frightened face of the Chinaman who had perpetrated the joke, I laughed again. I also felt quite pleased with myself for knowing so much more than this ignorant Celestial, and tried hard to persuade our two Russian guards that war had been declared. But, although also somewhat excited, they were too cunning for me.

"No, it's only practice," they said gruffly.

At twelve o'clock the firing slackened, and I came to the conclusion that I had had enough amusement for one night. I told the captain so as I gaily bade him good-night, adding that, although I had not been able to do anything in Chefoo, I was getting value for my money now. Just as I was falling asleep, I heard the firing recommence, and I noticed that somewhat heavier guns were now being fired. I also heard the whizz of shells, but even that failed to make me get up again, and I slept the sleep of the just until about 5.30 next morning, when the mate roused me to say that a Russian officer had come aboard and wanted to say something, but could not manage to make himself understood, as he only spoke Russian, a language with which the mate was not acquainted.

Without stopping to take breath, our chief officer went on to tell me that two big battle-ships had taken up their position right opposite the entrance to the harbour.

"A most extraordinary thing!" he added. "They must really have got a scare last night after all. The firing ceased, by the way, at about three this morning. These two battle-ships I speak of came abreast of the entrance at one o'clock. At about half-past one a number of young naval officers came aboard of us, evidently very flurried about something, and one of them tried to talk to me in French, but as he always relapsed in his excitement into his mother tongue, I could not make head or tail of what he said. Why didn't I wake you up then? Oh! Well, you see I didn't want to disturb you at such an hour. It can't be a very important matter, anyhow. Some d——d red tape or other. Usual thing with the Russians. No, I couldn't for the life of me make out what that fellow wanted. He got so muddled that he simply danced round the deck in pure madness, and finally went away, leaving behind him a fine rope with which he had made his boat fast to our gangway."

All this time I was trying to find the matches in order to strike a light, but before I had found them the Russian officer came to the open door, and as he took off his cap I saw by the reflection from the searchlights that his temples were glistening with great beads of perspiration.

He was polite, but seemed very excited. I asked him if he could speak German, and he answered in that language that he could, and then went on to speak to me in Russian. His words were:

"His Excellency the Viceroy has issued a decree ordering that no commercial ships leave or enter the harbour of Port Arthur."

In other words, the *Columbia* was not to attempt to enter the inner harbour or to go away to Chefoo.

After having twice repeated his warning and apologised for disturbing me, the naval officer turned abruptly and disappeared. I never thought of asking him if anything had happened during the night, and I dare say he took it for granted that we knew, and put our extreme calmness down to the fact that we were English.

I cannot say that I was in the least disturbed by this visit, for I saw nothing unusual in an order evidently issued with the object of keeping merchant steamers from getting into the way of the war-ships while the latter were engaged in manœuvres. What most disturbed me at that particular moment was—the cold.

I felt it in my bones as I stood there in my pyjamas, and the plan of campaign which I rapidly drew up and swiftly executed was to get under the blankets again as soon as possible. Having done so, the idea occurred to me that it might not be so abnormally early as it seemed, so I lit the candle and looked at my watch. It was about twenty minutes to six, so I got up again, put on some of the more necessary articles of dress, and went out on the deck.

There was now no firing, but the searchlights of the vessels were as busy as they had been when I had gone to bed the night before. The position of some of the battle-ships had changed, and, true enough, as the chief officer had already informed me, there were two big men-of-war lying close to the mouth of the harbour, with all their lights burning and their flashlights playing around them.

The lighthouse lamp had gone out, though it was still dark, but the guiding lights burned brightly.

"I cannot for the life of me understand," said the mate for the twentieth time that morning, "what they mean by placing these war-ships in such a position. Most extraordinary position, isn't it? Sure enough they *must* have got a bad scare last night."

Then we tried to warm ourselves by walking up and down the deck. The moon was now shining. There was a light southerly breeze, and a whitish mist lay on the horizon. The peacefulness of nature was in strong contrast to the agitation of man. It was long after day had dawned before the Russian vessels ceased using their searchlights, and by that time the practised eye of one of the officers of the *Columbia* had detected something unnatural in the position of the two warships lying at the harbour mouth. He was not very long in coming to a conclusion.

"They've had a collision or met with some accident," he said emphatically, "there can be no doubt about that. See the list that big one has got? Why, her name-plate is nearly touching the water. And the other has a list aft. Besides, they're both aground. There cannot be more than seventeen feet of water there."

"By Heaven!" he added, slapping his thigh in sudden excitement, "one of these Chinese boys told me just now 'two piecee ship strike together in night time,' and, dammit! you see he's perfectly right after all. There must have been a collision. But how the deuce did *he* know it? And what do they all mean, I wonder, by flying their flags at the mast-head? Can that be the *Retvizan*, one of the finest battle-ships afloat? I'll go in and get my Brassey."

It took us some considerable time to realise that two of Russia's best and biggest battle-ships lay helpless almost within a stone's throw of us. Then we all asked simultaneously: "What will the Japanese do when they hear of this?" And the answer each of us gave was that Japan would declare war at once.

By-and-by somebody suggested that perhaps the vessels had been torpedoed or had run on submarine mines, but that view was considered too far-fetched, and the general opinion was that there had been a collision.

I, for one, was so convinced that this was the only rational explanation that I wrote out a telegram to be despatched to the *New York Herald* from Chefoo, and gave it to the mate with instructions to send it off on his return to Chefoo by the *Columbia* in case I did not see him previously.

I did this because I felt sure that the tug would come along for us in a few moments and that I would have "tiffin" that day in Port Arthur.

After having made arrangements for the despatch of this telegram I came on deck again and found that the excitement of the ship's officers about the torpedoed vessels had only increased. It was generally recognised that the Russians would do all they could to keep the news back for some time, even if they had to cut all communication between Chefoo and Port Arthur and to administer repeated doses of quarantine to the *Columbia* and other British ships in harbour.

"In that case," quoth the skipper, dryly, "Old England may have some little suggestions to offer."

"But the Japanese who are left in Port Arthur will soon find out about it," said the mate, "and no power on earth will prevent them from carrying the news to Japan. They'd walk all the way to Corea, they'd go to sea in a 'sampan.' Japan is bound to know of this in a few days."

"And as soon as she knows of it, she'll strike," remarked the second officer; "the two fleets are now on an equality as regards battle-ships, and the Japanese are not likely to give Russia time to repair these two."

This was the tone of our conversation as we rapidly walked the deck in the faint, grey, chilly dawn of that bleak winter morning. We could never get away from the one point, and we were so overwhelmed by the magnitude of the disaster that we could only converse about it in monosyllables. These monosyllables generally constituted abrupt and sometimes profane exclamations expressive of the gigantic nature of the misfortune that had overtaken the Russian fleet, of the great chance the Japanese had got, of the certainty of war.

Never was there such unanimity of opinion on board a ship. It was so perfect that nobody listened to anybody else. Each jerked out explanations absolutely identical with those jerked out by his neighbour, and then, after brooding over his own remark for a few moments in silence and taking yet another long searching look at the disabled men-o'-war, repeated the same remark in another form. It did not seem to strike any of us at the time that this was an absurd form of conversation. Sometimes this monologue was varied by a new discovery.

"There goes a boat-load of wounded!" shouted the mate once. "That *must* have been a bad collision."

While the searchlights were still flashing on the face of the waters, and the dawn was still a sickly, pallid light in the east, fourteen Russian torpedo-boats splashed tumultuously past us on their way out. By the flashlights I could see the gloomy countenances of their commanders as they stood on the bridge wrapt in their great-coats, and I noticed that some of them levelled their glasses at us and inspected us carefully, as if they were not sure but that we might be a Japanese war-vessel.

"On what mysterious mission have they gone?" I asked myself, musingly, when they first dwindled into black specks on the water and then vanished in the misty portals of the dawn.

When the light had become stronger we noticed other things. We noticed that a large number of cables or chains connected the *Tsarevitch* with the adjacent shore, and that steam launches, tug-boats and lighters, filled with Chinese coolies, were fussing around her like courtiers around a wounded monarch.

We could also see that the forts had been manned during the night—rather a strange thing we thought. In some places where there were galleries, long lines of men were visible, and the heads of others peeping over the breastworks showed that the fortress artillerymen must have been at their posts all night.

On the highest point of Golden Hill Fort stood a large group of men, evidently high officers, all scanning the horizon with glasses. That group stood there throughout all the anxious hours that followed, in fact as long as the *Columbia* remained in Port Arthur. One of the group—a stout man standing a few paces in advance of the others, and never once taking his binoculars from his eyes, or turning round to say a word to his companions—resembled the Viceroy in the general contour of his figure, but on account of the distance I could not say for certain that it was Alexeieff. I afterwards found, however, that one of the Japanese passengers on the *Columbia* had arrived independently at the conclusion that it *was* the Viceroy.

By-and-by the sun rose, and, owing to the light mist that lay upon the water, it was very round and red, looking for all the world like a red-hot cannon-ball.

"That's an ominous sign," I remarked, with a superstitious shiver, for that rising sun recalled at once to my memory the flag of Japan.

In the rays of this sinister orb the windows of the houses in Port Arthur became red as blood. Against the ensanguined sun itself stood out the hulls and the masts of three vessels, apparently cruisers, lying motionless, about five miles off. These could not be Russians! What on earth were they? The ship's telescope soon conveyed to me the astounding information that they flew the flag of the Rising Sun. They were, in fact, the swift cruisers, *Yoshino*, *Takasago* and *Chitose*, and they were calmly lying there, trying to find out through their glasses the exact amount of damage that the torpedo-boats had done.

I shall not try to describe my sensations when I first saw the Japanese so close. I could not if I tried. I was thunderstruck. A tremendous electric shock seemed to go through me. I dropped the telescope. My breath left me. The deck sank beneath my feet. I was as one alone in interplanetary space, receiving an appalling supernatural revelation.

Millions of thoughts shot through my head every second. The first one was, of course, "It is war!" The second was, "Japanese torpedo-boats were in amongst us last night, and damaged these two battleships."

After pinching myself and smiting my head, and rushing a couple of times up and down the deck to make sure I was awake and sane, I turned to have another look at the torpedoed vessels, and noticed how the men were gathered together with white, scared faces on the deck. There seemed for the moment to be no captain, no officers, no order. The sailors were no longer important parts of a formidable fighting machine: they were a mob—a silent, scared mob—looking with terror towards the abyss from which the monsters of the night had emerged.

Some of them, it is true, still seemed to go about their duties in a mechanical manner, and I particularly remember seeing one man throw water over the side.

Finding that the captain had been shouting at me for the last five minutes, I entered into conversation with him. We agreed that these Japanese vessels could not be supported by the Japanese fleet. They were simply a few prowlers that had come with the torpedo-boats to do as much damage as they could and then rush off again. The Russians would be out after them directly. In true Anglo-Saxon style we minimised the miracle that had happened. We also left it to be inferred from our remarks that we had suspected all along that something like this was bound to occur.

No satisfaction was expressed by anybody on board the *Columbia* at the terrible blow the Russian Navy had received. There was something so pathetic in the helplessness and in the unnatural position of these tremendous engines of war, which had been so suddenly disabled, that we all remained looking on sadly,

ON BOARD THE *COLUMBIA*

in silence. It was like being an eye-witness of the downfall of Napoleon.

A Danish pilot employed by the Port Arthur Harbour Board now swirled past us in a launch. We asked him if the two battle-ships at the harbour mouth had been torpedoed.

"Three have been torpedoed," he shouted back; "there's the third on your right, the *Pallada*."

And, sure enough, we had been commenting previously on the suspicious list to port which that big cruiser had, and on her awkward appearance, which made her look as if she were aground. Everybody had had his doubts about her, but nobody had dared to express them. The English hatred of exaggeration had prevented him.

Before he was out of earshot the pilot had bawled to us to clear out at once, as the whole Japanese fleet was coming up, and, if we did not move immediately, we should find ourselves right in the line of fire.

The captain bellowed back that we had been told not to leave the port, and that any attempt to move might draw on us the fire of the forts, but by this time the pilot-boat was churning up the sea three miles away.

Meanwhile the Japanese cruisers had made a very long, leisurely survey of the Russians, and had then gone away slowly, whereupon the whole Russian fleet weighed anchor and started in pursuit. It is a singular instance of the effect of habit that, on weighing anchor, the Russian sailors very carefully cleared all seaweed, sand, etc., from the anchor chain, as if they could not have postponed that operation to a more convenient time.

Before steaming out, the Russian ships hastily threw overboard bedding and furniture, which were at once seized upon by eager Chinese "sampan" men. I noticed one man paddling ashore with something that looked like a ping-pong table, and several went very far out in their quest for booty.

These amphibious beings seemed to be the only people who were not thunderstruck by the appearance of the Japanese. To them it was simply "Yeebin whalaï" (The Japanese have come back), just as if ten long years had not elapsed since the Three Nations had made them haul down their flag from Golden Hill.

These Chinese boatmen all disappeared very quickly, however, when the shells began to fall. But no shells fell just then, for the Japanese cruisers had gone away, with the Russians after them. This was at about nine o'clock.

Admiral Togo probably wanted to lure the enemy outside and to fight them in the open ; but he did not succeed, for, on sighting the Japanese fleet, the Russians all returned to the harbour.

The attention of those on board the *Columbia* was temporarily withdrawn from these great events by the appearance of a naval doctor, who declared the quarantine at an end, but could give us no information as to whether we could leave or not. He said he would go ashore and inquire.

The Russian fleet returned at about ten o'clock, and, immediately after, there took place a flagrantly impossible event. Sixteen Japanese war-vessels, six of them clearly battle-ships, appeared in a long dark-grey line on the horizon. They appeared so suddenly that they seemed to have risen from the sea, or to have materialised from the mists of the morning. They were only five miles off, and at the mast-head of every one of them a Japanese naval flag shouted defiance. I felt that I was present at the inception of an historical event not less momentous than the fall of Constantinople. For the first time in the history of the world the pagan war-flag of the Sun Goddess was opposed in field of battle to the banner of the Cross.

I could not take my eyes off these menacing warships. They were not unfamiliar objects. I had lived under that flag myself. I had seen those battle-ships at Hakodate, Nagasaki, Ujina, Kobe. In the lovely Inland Sea they had seemed to me to be merely masses of ugly machinery, desecrating the landscape. Here, off the bleak, fortified headlands of Port Arthur, they harmonised perfectly with the sternness of nature. Evidently they had not been built for Miyajima or Shikoku. These floating fortresses had been built for Port Arthur Bay.

Things now looked desperate for us on board the *Columbia*, and our captain took down the quarantine flag and ran up the signal, "Will you give me permission to leave?"

The Russian soldiers we had with us got a little excited when they saw the quarantine flag taken down, and asked for an explanation; and the skipper, who was fast losing control of his temper, wanted to throw them overboard, rifles and all, but I restrained him and tried to pacify them as best I could. I also tried to distract their attention by pointing out to them the Japanese vessels on the horizon. They laughed at my simplicity, and said that these were Russian vessels.

No answer was signalled to the *Columbia*, but after a while a naval officer came aboard and requested us to "move." The captain furiously demanded if he might "move to Chefoo," but in a menacing tone the officer said no, he had better not attempt to leave Port Arthur until permission had been signalled to him from the shore. He might, however, have the kindness to move just a little out of the way, as a cruiser wanted to take up its position in the place the *Columbia* occupied. Then, after saying something in a low tone to the soldiers, the naval officer left the ship.

At this unpropitious moment, there approached us a "sampan" in the bows of which stood a gentleman whose putties, Norfolk jacket and bored *sang froid* all proclaimed him English. He informed the captain that he was a British military officer and would like to be taken to Chefoo; but the captain was in such a rage at his signals not being answered and at the mess he had got into generally, that he acted as Hotspur once did under similar circumstances, and not only refused to entertain the proposition but told his countryman, in the most violent language at his command, to begone instantly. The other looked for a moment as if he would come on board in spite of us, but at this juncture our Russian soldiers resumed their old trick of pointing their rifles at the "sampan" man, who thereupon retreated with great rapidity.

I must frankly say that I was glad this English officer did not get on board, for, if he had, I would never have made the journalistic "scoop" I did; but at the same time it is a pity, from a general point of view, that he was unable to accompany us, as, owing to his superior technical knowledge, he would doubtless have

ON BOARD THE *COLUMBIA* 63

made the most of the splendid opportunity we had of seeing the battle.

While the captain was giving orders to get under way, a sudden wild idea that it was all a mistake, a regrettable misunderstanding, flashed across my mind. "Let us be reasonable," I said to myself, "the whole thing is too dramatic to be true. Lurid events like this don't happen in these prosaic days. To-morrow we'll all be laughing about this scare, in the 'Saratoff.' The collision theory is right after all. Russia and Japan have arranged their little differences. The Japanese fleet is here on a friendly visit."

And my eyes sought the Japanese line-of-battle for some confirmation of this view. And the Japanese line-of-battle spoke.

At that instant—it was then a quarter-past eleven—there was a big bright flash from the starboard side of the *Mikasa*, then about five miles distant, and, immediately after, a vast, invisible Something rushed over the mast-head of the *Columbia* with the mighty sound of a railway train hurled into space, and every one on board, from the cook who had deserted his galley to the captain who had not yet left off swearing, ducked suddenly and reverentially.

It was the first shot of the Russo-Japanese War! The table had been overturned, the diplomatic chess-board kicked across the room, and one of the armed players had jumped to his feet and smitten the other on the face!

In the pause that succeeded that first shot, I felt, like the weight of Atlas, the awed, tense silence of the world. The child of the nations had drawn his tiny sword on the mighty behemoth of Muskovy! David had challenged Goliath, and, if he failed, his punishment would be such as to make the nations white with terror. If he did not fail, the consequences would be more terrific still. They would be the fall of the House of Romanoff.

No more proposals, counter-proposals, amendments to counter-proposals, mutual engagements, *notes verbales*, reciprocal recognitions, bases of understanding! No more delays, due to Count Lamsdorf being "very much occupied," to the Tsar being "absent at military manœuvres," to the Empress being sick, to the necessity of transferring the negotiations to Tokio, or to "the lack of a suitable formula!"

Admiral Togo has found the formula which *he* considers suitable, and, a thousand feet overhead, it now goes wailing and shrieking towards the doomed fortress!

Some seconds after, the shell, which was, I should say, a 12-inch one, burst with a terrific roar in the small space of sea intervening between the torpedoed battle-ships and a group of frightened-looking torpedo-boat destroyers.

The report of this gun was like the report of a pistol fired into a powder magazine, for the reply which it provoked was terrific. The Russian batteries thundered like gods hurling a tremendous anathema at some sacrilegious intruder. Golden Hill Fort howled in gigantic remonstrance. The electric battery bellowed forth thunder. On the middle batteries there was a deafening, interminable chorus of cannon. The guns on Wieyuen Fort and Tiger's Tail erupted like active volcanoes. Spouts of smoke poured from Liao-tau-shan, where smokeless powder did not seem to be used; and at intervals White Wolf Hill joined with a crash of artillery in this prodigious litany. That noise

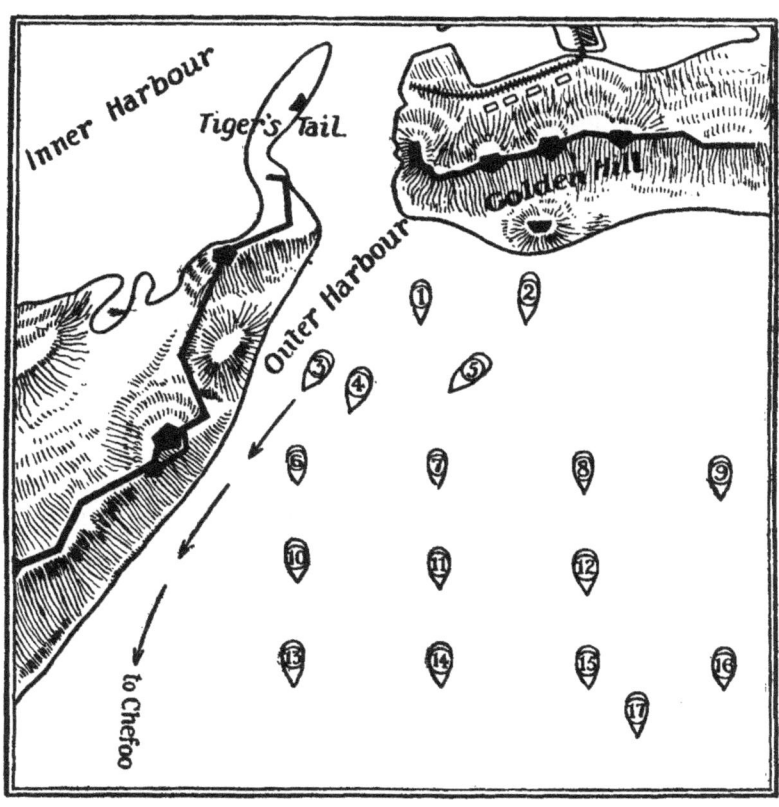

POSITION OF RUSSIAN WARSHIPS IN OUTER HARBOUR AT PORT ARTHUR AT THE TIME OF JAPANESE ATTACK

1. The *Rasboinik*; 2. the *Gilyak*; 3. the *Columbia*; 4. the *Novik*; 5. the *Boyarin*; 6. the *Petropavlovsk* (admiral's flagship); 7. the *Poltava*; 8. the *Sevastopol*; 9. the *Cesarevich*; 10. the *Peresvet* (vice-admiral's flagship); 11. the *Retvizan*; 12. the *Pobieda*; 13. the *Bayan*; 14. the *Pallada*; 15. the *Diana*; 16. the *Askold*; 17. the *Angara* (the volunteer fleet steamer which was converted into a cruiser).

seemed too great to be terrestrial; it pertained to the solar system. It was as if the seven thunders had uttered their voices. It was as if the five thousand isles of Japan were hurling themselves on us bodily. It was as if the earth had come into collision with Mars. With the voices and thunders and lightnings, it was like Armageddon.

It is difficult to measure things that pass all limit of measurement. It is difficult for a great writer, and impossible for a minor journalist, to give in writing an idea of what far transcends the ordinary. Nobody can get from books an accurate conception of the ocean, the Pyramids, the Himalaya mountains, the Grand Cañon of the Colorado. He must go and see them for himself. And nobody that has not heard a great cannonade can understand from books what it is. It towers above ordinary noises, as Fujiyama towers above the hovels of Hakone. What peculiarly struck me about it was its quality of stupendous and overwhelming vastness. But the supreme limit of noise had not been reached, for whenever the 63-ton guns at the entrance to the harbour went off all together with a vast shout like the crack of doom, all the lesser thunders were drowned; and through the air ran a giant, rending sound and a violent vibration, almost strong enough to knock me off my feet as I stood on the deck of the *Columbia*. On such occasions my knees smote one against another, and I felt inclined to throw myself prostrate on my face, as if I had heard the voice of Jehovah.

The first shell had evidently been intended for the torpedoed battle-ships, and it went so near its mark that it must have splashed them with spray from the big liquid column that shot from the sea at the point where the projectile touched the water. Near this point of contact there happened to be a Chinese boat, which must have been injured, for we saw the entire crew jump into the sea.

The Japanese did not pause to contemplate the effect of their first shell. All their vessels now opened fire, running south-west in a stately line. The air was filled with the whizz of high-velocity projectiles, hundreds of which seemed to pass over our heads every minute; the surface of the sea in our neighbourhood was dotted with columns of water, as the surface of a pond is dotted during a heavy rain-storm; and the din was intensified tenfold.

The *Columbia* was now moving, but, of course, I expected she would soon anchor again.

The Russian fleet divided into two parts. One part ran parallel to the shore on the right-hand side of the entrance, the other parallel to the shore on the left-hand side, all the vessels,—even the torpedoed battle-ships—firing continuously at the Japanese. On the whole, they seemed to manœuvre clumsily. Some of the war-ships revolved without changing their position, and the whole fleet was evidently placed at a disadvantage by reason of the cramped space and of the consequent danger of running ashore. The *Novik* and some other cruisers ran out pluckily until within a short distance of the enemy, whose torrents of shell sometimes hid them from our view. The *Poltava* and the *Diana* were wrapped in flames.

I must confess, however, that I was not calm enough just then to watch the fight with the amount of attention necessary to give a very detailed report of it. The reason of this was that we were running parallel to a line of Russian cruisers, which drew on us the fire of the Japanese. We were so close to the beach that I could have thrown a stone ashore, and were still going south. I wondered vaguely why we had not yet anchored, but was afraid to ask the captain, as he was now absolutely unapproachable. Besides, what did it matter? We could no more expect to escape those thick-falling shells than a man standing outside in a thunderstorm can expect to escape the drops of rain.

The skipper had now hoisted his biggest British ensign to the mast-head. "D—n them," said he in a surly tone, speaking more to himself than to us, and jerking his thumb upwards, while in his eyes there burned a lurid light which I took at the time to be the light of insanity, "d—n them, let them fire on *that!*"

This remark seemed to me to be one of those childish but infinitely mystic and significant things which, all unconsciously, dying soldiers sometimes say. Did the captain imagine that there was some potent, storm-quelling magic in the ensign that had won the over-lordship of all the seas? Did he think, for drowning men grasp at straws, that the Japanese might refrain from firing on that flag out of friendship or the Russians out of fear? If the former were the case he was mistaken, for the Japanese projectiles continued to fall very close. One fragment of shell made a small hole in the deck forward, another fragment tore the flag itself.

Before the engagement began I had been reflecting with exultation that there was a chance of my getting to Chefoo before any other war-correspondent; but when the shells began to sing through the air and raise huge pillars of water before, behind, and close to both sides of the ship, I forgot all about that matter, or if I reflected on it at all, it was only to curse my luck at falling in a fight which was not mine. For I regarded myself as already doomed. I thought of writing a farewell letter to one dear friend; but the reflection that letters never find their way from the bottom of the deep made me stop after the first few words.

What annoyed me most was the uselessness of my death. To die for a great cause is glorious. To die as a combatant on board one of those war-vessels would be an honour.

I felt, oddly enough, that if I had died as a regularly attached correspondent on board one of the Russian battle-ships, I would have been satisfied. Even if I had knowingly, willingly, sailed into the fray on board the *Columbia*, the prospect of death would not have been so horrible. But it was by the merest accident that I had got caught in this whirlwind of great events, that I had got mixed up in this gigantic contest of empires. Any fool might have done the same. I ardently longed to get outside the danger-zone so that I could bid my friends good-bye with a sad, sad smile, and then sail back again to meet my fate.

The only bright spot in this gloomy outlook was the conviction that my paper would manfully lie for me, would say that with eagle eye I had foreseen all that was going to take place, and had steered straight for the heart of the battle. I also reflected with melancholy satisfaction that I had certainly got the better of those Chefoo shipowners who had insisted, a few days before, that in case I chartered one of their vessels, even at a most exorbitant rate, I would have to agree that the captain would be at liberty to turn back in case he saw any of the rival fleets on the horizon.

But in truth my death was going to be miserable. A non-combatant, struck by a stray shell while running away from the fight on board a harmless merchant steamer—Good Heavens, what a fate!

I looked into the engine-room and was surprised at the regularity with which the cranks and connecting-rods were doing their duty. I looked around generally, and it occurred to me that the *Columbia* had shrunk to the dimensions of a row-boat. Compared with the iron leviathans which were battling around her in smoke and flame, she resembled a pet lamb that has got mixed up in a bull-fight.

I have a dim remembrance of moving about the ship with inconceivable rapidity. I fancied that if I remained still for a second a shell would surely fall on top of me. First of all I went aft as far as I could. I don't know why I went aft, but I had a kind of vague idea that if the front part of the ship were blown away, I could hang on to the rear. Here I found chief-engineer Smith, his face of a pallor which moved me more than eloquence, one side of it splashed with powder or some black stuff shot up by a shell that had burst near the screw, and the other side glistening with perspiration.

Mr. Smith did not seem to hear the banal, consolatory remarks I addressed to him; but in spite of his glassy stare and very preoccupied manner he showed that he was aware of my presence by telling me, in extremely emphatic language, the sort of fool I was for not having gone ashore in the doctor's boat. I did not, however, understand all he said, for, strange to say, he had relapsed in his excitement into the broadest of broad Scotch.

The Chinese crew looked as if they might, in their madness, do something desperate, but the Chinese passengers remained all the time crouched behind the little wooden structure that formed the saloon and the cabins, and seemed to think that they were quite safe there. One of them said to the ship's officers: "What for you standee out there in open? All right here," and seemed hurt and astonished when he saw that none of us accepted the invitation to get under cover.

There was always present in my mind the terrible certainty that there was no longer any cover, no more protection. A glance at the terrific splashes made by the shells that fell around showed me that, if one of those formidable missiles struck the *Columbia*, all was over with us.

Yet, in spite of this, I must say that I always breathed more freely for a second or so after I had got behind something, no matter what it was. I also had at times the strongest possible inclination to go below, to get down to the very keel of the ship, to go through the keel if possible, to dive to the bottom of the sea, coming up for breath in the intervals between the shells. The chief-engineer seemed to have the same inclination, for I once caught him hesitating at the top of a ladder, which he clutched with a grasp of iron. He did not descend that ladder, however. He said that he saw there was no good in doing so, and, indeed, there was a better chance on deck than below.

Between the cabins aft and those forward there was an open space, and I suddenly took it into my head to traverse this space in order to join the ship's officers, who were all gathered together at the other extremity of the boat. I did so, running as quickly as my legs could carry me, as if I were running from one certain shelter to another and might be caught half-way across if I did not hurry. Of course I did not reason about the matter. My legs simply ran off with me.

Outside the saloon, on the side facing the forts, I found our two Russian soldiers crossing themselves at a great rate and praying fervently. A few minutes before, they had gone forward with their rifles, and wanted the captain to stop the boat, but I had explained to them that we were going "nyemnozhko dalsche," just a little further, so as to be out of the way of the projectiles; that, in doing so, we were only obeying the orders we had just received from the last naval officer who had visited us, and that directly we rounded that point yonder we would drop anchor.

This, combined with something in the eyes of the Englishmen, pacified the soldiers, and saved us from a bloody struggle which I had, at one moment, regarded as inevitable. The soldiers seemed to particularly appreciate the idea of getting away from the shells, and when the latter fell like rain around us they were too much occupied in prayer to pay any attention to external things. After a while one of them completely disappeared, going down below, probably in obedience to that blind instinct of self-preservation which all of us found it so hard to struggle against and which the Chinese so cheerfully obeyed. He reappeared when all was over and we had almost lost sight of land, but neither he nor his companion caused us any further trouble.

On my reaching the "shelter" of the forward set of

cabins, I found, in the unprotected space in front of them, that is in the extreme bows, the captain and the rest of the officers grouped together, wild-eyed, pallid, and silent. The quartermaster was at the wheel.

The mate casually threw a rope's end overboard, with the object, as he afterwards told me, of having something to hold on to in case the ship was struck. At the same time I conceived the brilliant idea of throwing some woodwork into the sea and jumping after it. How fine it would be to swim ashore—we were, as I have already said, running very close to the land—with the assistance of this woodwork! As my imagination dwelt on this flattering prospect, a large shell dropped on the spot where I had imagined myself to be swimming and caused me to abandon the idea hastily.

I decided, then, to stick to the captain. At the same time I began to conceive an intense animosity for the Japanese in general and for Admiral Togo in particular, for how can one retain his good opinion of people who are throwing 12-inch shells at him? I thought it vile, treacherous. " O ! *won't* I ' roast ' them in the *Herald* if ever I get out of this ! " I told the captain what I would do, but did not catch his reply, for at that instant a shell exploded with a tremendous detonation right under the bow, splashing the deck with water and making the gallant little craft first baulk like a horse and then tremble violently from stem to stern. Everybody's face grew a shade whiter, and with a shiver that penetrated to the marrow of my bones I caught the dreadful words, "contact mine." The faces of the Chinese sailors grew livid, and it looked as if they would rush overboard, carrying the rest of us along with them.

I ran into my cabin and remember feeling astonished and hurt for the millionth part of a second on perceiving that things were just as I had left them on getting up in the morning—tooth-brush, soiled water in the wash-basin, bed unmade, pyjamas lying on the floor, half-smoked cigarette on the ash-tray, enlarged photograph of the captain's wife beaming at the head of the bed. Had everything been wrecked and had there been a smell of gunpowder in the air, and my blanket been standing on end looking like the ghost of Hamlet's father, I should have considered it the proper thing; but this common, comfortable vulgarity of a bedchamber that has just been slept in seemed monstrously out of place.

Glancing mechanically at the looking-glass, I was horrified to see reflected therein a face that was not my face at all, but that of a disinterred corpse. Then a terrific, vicious whiz-z-z-z-z overhead made me suddenly bury my head in the bed-clothes and stop my ears with my fingers, but hardly had I done so than an uncontrollable desire to get outside into the open air seized upon me. I felt that if I remained in that cabin a second longer I should smother. I felt that if I joined some group or knot of men I should be safe. Accordingly I fled from the room like one pursued by the furies. I went so quickly that I might have gone overboard had I not heard the captain say at that moment in his usual tones to his Chinese "boy" who was standing white-lipped beside him, and dressed, for some reason or other, in his best silk gown: "Boy, bring me some cigarettes! Hurry up! D—— you!

—! —!! —!!! —!!!! —!!!!!" whereupon the boy's tense face relaxed, as if he had been instantaneously cured of some painful malady, and he went away, smiling and assuring his panic-stricken countrymen, who were bunched behind him in the attitudes of men about to go mad, that it was all right. The skipper's lurid blasphemies had saved us from a mutiny.

One of the officers said he thought it best to run the *Columbia* ashore, but, as the shells were bursting more thickly on the beach and on the face of the cliffs than on the line we were taking, this plan was not adopted.

As a matter of fact we did the best thing we could under the circumstances. We ran between two lines of shells, the shells intended for the Russian fleet, which went too far, that is, which went beyond the Russian battle-ships, and the shells intended for the forts, which fell short, that is which fell at the point where sea and land met. I saw this afterwards.

The Russian battle-ships were frequently hit. One of the Japanese shells knocked a funnel off the *Askold*, leaving that vessel with four funnels ; another hit the *Sevastopol*, covering her with a dense cloud of black smoke, from which, however, she seemed to emerge uninjured. Several other Russian vessels were struck, but none of them seemed to be seriously damaged.

So much for the first line of Japanese shells.

As for the second line,—that intended for the forts,— a good many shells fell short, as I have already remarked, many bursting in the sea close to the shore and many striking the hillside and raising clouds of yellow dust. Two or three burst on the very summit of the forts, hurling up tons of earth, which hung out against the sky like a banner. One exploded a magazine on Golden Hill Fort, raising an enormous column of smoke.

While pouring in this rain of projectiles, the Japanese vessels kept sailing majestically south-west, afterwards wheeling round and returning along a line almost parallel to that by which they had come; and I dare say that if I had been in a place of safety I should have admired their perfect order and the grace with which they carried out their evolutions.

After forty minutes of the sort of experience that I have been trying to describe, the *Columbia* got clear of the rival fleets. For some time after we had got out of reach of the shells we still felt uneasy, for a shot from the forts or a Russian torpedo-boat might yet overtake us; but at last the battling navies and the headlands of Port Arthur sank below the horizon, and we were safe. The change was so sudden that for some time I had difficulty in remembering who and where I was. The air was so rarefied and the silence so profound, that I wondered if we were not floating in the clouds above the highest peak of the Cordilleras. My voice sounded singularly small, as if it were not I that was speaking but a diminutive person inside me, and, owing to the drumming in my ears I could not for some moments hear anybody else. I had a vague idea of having seen the skipper before. It must have been about a thousand years before. I wondered what he had been doing in the meantime. At present he was concocting a bowl of marvellous and potent punch. With Chinese unconcern the waiter was laying the table for luncheon. Good heavens! it was only half past one o'clock, and all these things had happened during the last four hours! The officers were affectionately examining the ship, just as you examine a favourite horse which has run away, smashed things, and had thrilling and admirable adventures. The bare-footed Celestial crew were picking up twisted fragments of projectiles with the happy smiles of children gathering shells by the sea-shore. A dim, far-away voice told the captain about his flag having been torn by a projectile. The captain did not curse. He smiled tolerantly, saying, " No matter! Haul it down, and let's have a look at the old rag!" We drank to the health of the rival fleets and of each member of the British Royal Family. Feeling sleepy and overcome, I finally went in the direction of my cabin, where I found that my almond-eyed attendant had made the bed and was now making things "all proper" as he expressed it. As I was falling asleep I heard a voice like that of an Oriental bonze chanting a litany in an unknown tongue. It was the skipper steadily working his way downwards through the Dukes and Duchesses of the House of Brunswick.

After a long nap I got up with my head as clear as a bell and found everybody telling everybody else that he had acted throughout in the most courageous manner. We fully expected to meet the Japanese fleet, but that caused us no anxiety. We did not meet it, however.

The Russian soldiers still remained with us of course. There had been some talk of putting them ashore on the Liaotung coast in an open boat, but as they did not seem to object to being abducted, we did not trouble ourselves any more about them. I felt sorry for the poor fellows, however, and went to see them. I found them sitting on deck with stolid, expressionless faces, across which the shadow of a smile flitted as I approached.

We happened to have on board three Japanese passengers, one of whom was from Dalny, spoke some Russian, and was, I should imagine from his cast of countenance, one of the many Japanese who were occupied along the Chinese and Siberian coast in *le commerce ambulant des femmes*. This Japanese was speaking to the Russian soldiers when I came along the deck. What he was saying I do not know, but I rather imagine that he was impressing on their minds the fact that their fleet had just got an awful beating.

I told the Russians that they were going to Chefoo, and that they had better see their consul there. They did not seem to know what sort of a "tchinovneek" a consul was, and, addressing me as *barin* (gentleman),—in the morning they had always used the contemptuous "thou" (Tui) and sometimes even *durak* (fool),—they innocently asked if there were Russian soldiers in Chefoo. I believe that the British consul in that Chinese port afterwards explained the fact of their appearance in Chefoo on board a British vessel to his Russian colleague, with the object of preventing, if possible, their being shot as deserters on their return to Port Arthur, and I think that they afterwards returned by rail to that fortress, but what happened to them there I cannot say.

I shall never forget the joy with which I saw again in the distance the calm harbour lights of Chefoo. An age of horrors seemed to have elapsed since I had seen them last. The captain anchored afar off, alongside a Russian steamer, which, in blissful ignorance of all that had just occurred, was getting

ON BOARD THE *COLUMBIA*

ready to proceed to Port Arthur with a cargo of cattle. He then sent me ashore in the ship's boat, so that I could send off my wire before any of the correspondents in Chefoo got the news. It was an hour's long rowing before we reached the pier; and then, though the boat with its Chinese crew immediately pushed off again, leaving only me and the chief officer of the *Columbia* on the land, a few quick sing-song monosyllables which passed between the men in the boat and the pig-tailed loungers about the quay betrayed our secret to the keen Celestial merchants of the town, and within an hour the Russian rouble had fallen to depths such as it had never before fathomed.

As I hurried towards the telegraph office I laughed hilariously at the utter sleepiness and respectability of this staid little outpost, which reminded me strongly of an obscure village in England on a wet Sunday afternoon, for I knew that I carried news that would stir it like an earthquake. The telegraph office was as silent as a church on a week-day. An invisible clock ticked loudly, and an old woman was explaining a telegram to a pale, bored-looking clerk, who gazed at me reproachfully when I came in, judging doubtless from my appearance that I was drunk. In ten minutes more that clerk rushed out from his sanctum with flushed face and gripped me in silence by the hand. I wound up that night in the Japanese Consulate, where Commander Mori, of the Imperial Japanese Navy, was displaying to an enthusiastic audience, which included Mr. Brindle of the *Daily Mail* and Mr. Denny of the Associated Press, a British flag torn to rags by a shell. It was the flag which had fluttered at the masthead of the *Columbia* on her mad race from Port Arthur.

CHAPTER V

INSIDE PORT ARTHUR

I SHALL now try to give some account of what was happening at this time inside Port Arthur.

On Monday, February 8, the stranger who landed in that fortress-city found himself immediately in an atmosphere charged to the highest degree with electricity; and, no matter how languid he may have felt on coming ashore, he soon became, like all those around him, excited, nervous, full of expectation and vague dread.

It might almost be said that the change was brought about more by something in the atmosphere of the place than by anything that was heard or seen, for nothing was to be seen save groups of excited people,—ladies, shop assistants, Chinese "boys," "izvoshcheeks," etc.,—gesticulating wildly on the pavement, and nothing was to be heard save a babble of confused and incomprehensible talk, in which, owing to frequent repetition, the words "Yapontsi" (Japanese) and " voina " (war) alone fixed themselves in the memory.

The " Saratoff" was so thronged with people that no standing room was left, and the Russian waiters had had to cease in despair the cry of "seichass" (immediately) with which they had previously been in the habit of making customers wait for hours before being served. They had evidently come to the conclusion that, on such an occasion, it was useless for them to hold out even the faint hope signified by "seichass."

The congestion was great. The very limited resources of the "Saratoff" were, in fact, overtaxed, and Pankratoff, the Armenian proprietor, looked on helpless and dumbfounded, through his enormous moustaches, like a torpedoed battle-ship looking at a fleet of the enemy's transports. Besides, nobody ever thought of eating, everybody was too busy talking.

The "izvoshcheeks" had gone on strike a few days before, so that crowds of people collected in the middle of the street undisturbed by the fear of being run over by one of these rapid vehicles. Suddenly there was a movement among these crowds of people. An "izvoshcheek" appeared, a sorry-looking specimen. The people fell back from it on both sides and stared. Why? Was an "izvoshcheek" such a curiosity as all that?

The soldiers and policemen saluted the "izvoshcheek." A hush fell on the crowd of gabblers. Something very unusual was taking place. The people in the rear craned their necks. The "izvoshcheek" came nearer. What was it, anyhow? It *was* something unusual.

Seated inside the vehicle was a figure which excited an odd mixture of feelings—an object which, while slightly ridiculous, was at the same time portentous. Some boys laughed. The brows of the elders clouded.

The person who caused these conflicting feelings was Mr. Midzuno, the Japanese consul from Chefoo. Mr. Midzuno was dressed in his gorgeous official robes, which gave him something of the air of an Armenian patriarch ; but his face and figure contrasted strongly, almost ludicrously, with his ceremonial dress, for, like most of his countrymen, he is small, slight and boyish-looking. He would have looked all right in knickerbockers and a Norfolk jacket. Opposite Mr. Midzuno sat the constable of the Japanese Consulate in Chefoo, a clean-shaven, square-jawed man of medium size, who was also clad in his robes of office.

Some residents of Port Arthur recollected dimly as they gazed on the swarthy face of the "constable" that they had often seen him in Port Arthur before. He had always been in civilian dress on such occasions, sometimes in very shabby civilian dress. Well, perhaps on those occasions he had been merely running to earth some law-breaker. At all events he could have been doing nothing serious, for, although in social life the constable is sometimes a formidable personage, he is not a factor of any particular importance in international politics. I shall, therefore, say nothing further at present about Mr. Midzuno's "constable."

Behind the carriage came a motley collection of Japanese, those that had not yet fled from Port Arthur. The men did not form a striking procession. In shabby, ill-fitting European clothes and ancient hats, they looked like a collection of bankrupt tailors. Behind them came a number of richly dressed Japanese women, many of them young and handsome, and most of them smiling right and left at the Russian officers, with that excessively light and easy manner which marks the woman of a certain class all over the world.

Many of the men belonged to a profession in which a considerable number of the Japanese settled along the Chinese and Siberian coast were actively engaged; they were professional procurers. I have since heard that some of them combined this profession with the more honourable one of officers of the Imperial Japanese Staff, but I do not know whether this is a Russian calumny or not.

Some of the women were "amahs" (nurses), and had been employed in the families of the leading naval and military people in the port. Whether or not they picked up any valuable information in this way I do not know, but I am inclined to think that, especially in their cups, Russian officials sometimes forget that Japanese women have got sharp ears and unusually active brains.

Mr. Midzuno had chartered an English steamer, the *Foochow*, and came over in her from Chefoo in order to carry all his countrymen out of Port Arthur and Dalny. He had first spoken on this subject to Mr. Tiedelmann, the Russian consul in Chefoo; and Mr. Tiedelmann, while protesting that there would be no war and that, even if war did take place, the Japanese in Liaotung would never be molested, extended every facility to his brother consul, that is he got the quarantine abolished in his favour at Port Arthur and he gave him a special pass which relieved him from a lot of troublesome formalities.

"But excuse me," cried Mr. Midzuno, when this had been done, "my constable is going with me. Please give him a special pass also."

Mr. Tiedelmann was only too happy to do so. He laughed lightly as he did it. The consul of his

Imperial Majesty the Emperor of Japan evidently meant to do this big "bluff" in style. Well, there was no harm in humouring him.

In Port Arthur the consul and the constable were treated with true Russian hospitality, the consul at the tables of the great men of the place, the constable in the sculleries. The consul saw Mr. Plançon, the head of the Diplomatic Bureau in Port Arthur, and had an interesting conversation with him. He lunched with the Governor of Kwantung Province. Some of the military and naval leaders of the Russians were present at this lunch, and, in the good old Slavonic style, a considerable quantity of champagne was consumed in toasts.

Consul Midzuno beamed with delight, but insisted on going away early. He probably knew what Russian luncheons mean. Besides, important work remained for him to do. Accordingly, he left by the *Foochow* in the afternoon, went to Dalny, got all the Japanese who had been left in Dalny aboard, and then steered for Chefoo.

Eighteen miles off Port Arthur he met the Japanese squadron and, when abreast of the flagship, the *Foochow* lowered a boat, and in a short time the consul and his constable were in Admiral Togo's cabin. Here the constable laid before the admiral a chart on which the positions of all the Russian vessels were marked, and told him of the careless watch that was being kept.

The admiral asked many questions about things which only a naval man will think of, and these questions were answered with remarkable lucidity by the "constable." No champagne was consumed, no "saké" even; but as the *Foochow* steamed away, her cargo of refugees cheered for the Mikado and his fleet. That was all the show of enthusiasm there was, and I dare say it was unsatisfactory from a European point of view, for the Japanese do not know how to cheer.

In fact there was a hard, businesslike air about this remarkable meeting, which must have contrasted strongly with the enthusiasm of the Russian officers in Port Arthur, when, at about precisely the same time, they drew their legs under Admiral Starck's hospitable table in order to commemorate Mrs. Starck's birthday.

Admiral Togo kept the chart the constable had given him, and it soon turned out useful. Meanwhile the consul went home, and when the *Columbia* came flying full-speed from Port Arthur the following evening, neither he nor his constable was astonished at the news it brought.

However, in order to celebrate the occasion worthily, the constable laid aside his humble garb and appeared in the consular drawing-room in the uniform of a Japanese naval commander. And he is a Japanese naval commander. He had been for a long time stationed at Chefoo, picking up hints, visiting Port Arthur himself, and sending trustworthy agents out in all directions, with the result that in the end he got to know more about the Russian fleet than Admiral Starck knew himself.

On the evening of February 9, the consul told the present writer the above story, and the constable nodded corroboration. The latter afterwards got a pencil and a piece of paper, and, without reference to any maps, drew, in the bold, sweeping style of drawing that the Japanese have all got, a remarkably accurate chart of Port Arthur, afterwards jotting down the ships—names, tonnage, armament and all, without an instant's hesitation. He then explained to me all that had happened, and how it had happened. I had been there and he had not, but he knew considerably more about the fight than I did. All I could tell him that he didn't already know for certain, was the number of the ships actually torpedoed.

"Constable" Mori remained at Chefoo for a long time after, very quiet, but with his eyes and ears open. Owing to his command of the Chinese language, to his system of espionage, whose ramifications extended even among the Chinese junk-men and sampan-men, and, above all, to the superhuman zeal with which, like all Japanese, he threw himself into his work, he thwarted almost every plot hatched by the Russians in Chefoo, and having for its object the maintenance of communications between that place and Port Arthur. A friend of mine, an employee of the Chinese Maritime Customs, once discovered, by accident, a link in his marvellous intelligence system.

He was sailing in a steam-launch at some distance from Chefoo, down near the headland which is crowned by a Chinese fort, when he observed a large, black object in the water. It was evidently a boat, but it showed no lights, it was in an unusual place, and it was of unusual shape for a merchant vessel.

My friend's profession necessitates his being always on the look-out for smugglers; in fact, he had undertaken this nocturnal expedition with the object of ascertaining if there was any truth in the reports he

INSIDE PORT ARTHUR

had heard about strange vessels being seen at night in this particular locality. Therefore, he watched the vessel narrowly, and soon perceived that she was signalling with the shore. When the signalling had gone on for a little while, my friend decided that it was time for him to interfere, and accordingly he steamed towards the mysterious intruder. He never overtook it, however.

As soon as its sensitive ears heard the swish of the approaching launch, the strange barque shot off at eighteen knots an hour—my friend is prepared to swear it could not be less—the red fire inside being reflected in the smoke from half a dozen short funnels. The stranger was a torpedo-boat, and, far out, she joined nine or ten dim, unlighted shapes which were far too large to be torpedo-boats; and, soon after, the whole fleet disappeared.

I asked my friend to ascertain who had been signalling from the shore that night, and he went to the signal station to inquire, They told him that it was a man from the Japanese Consulate.

Meanwhile the good people of Port Arthur were disturbed in their sleep or in their revels on the night of February 8 by a sound of firing, which they put down of course to practice. Mr. Plançon has since told me that on hearing this firing he simply turned on his side and went to sleep again, so convinced was he that it was nothing in particular. Next morning, however, there was wild excitement in the air. The Japanese had torpedoed three battle-ships in the darkness. The fleet of the Mikado was outside. The place was going to be bombarded. If the people had been excited before, they were doubly excited now. They crowded in the street facing the harbour, straining their eyes towards the horizon. The Viceroy must have told his *entourage* to show themselves in public in order to calm the excitement, for soon Mr. Plançon, Colonel Versheening, the Mayor, General Stoessel and other notables rode through the streets speaking affably to everybody and smiling mysteriously when questioned about the affair of the night before, as if to intimate that it was all a little surprise which they themselves had sprung on the town. Towards midday, however, when the guns began to boom again, a sickening fear clutched at every heart, and when a Japanese shell fell plump in the street nearly opposite Clarkson's, making a hole that you could bury a mule in, wild-eyed panic seized upon the people. It was as if the Judgment Day had come.

One of the first shells fell in front of the office of Baron Ginsberg, whose timber concession on the Yalu had had a good deal to do with the war.

On the very day before the bombardment, the baron, who, although a Jew of humble origin (his real name is Mess), and whose right to call himself baron is doubted, is a personal friend of Admiral Alexeieff, declared that there would be no war, and evidently believed what he said.

The departure of the Japanese inhabitants looked bad, but did not damp the cheery optimism of the great Jewish capitalist, who opined that it was all "bluff."

When a large shell fell in front of his office, partly demolishing it and making a big hole in the ground, the baron changed his mind about it being all "bluff," and suddenly disappeared from view. He was after-

INSIDE PORT ARTHUR 89

wards discovered cowering in the corner of a third-class railway carriage by one of his own employés, who was so affected by the sight that he jumped into the same train, and went off with practically nothing but his pocket-book and the clothes he had on his back. The number of sudden disappearances of this kind was large.

The prosperous restaurant keeper with the big moustaches also vanished after the first shell, having evidently gone underground, for he as suddenly reappeared again a few days after, as did also his door-keeper, a stout phlegmatic individual, who helped you on with your overcoat, accepted tips without hesitation, no matter how large the amount, and seemed the most unlikely man in the world to be disturbed by anything. But it was the dignified people that bolted on this occasion with the most undignified haste. A week later I met some of them at Chin-wan-tao, a hundred miles from Port Arthur, still running, still breathless. I don't believe some of them have recovered from the shock yet.

I do not blame them, however, after having heard, from one of those who did not bolt, a description of his sensations on feeling that in all Port Arthur there was no longer any protection for him, that the strongest roof could resist the shells as little as a paper screen, and that a projectile might fall anywhere.

The *Novi Kraï* newspaper was, as I have already pointed out, perhaps even a greater opponent of the Japanese than Baron Ginsberg: and consequently it was but poetic justice, I suppose, when a Japanese shell broke all the windows in its office and wounded the manager. Although most of its staff and compositors were drafted into the army, the *Novi Kraï* continued to appear until the end of the war.

The overcrowding on the trains that carried away the first batches of fugitives was almost incredible. Inside the carriages, people were packed on top of one another like herrings, outside they crowded the steps all night. After leaving Port Arthur the conductor requested the gentlemen to leave the train to the women and children ; but the gentlemen pointed out forcibly that many of the women carried large packages, which should be thrown out of the windows, and inveighed with tears in their eyes against the cruelty of separating husbands from wives and brothers from sisters.

Finally, they carried their point and were allowed to continue their journey. Some of these "gentlemen" were in such a state of panic that, as I have already remarked, even in Newchwang, Shan-hai-kwan and Ching-wan-tao they hardly felt themselves to be secure. It was strange the effect this panic had on some people. Silent men became loquacious, guarded men freely disclosed their vulgarity and self-conceit. Most of them seemed to attach too much value to their lives. For example, one obscure individual requested me to telegraph to Europe, as an item of news that would profoundly interest the public, the one fact that *he* was safe.

On the busy little commercial world of Port Arthur the shells of Togo had something like the effect of a Gabriel's trumpet. Business people, friends of mine, who had for a score of years or so been accustomed to sit behind desks with pens in their hands and ledgers before them, had it suddenly borne in on them that there are other things in life besides pens and ledgers and £ s. d.,—that there is war, and death. One of them was found, hours after the Japanese had withdrawn, rushing northwards without hat or coat. A clerk of the Russo-Chinese Bank disappeared, absent-mindedly, with a very large sum of money. The manager of a big firm seized all the spare cash in the till and departed with the observation that he would stand a good deal, but was "blowed" if he would stand *that*.

On the whole, the genial and energetic merchants of Port Arthur did not cut a particularly heroic figure when they heard the voice of the guns. They scattered like a flock of sheep which have heard the roar of the lion.

PART II
WITH THE ARMY

CHAPTER I

I JOIN MISHCHENKO

I DID not remain long in Chefoo, which, after its first rude awakening on the night of February 9, had become one of the drunkenest places in the Far East, but went on to Newchwang and afterwards to Mukden. From Mukden I went to Liaoyang and from Liaoyang to General Count Keller, and afterwards to the famous Cossack leader, General Mishchenko, whose brigade I joined in preference to any other section of the army because I had always heard Russians talk with bated breath of what the Cossacks were going to do to the Japanese.

General Mishchenko, who looks like a typical old Hungarian hussar, with reddish, protuberant nose and grey hair and moustaches, kindly asked me to stay at his headquarters, eat at his table, and put up wherever he put up.

After a few days he insisted on calling me, after the kindly Russian fashion, Franz Yakovlovitch ("Francis son-of-James," James being my father's name), and, as his officers and men were all very amiable, my sojourn among those famous horsemen forms one of the pleasantest experiences in my life.

On the day after I joined Mishchenko, I went out on a reconnoitring expedition, and, as soon as I returned to camp, the battle of Ta-shih-chiao began. Throughout the battle I remained with the general on the artillery position; for, instead of being allowed to worry the enemy with his Cossacks, Mishchenko had been ordered to remain at a point on the extreme left flank and try to do all the damage he could with his artillery, and these tactics he pursued until the close of the year. In fact Mishchenko is not a cavalry man at all; he is an artillery officer. I may here remark that the Cossack is very fond of cannon, and makes a skilful artilleryman.

After the battle we retreated in good order, fought an action of the same kind at Haicheng, and again retreated.

Then came the battle of Liaoyang, which I watched from the top of Shushan hill. Everybody knows that Shushan is a triple-peaked hill, 426 feet high, a few miles to the south of Liaoyang, and that during the battle it was occupied by General Baron Stackelberg, with whom, instead of with Mishchenko, I had decided, by way of a change, to see this fight. On August 30, I ascended Shushan, and found the top cut up by trenches and traversed by wire entanglements, while at its base were *trous de loup*, fougasses and every other species of field defence one can think of. In the neighbourhood there were over a hundred guns in position.

On the level ground, almost a thousand yards to the south-west of it, ran a trench filled with Russian soldiers, and towards this trench I saw the khaki-coated Japanese advance, evidently with the intention of turning the hill. When I say that I saw the Japanese I mean that I saw here and there a khaki-clad figure showing clearly for a second or so against the green

I JOIN MISHCHENKO

fields. These infrequent glimpses were enough for the scores of trained eyes that were watching from the top of Shushan. Bang! bang! bang! went half a dozen batteries at once, and a row of fleecy shrapnel cloudlets hung low over the kiaoliang fields. One shell caught about a score of men as they crossed a road that ran between the trench and the railway, and killed all of them. The picture of that heap of corpses, that muddy road, that trench with its bristling rifles, and that railway line, is so branded into my mind, owing to the number of times that I looked at it through my telescope, that there are few spots on this earth which I know so well. Another object which I seem to have known from earliest infancy is a small wooden house built alongside the railway track and evidently intended for railway men. Outside this house, which was only about fifty yards distant from the nearest Japanese, were a few Russian soldiers, whose position was precarious, for they could not get away without being exposed for several hundred yards to the fire of the enemy. It was almost comical, however, to see how they kept peering round the corner to see if the enemy were advancing.

Meanwhile the latter crept forward slowly, oh! so slowly! until they were within almost a hundred yards of the trench. I thought that they would then make a wild, dramatic rush forwards, but, instead of that, they lay almost twenty-four hours so well hidden that they must have burrowed their way into the ground, for the Russians had beaten down all the kiaoliang for hundreds of yards in front of the trench.

A gigantic pounding and booming went on all this time, but I had no key to it. It was like listening to people squabbling in an unknown tongue. Feeling that war was a delusion, I went to sleep that night in a Chinese hovel at the foot of Shushan; but half an hour or so after dozing off I suddenly awoke with the roar of imaginary cannon in my ears, and was more startled by the great silence than if a whole battery had been thundering beside me.

About the middle of the night I was awakened by the rattle of real musketry, evidently very near. Some of the Russian officers who were sleeping in the same hut with me got up, lighted candles, and moved about uneasily, in the attitudes of men listening for the approach of a visitor; but none of them went outside, and finally the firing died out, and we all went to sleep again.

At daybreak on Wednesday morning, August 31, I was awakened by a cannonade, so loud and so continuous that I rushed out of the house in a panic. The scene was enthralling, It was a beautiful dawn. The sky was perfectly clear of clouds. The moon shone brightly, and alongside it burned one brilliant star. There was just enough darkness in the air to set off to the best advantage the bright, continuous flashes of shrapnel, and enough of the rosy light of dawn to make the smoke of the bursting projectiles look like the soft fleecy cloudlets from which angel heads emerge in a famous painting of Murillo. Over the whole scene was spread the *estilo vaporoso* of that great master. It was a morn on which the Holy Child might have appeared to St. Antony.

I climbed Shushan, and gazed from that elevated point on a scene of rare beauty. The great plain of the Liao-ho was covered with a layer of mist which, touched by the rays of the sun, had the appearance of a silver sea, out of which rose on the north the famous old pagoda of Liaoyang and the glittering walls and gates of what almost seemed to be the Holy City. In an hour or so this great white carpet had been rolled up for the day, and the rich plain was flooded with sunshine, but as yet no living thing was visible. The spectators were present, but the stage was empty.

On the central peak of Shushan General Baron Stackelberg had installed himself in a ruined Korean tower, from which ran a number of telephone wires. I was on the eastern peak with Colonel Waters, the British military *attaché*, and Captain Reichman, the American *attaché*. An alleged bomb-proof had been constructed close by for the use of the *attachés*, but we all preferred to shelter ourselves behind a huge mass of rock which projected on the southern side of the peak, and over the shoulder of which we had a very good view of all that was going on below.

Bullets had whistled overhead all day on Tuesday, and many shells had exploded against the southern face of this rock. We therefore thought that the place was not quite safe, which was true, for on Tuesday alone 3000 men had been killed in that part of the field by shrapnel. On Wednesday we had still more reason to think so. Early that morning Colonel Waters had cheered us with the intelligence that the Japanese would infallibly work round on the west, and shell us from that direction; and, sure enough, at 11 A.M. Captain Reichman saw the flash of a Japanese gun due west of us. It seemed at first, however, as if shrapnel, the invention of the white man, shrank from rending its parent. It was marvellous and incredible how it missed. It seemed to choose every open space it could find, but at last its yellow master forced it to obey.

Shortly after eleven o'clock, shells began to burst in rapid succession on the north side of the rock. Soon it had become a regular downpour of exploding steel, and all the people that were on the mountain trembled. Black masses of smoke seemed to spurt out of the earth like geysers. Snowy puffs of shrapnel surrounded the summit. Balls whistled past like an equinoctial wind. Batteries big and little thundered and shrieked. We realised with horror and dismay that Shushan had suddenly become the pivot of the battle, the centre of the whole gigantic contest. It was a bombardment of hell. The roar waxed louder and louder, and the whole mount quaked greatly. It seemed as if the Japanese meant to pulverise it. I could not hear myself speak, but I fancied I could hear the pounding of my heart. I developed an intense desire to get away, but I could no more let go that rock than a drowning man can let go a straw that he has grasped. I had squeezed my person into the smallest possible compass at its base, and every time a shell burst close to me I backed up against that hundred-ton cliff with such violence that I feared I should knock it down. For days afterwards I was unable to account for those bruises on my back. I knew that it was dangerous to be near that rock, as the Japanese were probably using it as a mark to shoot by, but I saw that the path leading down the hill was more dangerous still, for shells were bursting on it every few minutes. The old Korean tower which sheltered General Stackelberg was hit again and again, and the telephone wires were cut in a dozen places. Colonel Waters got a bullet hole in his cloak. Before

I JOIN MISHCHENKO

long we saw General Stackelberg totter feebly down the hill, upheld on either side by two officers and followed by a retinue of bursting projectiles. He had sustained a concussion, his face was as white as paper, and he was barely able to walk.

The departure of the general made a most gloomy impression on me. I felt as some of the inhabitants of Sodom must after all have felt in their secret hearts when they saw the wise man Lot go forth from their city.

A curse appeared to hang over that mountain. Everybody seemed to have now deserted it. I felt it tremble beneath me. "God knows what's going to happen now," said I, for the twentieth time in forty minutes. "Hadn't we better clear out of this?" I was fully convinced—although I did not like to say so in presence of the military men—that the enemy had undermined Shusan and that it would go sky-high in a few moments. I fancied I heard the subterranean sound of picks.

"These Japs will storm the hill," whispered Captain Reichman hoarsely, adding, with extreme emphasis, "No d——d thing can stop them!"

I glanced quickly over my shoulder, for there rose before me a swift vision of a wave of roaring fanatics with blood-stained bayonets cresting the rock above us.

Previous to this I had been wounded in the hand, and at last I decided to leave this doomed peak, which the Japanese seemed bent on smashing to atoms. A Russian column had now come round on the right. We could hear their brass band playing and their wild "Ura! ura! ura!" but it was impossible to look at them over the shoulder of the rock, as shells were bursting there every minute. I would have given a year of my life for one glance at the spectacle below— the most terrible of all war's terrible sights—the spectacle of a great bayonet charge; but the price demanded was too high. It was my life itself.

In the intervals between the explosions we heard behind us a sound as of broken potsherds. It was caused by shell-cases and fragments of shell rolling down the rocky face of the mountain. The colonel, the captain and myself finally decided to make a combined rush for it. I broke away, however, with the intention of rescuing an ink-bottle and some writing-paper which I had left in the bomb-proof; but, while I stood hesitating outside, uncertain whether to enter or not, a shell burst with a deafening roar in the very doorway.

Amid the resultant smoke and dust I saw several pairs of soldiers' legs, but did not stop long enough to see if they were connected with bodies or not. I must have flown down that mountain like a bird, for two minutes afterwards I found myself sitting on the plain at the base of it, about half a mile off. I was covered with clay, had lost my hat and one boot, and was getting my hand re-bandaged in a German-speaking Red Cross Hospital, which consisted of several large straw mats spread on the ground and covered with half-naked, moaning men.

The neighbourhood was littered with bandages, top-boots that had been cut from wounded legs, and strips of dirty and blood-stained shirts and "rubashkas." The mats were splashed with blood, and on the ground alongside them lay two soldiers whose wounds were so bad that they were unconscious and had only a few moments to live. Their faces were covered by a piece of a muddy bag to which clung some oats, and I noticed that the breast of one of them rose and fell.

Others—dead men—presented a terribly squalid and repulsive appearance as they were thrown into carts. A line of Red Cross vehicles stretched without a break from Shushan to Liaoyang.

Some wounded officers were being held out like little children, as, with pitiful moans, they discharged the offices of nature. I suddenly found that I was sitting in a large black hole in the ground. It had been made by a shell, and other shells were falling all around. Some vindictive god seemed, like the executioners of St. Sebastian in the famous painting of Pollaiuoli, to be purposely planting his dread missiles in such a way as not to injure us mortally, so that we might experience the greatest possible measure of anguish before receiving the final, irrevocable blow.

Finally, Colonel Waters and Captain Reichman left me in order to follow Stackelberg, and, lest I forget it, I take this opportunity of thanking these two brave men, representing the two great sections of mine own people, for the kindness they showed me on this trying occasion.

It was now six o'clock in the evening, and the Japanese were about to deliver their grand attack. We had been caught in the preparatory artillery fire which was concentrated on Shushan, and which Colonel Waters, a calm, well-read observer, declares to have been the hottest artillery fire in the history of the world, "as hot," he says, "as the musketry fire in a skirmishing line."

When I viewed Shushan from the foot of the hill I failed to understand how we had managed to escape alive. The mountain stood out dark and lone against a blood-red patch of sky. The gathering darkness menaced it. Its triple summit was encircled by a crown of bursting shrapnel. Girt by thunders and lightnings, it recalled the Biblical description of Sinai. Some terrible god seemed to have descended on it in fire and smoke. The ruined tower was struck every ten or twenty minutes, and, each time, a cloud of dust and smoke shot upwards from it like the cheer of a great multitude.

I watched it, awe-stricken, as a man who escapes from a wrecked ship watches the waves rush foaming over the masthead. Surely, I said to myself, nothing, whether it be beast or man, can live in such a downpour. The sky was filled with a soft, translucent mist, which I had hitherto supposed to be characteristic of a Japanese evening alone, and a picket of Ural Cossacks, who had happened just then to ride along some rising ground to the west, were glorified for a moment into archangels as they passed through this delicate veil of vapour, and as the picturesque outlines of themselves and their horses and lances stood out clearly against the gorgeous west.

In that blood-red sky, apparently right over the heads of the Cossacks, but in reality some versts to the south-west, there were suddenly three beautiful flashes of white light, as if a magnesium ribbon had been burnt—no, there were four, five, six, seven— seven beautiful bursts of shrapnel light, which were instantly succeeded by small puffs of brownish yellow smoke that dissolved gracefully.

In the north-west hung a huge black bank of clouds, presaging a thunderstorm; and against this inky background the lightning played almost perpetually. As yet there was no thunder, but the thunder came later.

The approaching storm brought on night prematurely; but the sunlight which was quenched was replaced by the red flare from two villages near Liaoyang, which the Russians had set on fire.

Half-way between Liaoyang and Shushan, but a little to the west, is a grove of trees, under which General Kuropatkin, mounted on a white horse and surrounded by his staff and his body-guard of Amur Cossacks halted while the Russian reserves advanced against the Japanese who were threatening their right flank.

Meanwhile the roar of the artillery had redoubled in violence. Darkness was closing in, and the guns thundered with great wrath, because they knew that they had but a short time. And when they had reached a pitch of loudness that seemed impossible to be exceeded, some big angry battery would suddenly and unexpectedly give vent to a series of terrific shrieks that seemed calculated to split the mountain from base to summit.

At length the long-threatening thunderstorm burst, and, as if awed by the wrath of heaven, the earthly artillery gradually ceased, the last flashes of the shrapnel bursting in the darkness above Shushan as if to emphasise the importance of that position. A diminished rifle-fire afterwards continued at intervals, but finally there was silence.

As the village at the foot of Shushan in which I had slept the night before, was on fire, I determined to return to Liaoyang in the darkness, not thinking of what an extremely dangerous thing it was to do on such a night. The rain was coming down in torrents, and my horse had not floundered far through the sticky mud when I heard a voice cry: " Kto idyot ? " (Who goes there?) I answered: " Svoï " (of yours), as I had been accustomed to do in Port Arthur; but, whether it was because this was not the password or because of my foreign accent, the sentry refused to let me proceed. "Nelzya!" (Impossible!) he said, and when I pressed him he kindly pointed out to me another road, a road which led to an intrenched position, where I stood a good chance of getting shot if I employed my "Svoï."

I thanked him, and went in the direction indicated, but I had not gone far before I was brought to a halt by another "Kto idyot?" more emphatic than the previous one. My password was an even greater failure this time, for it led to my immediate arrest. In fact if I had told the sentry I was a Japanese officer he could not have shown greater promptness in arresting me. He rushed forward, and, catching hold of the bridle of my horse, questioned me further.

"Who are you?" he asked fiercely.

"A war correspondent," I answered mildly, aware that among military men it is not a name to conjure with.

"A war correspondent?" he repeated, with the air of a man who has had a new word added to his vocabulary. "Are you Chinese?"

I told him my nationality, but he was still dissatisfied.

Having made me dismount, he passed his hand over my chin, and, finding that I had no hair on my face, he jumped back with an oath and was near bayonetting me on the spot. I must surely be a Japanese. On my imploring him to bring me to some of his superiors, he at last conducted me to a place where I was told that I would find a captain. With him went several rough voices, the owners of which I could not see.

I was glad that he consented to conduct me to the captain, as I had now fully realised my danger, and had seen that it would take very little to make these frightened, ignorant men shoot or stab me. "The captain," I said to myself, "will understand the situation perfectly, and release me at once." In this I made a great mistake, for the captain turned out to be twenty times as scared as the soldiers. He was standing with a number of men in a post a few paces off the path on which I was walking with my guard; and when I heard his high-pitched, nervous voice call out in the darkness asking us what was the matter, I began to fear that it was all up with me, and my imagination became feverishly active. I felt a bayonet thrust savagely into the pit of my stomach, I felt the point come with a terrific jar against my backbone. I was smashed brutally over the head with a clubbed rifle. I heard my skull give way beneath the blow. I saw myself lying on the ground, in a dying condition, my bandaged hand twitching feebly. I saw in the newspapers a brief paragraph which said that I had been killed by a Japanese shell.

When the circumstances of my arrest were related to the captain he became frenzied with excitement.

"Bring him in! Bring him in!" he cried, waving his hands like a maniac. "He's a spy. He's a Japanese. See that he has got no weapons. A revolver. He's sure to have a revolver. Search him carefully. Hold his hands tight. He's a dangerous fellow."

A soldier now got on each side of me and held my arms, at the same time guiding me along a narrow passage which ran between two deep trenches. I saw that I was being brought into a covered work with parapets, traverses and bomb-proofs. A sentinel casually waved a lantern towards a row of black yawning *trous de loup* with sharpened stakes at the bottom. I felt all the terror of a man being led into an *oubliette*. The rear was brought up by the excited captain, who kept gesticulating and ejaculating all the time.

As we passed over a narrow plank traversing a deep ditch, and descended into a small court beneath the surface of the ground, I felt that my life was in great danger, and I was confirmed in my worst fears when, in the light of the dark lanterns that were flashed in my face, I saw the captain. He was a thin, nervous-looking man, with a sparse, sandy-coloured beard and grey eyes that bulged in his head as he looked at me. I realised that long-continued fatigue and excitement, combined with want of food and sleep, had reduced him to a condition of nervousness little removed from lunacy; and unfortunately his nervousness had evidently infected the ignorant soldiers, who formed a ring around me, and on whose white, scared faces I

I JOIN MISHCHENKO

could read no more trace of pity than a tiger might see on the faces of a ring of hunters.

Fortunately, a different type of officer happened to be in the fort at the time. This was the chief of staff of the Second Army Corps, as well as I can remember, an urbane, highly-refined, cool-headed officer, speaking French and German as fluently as he spoke his mother tongue. It took me about three minutes to satisfy this officer that I was what I pretended to be ; and then, over a glass of wine and some biscuits, he informed me that all Englishmen were mad for exposing themselves to danger when there was no necessity for it, and explained to me, in a tone of philosophic aloofness, the greatness of the risk I had run.

"These soldiers," said he, waving his biscuit in a semicircle, "are from Europe and have not been long here, so that they know nothing of correspondents. Then, your dress and the fact that you are a foreigner found in the heart of a Russian encampment on the night after a battle and while the enemy are expected to make an attack at any moment, might well have cost you your life.

"I am surprised," he added, in a dreamy, meditative tone, "that you were not shot, especially as two Japanese officers accompanied by some Chinese did actually enter our camp last night and were killed. Hullo ! What's that ? "

At this moment the silence of the night was brusquely torn by a volley of musketry, followed instantly by another and another. Outside, it was as black as pitch, the rain was falling fast, but the continual flash of the rifles lit up white faces which gleamed in the distance like foam on the crest of a breaking wave. The Japanese were coming on, coming on, coming on.

Between the startling r-r-r-rip! r-r-r-r-rip! r-r-r-r-r-rip, r-r-r-r-r-rip! of the volleys there comes to us faintly the notes of a distant, savage chant of *banzaï! banzaï! banzaï!*

It is like the cry of wild, invulnerable tribes! It is like the defiant shriek of Dervishes! It swells on the air like a fierce Oriental Marseillaise. In this abrupt, staccato roar is something foreign, repugnant, disquieting. It does not belong to the European brotherhood. It does not come from Christian lips. It does not even seem to come from human beings. It reminds me of the fierce Allah il Allah! Allah il Allah! that I used to hear in Mahommedan cities. It recalls the mad monotonous chant of Hosein el Hosa! Hosein el Hosa! on the anniversary of Kerbela. It evokes memories of India. It recalls the horrors I had heard in my cradle of Nana Sahib and the mutineers of Lucknow. With a start I recollect that these faces, which shine white in the flash of the Russian rifles, are the faces of Orientals, that this cry is for the blood of white men. It is not the cry of Frenchmen or Germans. It is something infinitely more disquieting and significant. It is the cry of that strange and monstrous Asia with which Europe has been at feud for thrice a thousand years. It demands vengeance not only for Port Arthur but for Kagoshima and Shimonoseki, nay, more, for Salamis, for the Pink Forbidden City, for the Red River, for Plassy, for Kandahar, for Mindanao.

Oh, England! Oh, my country! What deed is this thou hast done?

I JOIN MISHCHENKO

Meanwhile I most fervently thanked God that I had come into contact with the excited captain *before* this attack began. The officers around me were naturally excited by these terrible sights and sounds, and, rising unceremoniously, told me that I was free to go wherever I liked. But I was now in no mind to go, and I pointed out to them that if, according to their own account, I stood a good chance of being shot by a sentry before this attack began, I stood a still better chance now that the Japanese bullets were actually whistling overhead and the sentries were all in a state of intense nervousness. They said that they would send a soldier with me to the main road, a few hundred yards off; but I answered that this was not good enough, the soldier would have to come with me all the way to the city, else I would rather prefer to sleep in the trench all night. Without deciding one way or another they went away, leaving me sitting there; but in about an hour the chief of staff came back and told me that on account of the seriousness of this attack, he was going personally to headquarters in Liaoyang. Would I come with him? Of course I would go with him.

We reached the town without any mishap, and, on the way, my companion genially pointed out to me four different places where I would have been shot if I had tried to pass alone without the countersign.

About the time I was arrested, the Russians evacuated Shushan.

Next morning I went east with Mishchenko, to cut off Kuroki. I was with Rennenkampf in the attack on Pen-shi-hu, in October, and on this occasion I crossed the Taitsze river with a band of Cossacks, who advanced further south than any other section of the

Russian army, and succeeded for a time in severing all connection between Kuroki and the gallant little Japanese force that held Pen-shi-hu. After the battle of the Shaho I again joined Mishchenko. I had now two Cossack orderlies ("vyestovoï"), one Philipoff, a Siberian from Verkhnyudinsk, whose business it was to ride with me; and the other a Buriat, who was charged with the care of my baggage.

Philipoff was a lad of twenty-two, and he reminded me very much of a strong, healthy, farmer's son in England, only that he was not quite so clean. In the morning, it is true, his face shone like a schoolboy's if water was handy and it was not too cold, and he always kept his teeth as white as if he were a Japanese; but I never knew his ablutions to extend as far as the back of his neck, save when he went to the steam bath which the Cossacks always established in a village where they were likely to remain any length of time.

Philipoff had the usual big sword, top boots, trousers with a broad yellow band running down each leg; and, cocked on his peculiar Cossack saddle, with a rifle at his back, this youngster was worth more to me than a cartload of duly stamped and sealed official documents. In short, he was a passport to every place over which the Russian eagles waved. Other correspondents, who had got all sorts of special permits, but who had no Cossack, were arrested at every step by soldiers who could not read; and even the *attachés* were not half as grand as I, for they had only got clumsy infantrymen whom they themselves supplied with horses.

Philipoff had left a young wife at home, but had as

FRANCIS McCULLAGH AND HIS COSSACK PHILLIPOFF

yet no children. The down of boyhood was still on his lip, and, except where horses were concerned, he was as simple as a child. As soon as he was placed under my orders he cautiously entreated me to take him to see Mukden, the glories of which ancient capital he had only as yet contemplated from the train which had brought him, some months before, from Harbin to Liaoyang. His longing to gaze on the ancient seat of the Manchus was like that of Jude the Obscure to see Christminster; and, of course, I at once brought him to Mukden, where he was as happy as if it were Paris. I was at first afraid, after all the terrible things that I had heard about the Cossacks, that he would promptly get drunk and perhaps assault me; but never once during the six months we passed together did this Russian lad get intoxicated or give me the slightest cause for dissatisfaction. He confessed to me, however, that he had got drunk once in his life, *i.e.*, at his "knyazhenetsky stol" (princely table), which high-sounding name the Cossack gives to his wedding-breakfast. He never tried to make a "kopeck" of profit on the many commissions with which I charged him, and he used to tell me how disgusted he was at the way Chinese "mahfus" (grooms) of other correspondents defrauded their masters and starved their masters' horses. I think it is not egotistical of me to say that my horses were always in the pink of condition, for it is Philipoff that deserves the credit.

From all that Philipoff told me about the Transbaïkal Cossacks, and from what I saw of them with my own eyes, I came to the conclusion that these much-maligned horsemen are gentle, inoffensive farmers' sons, who do not like war at all, who are apt to fall asleep at any time in the day (Pushkin notes that characteristic in his " Prisoner of the Caucasus "), and whose only ambition is to till their fields, sing songs, and live happily with their wives, for all of them are married. And yet these simple lads are the folk of whom a Frenchman wrote in 1814, "le viol, le meurtre, le fer, le vol, le pillage, l'incendie, le carnage, tous les maux de la terre, leur sont familiers. Le récit de la férocité de ces barbares fait frémir la nature."

As for their officers and for Russian officers in general, they are an extraordinarily hospitable and genial people. It would almost seem as if Russian officers were influenced by that beautiful superstition, which still prevails among the Russian peasants, that one must never refuse to offer hospitality lest he repulse angels unawares.

Scores of times throughout the course of the war, I lost touch with Mishchenko's detachment, and in such cases I had to rely on the hospitality of strange officers whom I happened to meet with. As a rule I did not know these officers, and my "udostoverenie" gave me no claim on them whatever, but nevertheless their treatment of me was invariably very kind.

Again and again have I arrived when the officers were making a meagre dinner of a few tins of Russian preserves—a quarter of one small tin, say, to each man—and, although I have never been regarded as an entertaining individual, they always hailed my advent as gladly as if I had brought them a fresh supply of provisions and a case of vodka.

I sometimes stumbled on them in the early morning at an hour when no society tolerates callers, and when some of them were in bed and some of them walking about in their pyjamas, but it never made any difference in the manner of their reception. On such occasions they did not shake hands—for in the morning the Russians do not shake hands until after they have washed—but the loud, cheery tones in which they said, first, " Z dobrym utram " (good morning), and then, without pausing to take breath, "stakan chaï pajaluista?" (a cup of tea, please?) were as brimful of friendly feeling as they could possibly be.

On such occasions I have seen officers produce cherished stores of sweetmeats, a precious tin of butter, or a last box of chocolate—objects worth their weight in gold at such a time—and place them in front of the visitor whose name they did not know, and whom they never expected to encounter again. If these pages happen to meet the eyes of any Russian who has thus befriended me I hope he will take this as an expression of my warmest thanks.

Another characteristic of the Russian officer is his high spirits and his marvellous health and vitality. He seems to be simply bursting with vitality and overflowing with animal spirits. In most of the messes the officers are large-limbed, young, ruddy-faced, bright-eyed, and to hear the racy, enthusiastic, jovial way in which they recount their experiences would make the most confirmed old misanthorpe feel cheerful. Their hearty laughter is infectious; and their gaiety does not depend on good food and good drink, for I have found them as cheerful after dining on a few fragments of stale bread as after a champagne lunch.

CHAPTER II

BEFORE MISHCHENKO'S RAID

DURING the battle of the Shaho, Mishchenko had been stationed near the village of Fudyapu, on the banks of that river, a few miles south-east of Hwang-shan; and, instead of doing anything with his Cossacks, he had been chained, as usual, to a bare hill-top, where his horsemen were quite useless.

In November he left this village, and went into the reserve at a hamlet called Mudzetun, a few miles south of the Hun river. With their usual ingenuity, the Cossacks had marvellously transformed this erstwhile Chinese village, so that it had become as Cossack in appearance as Verkhnyudinsk or Arshinsk, the only evidence that it had ever been inhabited by Celestials being a small Buddhist temple on the roadside.

The streets were carefully swept every morning. The numbers of the different "sotnia" living in this "stanitza" had been painted in white on the mud walls bounding the little courtyards, while the inside of all the houses had been carefully washed and papered with back numbers of Russian journals, among which the illustrated supplements of the *Novoe Vremya* were conspicuous. The houses were heated by means of "*kangs*" and of small tin stoves constructed, after a European model, by the tin-smiths in Mukden. The sanitary

BEFORE MISHCHENKO'S RAID

regulations were strict, and one of the huts had been made air-tight and converted into an excellent Russian bath-house.

The weather was now cold, but glorious. The ground was hard as iron; there was little snow; and, though there was plenty of sunshine, the cold wind pierced one to the marrow, unless one followed the example of the Russians and wore a pile of furs, which gave one the appearance of a small elephant.

Bearded men suffered a good deal of discomfort from this cold, because the vapour from their mouths formed into icicles, the removal of which from their moustaches and beard was rather painful.

A stream ran through our village, but it ran underneath a coat of ice, thick enough to bear a railway train. Every day the Cossacks cut holes in this ice to allow their horses to drink. The water for their own use they got at the village well, where, in accordance with the Russian custom, a soldier always stood on guard. In an enclosed space behind the houses, the horses were piqueted and fed on straw.

While walking one morning through our village of Cossackville, I was surprised to see five or six wretched-looking Chinese standing by the frozen bank of the stream collecting the entrails of the cows and sheep that the Cossacks had just killed for dinner, and, for a moment, I was as startled at seeing these Celestials as a New Yorker would be at seeing a Red Indian stalking in paint and feathers through his back yard.

Some village dogs had collected near them, partly for old acquaintance' sake—these gentlemen having probably been the aldermen of the hamlet under the

Chinese *régime*—and partly, no doubt, for the sake of the eatables.

When the Cossacks entered into possession of the village, these dogs had left it in a body, and they had afterwards lived in the fields at a respectful distance. They were not hostile, however; they were only puzzled. Some of them had given hostages to fortune in the shape of pups, which the Cossacks took care of, and all of them seemed to see more or less distinctly that the newcomers were not wholly bad. They therefore refrained from barking at the Russians, and were probably open to an offer to come back on the old terms. But the Russians did not want them back, and I am afraid that the rigorous winter thinned their number. Often when I went out riding I found two or three of these poor animals frozen to death. In Mukden, Chinese beggars picked up these dead dogs, whose skins they sold, and whose flesh they ate.

The case of the Chinese was indeed hard, for the whole country between the Shaho and the Hun, over a line extending eighty or ninety miles, had been swept clear of them, and the population of Mukden had consequently swollen to five or six times its usual size. Day after day I met the inhabitants of outlying villages coming in, sometimes with a mule and a few pots and pans, sometimes with nothing at all. Often I met a number of sturdy young men carrying on a door their aged grandmother or great-grandmother, one of those extraordinarily ancient people only to be found in China, where old age is worshipped. Once I met a cheerful young farmer carrying his two little children, each swung in a basket about the size of a hat-box, balanced over his shoulder, one in front and one behind. That poor fellow had lost everything in the world save these two children, but he was quite happy.

The Cossacks never practised firing at targets, or in any other way; but every morning they had cavalry drill on the village green, and sometimes, on returning from this drill, they would burst into a lively, rattling chant, which had always the effect of making me issue forth into the ice-cold, crisp morning air, radiant with sunshine, and, after the over-heated "fanza," pleasant to the taste as iced champagne in summer time. In fact the amount of singing they did was extraordinary, and it was excellent singing. Sometimes they sang that beautiful national chant,

> Mnogo lyet, mnogo lyet,
> Nashe Pravaslavny Tsar!

> Many years, many years
> To our Orthodox Christian Tsar!

although a considerable proportion of them were neither Orthodox nor Russian, but Lamaïsts of pure Mongol blood, and with a strikingly Japanese caste of features, which, by the way, led many of the newly arrived European troops to shoot or arrest them pretty frequently at this time.

There is a striking contrast between the bloodthirstiness of the Cossack's reputation and the peacefulness of his songs, which principally deal with love and home, and seldom with war.

Some of them are old and famous. The following is a free translation of the first stanza of a popular ballad, said to be more than two hundred years old, but, nevertheless, only too applicable, alas! to the recent war:

> A Cossack rode out to a distant countrie,
> To a distant countrie, with his "sotnia" so gay,
> And in vain his fair "kazachka" looked o'er the lea
> From the rise of the sun to the close of the day;
> For her young Cossack lover she never did see!
> He died in the snow in that distant countrie. . . .

Below I translate the first verse of a song which was composed by the famous Cossack leader Davidoff at the time of Napoleon's disastrous retreat from Moscow, and which was chanted by the Cossacks as far as the gates of Paris. Like most Cossacks, Davidoff was a hard drinker, and his ballad bears witness to that fact The first verse runs as follows:

> Happy he who in the strife
>   Bravely, like a Cossack, dies;
> Happy he who, at the feast,
>   Drinks till he can't ope his eyes.
>
> *Chorus:*
> Silver on the horse's feet,
>   Half a farthing for the master,
> Good oats for the charger fleet;
>   A crust for you—you'll ride the faster.

Davidoff certainly interests me, for it is not often you find a great cavalry leader who is at the same time a good ballad-maker, and I should like to get more of his rousing songs.

The collector of Cossack ballads will notice that there is nothing that in the least resembles Béranger's well-known song, "Le Chant du Cosaque," in which the

Cossack is made to declare that he will trample down sceptres and—the Cross:

> *J'ai pris ma lance, et tout vont devant elle*
> *Humilier et le sceptre et la croix.*

As a matter of fact, the Cossack is the strongest supporter the throne has got, and, if the Tsar is overthrown, the revolutionists will have to reckon with the rider from the Don as the French revolutionists had to reckon with the peasants of La Vendée. Many of his songs are religious, and the expression "a man without a cross" (*i.e.*, a man who does not wear a crucifix around his neck, as all Orthodox Christians are supposed to do) is, in his mouth, a term of reproach.

Some of the Cossack songs relate to "the King Napoleon," who, in "the year twelve," and at the head of "the army of twenty nations," invaded "holy Moscow of the snow-white walls."

In fact, Napoleon, or, as the Cossacks call him, "Poleon," seems to be the one foreigner, Julius Cæsar, Belisarius, and scriptural characters excepted, with whose name the Cossack is familiar, and this is exactly as it should be, for it was the Cossacks of the Don that first conquered that mighty conqueror. Davoust, Ney, Eugene, even that brilliant horseman Murat, are all alike unknown to them, and of England they know as little as the average Athenian knew of the inhabitants of Ancient Britain. I remember once overhearing two Cossacks discussing me shortly after my arrival in Mishchenko's camp.

"An Englishman!" quoth one of them in astonishment, "why, he is quite clean and civilised like ourselves!"

The great hero of Cossack song is "the Cossack Platoff," who led the horsemen of the Don in the wars of Napoleon I. Him the Tsar sends disguised as a merchant to "the Frantzouz." He goes to the Court of France, and is questioned by "the daughter of the Frenchman Arina," who asks him to show her the portrait of "the Cossack Platoff," whereupon he shows her his own portrait and instantly flees, remarking, somewhat ungallantly, to the young lady as he mounts his faithful steed, "Ah, crow! French brigand! You can never alive take the Cossack Platoff!"

Naturally Yermak is revered by his children, the Transbaïkal Cossacks. One of their songs represents him as going to ask pardon of the Tsar before embarking on the conquest of Siberia;—

> On Mother Volga,
> On the Kama,
> Live the Cossacks, live the Freemen,
> Cossacks of the Don,
> Cossacks of the Caucasus,
> And they have for Ataman
> Yermak Timofeëvitch.
>
> Like a silver clarion
> Sounding in the wilderness,
> Sounds the voice of Yermak,
> Yermak Timofeëvitch,
> And it says, "O brethren!
> Winter now is coming on,
> And no resting-place have we!"
> Says Yermak Timofeëvitch.

He asks his men if they will go to the Volga, " where people treat us as brigands," to the Jaïk which " is far,"

BEFORE MISHCHENKO'S RAID

or to Kazan, " under whose walls is encamped Ivan the Terrible." They finally decide to go to the banks of the Itych, to the town of Tobolsk, but first they must ask pardon of the Tsar.

Accordingly Yermak advances at the head of his men. " Slowly and respectfully " he traverses the inner court, the vast court of the Tsar. He approaches the red staircase. He dismounts from his horse. " Slowly and respectfully " towards the white palace of the Tsar goes Yermak Timofeëvitch. " Slowly and respectfully " enters he the palace. The Terrible is seated on his throne, surrounded by his Boyars. Yermak addresses him :

> Health to thee, O little Father !
> Health to thee, most Christian Tsar !
> Ivan Vassilÿevitch !
> I am Yermak.
> I ask pardon
> For the crimes I have committed
> On the sea and on the highway.
> I have seized ships full of pearls,
> Ships of Mussulman and Persian ;
> Even vessels of the Empire
> Have I captured, have I plundered,
> But these vessels of the Empire
> Bore not, Tsar, thy coat of arms.

The Tsar, puzzled, asks himself aloud what he is to do with this man, and one of the Boyars expresses a decided opinion that hanging, or even decapitation, would be too good for him, whereupon Yermak Timofeëvitch draws his trusty sword, and cuts off that Boyar's head at one blow.

On the footstool the head bounded,
Rolled adown the spacious chamber.
To the door fled all the Boyars,
Tumbling over one another.
Yermak feared he had offended,
Had, perhaps, been somewhat hasty.

But, though the song does not say so, we are left to conclude that this little outburst of temper won the Tsar's heart, and led to Yermak being entrusted with the conquest of Siberia. As a matter of fact, Yermak did not see the Tsar until he had already conquered Siberia; but if there is one thing more than another that distinguishes the ballads of the Cossacks, it is their sublime inaccuracy.

It is not generally known, by the way, that Yermak Timofeëvitch is honoured by the Greek Church, which solemnly prays once a year for the repose of the conquistadore's soul. In fact, he is almost regarded as a saint by the Cossacks, who, in this respect, treat their hero with more respect than the Spaniards treat Cortez or Pizarro, or than the English treat Clive or Warren Hastings.

In one of their songs, wherein a soldier is lying dead and his black horse is bending over him, all the Cossacks join, after every second line, in a wild barbaric chant of "Akh! Moï Bozhin'ka! Akh! Moï Bozhin'ka!" which is extraordinarily weird and effective. Another favourite subject is a Cossack youth languishing in a Moslem prison.

There are continual references to the great rivers along which most of the Cossacks live. In fact, the Don Cossacks regard the Don as the early Romans regarded Father Tiber; it is almost a divinity. They call it Don Ivanovitch (Don, son-of-Ivan, for the Cossacks have a tradition that the Don is the offspring of Lake Ivan), much as the Japanese peasants call their famous mountain Fuji San (Mr. Fuji), and generally designate it as "the quiet Don Ivanovitch," by way, I suppose, of contrasting it with the unquiet peoples who roam its banks.

Cossack ballad-makers refer often in their songs to beautiful girls, differing greatly in this respect from Japanese ballad-makers, who would as soon think of referring to the binomial theorem.

The Cossack song lays great stress on a free life, independence, and contempt of death.

It does not seem, however, to show any extraordinary respect to the Tsar, or at least to his representatives, some of whom the Cossacks decapitate and cast into the "quiet Don Ivanovitch," addressing insulting remarks to them as they float down the stream. No Tsar has ever been so reverenced by the Cossacks as Stenka Razin, who for years defied St. Petersburg and devastated all the country between the Volga and the Don.

I once heard recited at the camp-fire a splendid ballad which a poet, called Zhukovsky, I think, composed in the Russian camp on the eve of the battle fought on the Tarutina during Napoleon's invasion of Russia. It begins with a powerful description of night in camp—

> Na polye brannom teesheena ;
> Ognee mezhdu shatramee !

> Silence rests on the battlefield,
> Fires burn among the tents.

But the best thing in this ballad is the invocation of a dead hero, an invocation which Béranger, by the way, borrows in his *Chant du Cosaque.*

"Who," asks the poet, "is this tremendous giant, this horseman from the North, that glares with terrible eyes at the camp of the sleeping enemy?

"Ghosts fly with fearful cries from his path, which, far as the snowy fastnesses of the Alps, is strewn with thunderstorms.

"The Gaul grows pale. Beneath this baleful glare the Sarmate trembles in his tent. Woe! woe! to the foeman! 'Tis the spirit of our terrible Suwaroff!"

Naturally enough, the Cossack does not forget to mention the horse in his ballads. In fact, he manages to introduce him into the most unlikely subjects. One of the Russian marriage songs begins, for instance, as follows:

> Mátushka! What makes that dust on the plain?
> Sadár'nya! What makes that dust on the plain?
> My daughter! the hoof-beats, the hoof-beats of horses!
> Sadár'nya! the hoof-beats, the hoof-beats of horses!

Of course the lover is astride one of the horses, although the fair one is not supposed to know it.

Again, in another marriage song:

> 'Tis not a falcon flying through the sky,
> 'Tis not a falcon with its feathers blue,
> 'Tis a bold youth who gallops bravely by.

When winter came on, some of the "skazki" (stories) those Cossacks used to tell during the long nights around the samovar were calculated to make one's flesh creep, stories of the old days when a Cossack who had murdered another Cossack (if he killed a person who was not a Cossack, it did not seem to be regarded as murder at all or even manslaughter) was buried alive underneath the coffin of the man he had murdered. Sometimes the ghost of a murderer used to appear with the coffin of the victim on his back, and to pursue any one who passed his grave by night, and the fear of being chased in this frightful way was sufficient to prevent the boldest horseman from approaching the haunted spot.

I first heard this story one night immediately after the battle of the Shaho, and in the middle of a desolate valley where some ten thousand men had just been killed, and I could not help thinking it strange that not one of the Cossacks, who, in Russia, would be frightened to death if asked to pass the grave of a murderer by night, was in the least disturbed when told to traverse alone, at any hour in the twenty-four, this valley of dead men's bones. The Cossacks seemed no more to expect ghosts to appear in a battlefield than in a butcher's shop.

In the Cossack "skazki" the dead are sometimes represented under an altogether dreadful aspect, horrible stories being told of corpses, animated by demons, rising at midnight and attempting to rend their watchers. Warlocks, vampires, and all that terrible brotherhood trouble the Cossack imagination, and sometimes, especially on a dark night, one gets quite unnerved by a course of these stories, which are so different from the sunny myths of the Japanese. As for the songs and superstitions of our Mongol and Caucasian contingents, I have neither the space nor the knowledge to deal with them.

The only outdoor exercise the Cossack got at this season, besides his daily drill, was attending to his horses and stacking up the straw and "kiaoliang," which was conveyed to Cossackville from villages to the north of Mukden in long lines of Chinese carts. This spectacle of the men building up stacks of straw was very peaceful and rural, and harmonised well with the sound of the hammer, which was always ringing on the anvil in our village smithy, but not, I am sorry to say, converting swords into plough-shares.

As for outdoor sports, there was not such a thing as a football in the entire army, and the only exercise the officers got was riding into town or practising pistol-shooting for bets. Indoors they read Anton Tchekhov, Turgueniev, Grigorovitch, Pisarov, and heavy reviews giving a very complete account of foreign literature. Many of them took in the leading daily papers of St. Petersburg, and several received technical reviews, periodicals dealing with military matters, with the horse, etc. On the whole their reading was solid. They also played cards, but they were not happy till they had got from Harbin a gramophone, which reeled off Russian songs during mealtime. Sometimes a rattling old Cossack tune would so excite the younger members of our community that they would jump up from table and dance the "Kazatchok."

I still seem to hear this gramophone grinding out select pieces from Glinka's "Life for the Tsar." Meanwhile the steaming "samovar" purrs gently on the table, swift justice is being done to the "pirogi" (patties) and "caviare." The "borsch" is carried round by the boyish Zeemeen, whose wide

BEFORE MISHCHENKO'S RAID 129

kaftan is confined by a narrow belt studded with bright brass rivets like a prison door, whose head is crowned by a huge wolf-skin busby, even in the dining-room, and whose feet are always encased in high boots. We are also waited on by the jocose, mysterious-looking Buriat, Munkusha, whose name everybody pronounces in a different way.

Owing to the fact that I wore no uniform, I was for a long time a puzzle to the Cossacks.

Philipoff once said to me, "I suppose, Vashe Blagarodie (one of noble birth), that before entering the service of his Most Gracious Majesty the Tsar, our Gosudar, you had to renounce allegiance to your own Gosudar?" And when I told him I had done nothing of the kind, he attempted to cheer me up by saying that I would probably get a decoration anyhow.

The Cossack never wearies of talking about decorations, and speculating on the order which he himself will receive when the war is over; and when he does receive an order he seems to wear it continuously day and night.

The Cossacks and the Russian soldiers generally are treated far more gently by their officers than the Japanese soldiers are by theirs. When I was in Japan there was a regular epidemic of suicide among soldiers, the result of ill-treatment on the part of officers, who were not brutal, however, but only over-zealous and over-anxious to imitate the German system to the letter. During my stay with the Russians I never saw anybody ill-used except in two cases. In one case all the orderlies in a houseful of officers got drunk, for which offence one of them—the worst

—was sent to the guard-room. As it was extremely cold, however, Essaoul Cheslavsky, the officer on duty, gave orders that the prisoner was to be released in three or four hours. In the second case a Cossack, who formed part of an expedition which I accompanied, got intoxicated on some liquor which he had obtained in a Chinese house, and for this he was made to dismount and go for some distance on foot.

CHAPTER III

A CHRISTMAS WITH THE COSSACKS

Towards the end of 1904, Mishchenko's whole force, now consisting of 7500 horsemen, including Cossacks, dragoons, mounted infantry, horse artillery, and Caucasian volunteers, suddenly moved from their quarters at Mudzetun to Suhudyapu on the Hun river, about a dozen miles to the south-west of that city, with the object, as afterwards appeared, of making southward raids during the winter and cutting the Japanese line of communications.

At this time my position was rather difficult. Whether because of these raids being in contemplation and of the General Staff being unwilling that I should take part in them, or because some other correspondents had complained repeatedly about my being allowed to have mounted orderlies and to circulate generally wherever I liked, while they were now forbidden to leave Mukden, Colonel Pestitch, the censor, made repeated efforts to detach me from the Cossacks.

One day I rode into Mukden and found some of my *confrères* of the Press very angry because the censor had made them all promise not to leave the city. They had asked him if this promise was also to be exacted from me, whereupon he said " yes," and gave them to understand that he was just lying low, waiting for me, and that as soon as I had entered the gates of the city he would pounce upon me, separate me from Philipoff, and make me remain in Mukden like my colleagues. This news greatly disquieted me, for I knew that the censor was living with his friend, the Russian Resident of Mukden, under whose orders were the soldiers who guarded the gates, and that these soldiers had received instructions to let no correspondent pass. I was caught, then, like a rat in a trap! But I determined to make a dash for freedom before the censor had got wind of my arrival, and accordingly sallied out. If I had left the city as usual by the south gate I should probably have been stopped, but, attended by my faithful Cossack, I galloped through the west gate, and, owing to my Russified appearance, to the headlong speed at which I rode, and to the fact that it was getting dark and that I wore no brassard, the soldiers at the gate were so impressed that, instead of arresting me, they called out the guard and gave me the military salute. I had determined to gallop past them in any case, and once outside the walls, it would not have been easy for them to catch me.

I had no difficulty in finding my way back to Mishchenko, for a huge chunk of country to the north of Mukden was now traversed by broad roads, running east and west, north and south, and marked at every crossing with finger-posts pointing out the way of retreat, like the signs in the American theatres pointing to the fire exits.

When I reached the Cossack camp and told my friends of my outlawed condition, they greeted me with as much enthusiasm as their fathers on the lower

A CHRISTMAS WITH THE COSSACKS

Dneiper would have greeted an outlaw flying to the Sitch; and I think that if the censor had sent any emissary to bring me back, that emissary would have run a serious risk of being hanged.

I found that the Cossacks had now got huge "papakhas" or wolf-skin busbies with stripes of cloth of gold on the crown—a very ancient style of Cossack headgear, which greatly altered their appearance for the better, and of which they were as proud as a lady is of a new bonnet or as an Assam buffalo ought to be of his horns.

A few days later, a further change was made in their appearance when "polshuboks" were distributed amongst the men. These "polshuboks" were pelisses made of untanned white bearskin with the wool inside, fitting very tight, fastened down the middle of the breast by means of hooks, reaching nearly to the knee and smelling abominably. Philipoff brought me one, and it gave the finishing touches to my "Kazaksky" appearance.

I found that the Cossack officers had changed too, but in a different way. They had all become very studious, and were taking a particularly keen interest in nitro-glycerine and the blowing up of railway trains and bridges. They even had night schools, in which lectures on this fascinating business were given by an anæmic-looking young officer in spectacles, who had been sent to us by the General Staff. I attended some of these classes, for I found it distinctly interesting to watch this pale-faced professor show the students seated around him how to wreck railway property and derail engines. It was like attending a meeting of anarchists. The object of the whole thing was of course clear to me. We were going to send out expeditions to wreck the railway,

Meanwhile a large quantity of nitro-glycerine arrived in camp, and was stored in an empty house next to the one which I occupied. A sentinel was placed at the door of this house, and one of the duties of the officer of the day was to go to this sentinel the first thing in the morning and get him to repeat a long string of cautions like a child repeating the ten commandments. He was not to allow any one to enter the hut with a light, with his boots on, etc.; but, in spite of all this care, I half expected, from what I knew of "the careless Cossack" (as Pushkin calls him), to find myself travelling rapidly skyward some fine morning, owing to the explosion of the whole magazine.

Hearing, the day after my arrival in camp, that a party of two hundred men under Colonel Plaoutine was going to cross the Liao river next day, I determined to accompany it, for it would be rather difficult for my friend Colonel Pestitch to get hold of me in case I was away down somewhere in the rear of the Japanese army. The only other foreigner who joined this party was Lieutenant Ferdinand Burtin, a young French officer from Algeria, who had some time before joined Mishchenko's detachment as a volunteer, with the rank of "sotnik" or centurion.

Colonel Plaoutine's instructions were to cross the Liao river, which is the frontier of China, to proceed south as far as Davan, see if there were any Hunghuze in that district, or if the Japanese had been establishing any depôts there, then march westward as far as the Kupanze-Tsinmintun railway and ascertain if that line were carrying any contraband for the Japanese.

A CHRISTMAS WITH THE COSSACKS 135

His instructions went no further than this. He was not told to stop any train, or to arrest anybody; he was told, however, that he was not to allow himself to be over-powered. As a matter of fact, he went much further south than his instructions warranted. These were the ostensible objects of the expedition, but I suspected that a deeper object, unknown even to Plaoutine himself, lay behind, and at once wrote to the *New York Herald*, in a letter which was published about a month afterwards, saying that the real aim of the Russians in making this raid was "to reconnoitre the extreme left of the Japanese, with a view to sending Cossack expeditions that way in order to cut the railway south of Liaoyang."

Before we started on this foray there was a good deal of excitement among the Cossack officers who were to take part in it, at the prospect of coming in contact with the Chinese troops or with the English officials on the railway. Everybody wanted to join in this expedition, and, late on the night of December 20, while the Russian officers were discussing the perilous ride in front of them, three lads, all of them about fifteen years of age, who had run away from home in order to join Mishchenko, came to our leader and implored him to grant them permission to go also. A vivid representation of the long rides in front of them and of the risks they must undergo, seemed only to whet their appetite for the adventure. In their eagerness for danger they reminded me strongly of English or American lads. They were Russian Tom Sawyers or Huckleberry Finns. But, for some reason or other, they did not turn up next day.

The officers themselves thought that the danger

from the Hunghuze would be great, and that if they attempted to enter any station where an Englishman was station-master, there would be a row, which might run like wild-fire round the world, and in which not only Russia and England but other nations as well might be involved.

They seemed greatly to relish, however, the prospect of coming directly into contact with these Englishmen, so troublesome, but so hard to get at; and the railway was always alluded to by them as the "English railway."

As is well known, of course, this Tsinmintun line had originally been almost an English strategic railway, run up from Shan-hai-kwan to a point as far north as Mukden, in order to counterbalance the Russian line on the other side of the Liao-ho, and to place the English in a position to watch Russia's descent from the north, and, if possible, to stop it. The previous relations of the Russians with the directors of this Chinese railway had not been of the most pleasant character. On July 8, 1900, they had grabbed the whole line and turned out Mr. Claud W. Kinder and his staff, a step which was somewhat resented in England, owing to the fact that the line had been chiefly constructed by British capital, and was, to a large extent, mortgaged to British bondholders. At Yinkow and elsewhere they had seized fifty miles of railway material, and all sorts of machinery and stores, and sent them all on to Port Arthur, and they behaved everywhere in the same rather high-handed fashion.

One thing that served to make the expedition popular among the Cossacks was their expectation that, unless they came in contact with the English, it would not be those stubborn Japanese that they would be called upon to fight, but the Chinese.

"I like fighting the Chinese soldiers," quoth Philipoff. "As soon as they let off their rifles they run away. And, glory be to God, in China I have now, one of noble birth! a chance of getting a better horse!"

And, as a matter of fact, during this raid, Philipoff once brought before me a Chinese farmer, who was feverishly anxious to swap his good horse for Philipoff's bad one; but as I was afraid that pressure had been brought to bear on the Celestial, I would not consent to the transfer.

Anyhow, whatever were the reasons, the fact remains that every one who went on this expedition was keenly envied by those who stayed behind. I myself was among the envied ones, for to my own surprise I was allowed to go. When I applied to Mishchenko for permission to accompany Colonel Plaoutine, I hardly dared to hope that permission would be granted me, but granted it was, instantly and cheerfully. It was rather a damper, however, on my enthusiasm to receive immediately afterwards a small packet containing an antiseptic bandage for wounds, and to hear the regimental doctor hurriedly explain to me how to use it, and assure me that I would probably need it before I came back.

Below I give a plan of our wanderings. The reader is warned, however, that he must not look upon it as a map, my object being only to give him a general idea of our route, and of the respective positions occupied by the villages which we visited.

We first crossed the Hun river and went to Erdagow, where we passed the night. Next day we crossed the Liao river at Kolama. This frontier stream is here very unimposing, flowing as it does through a

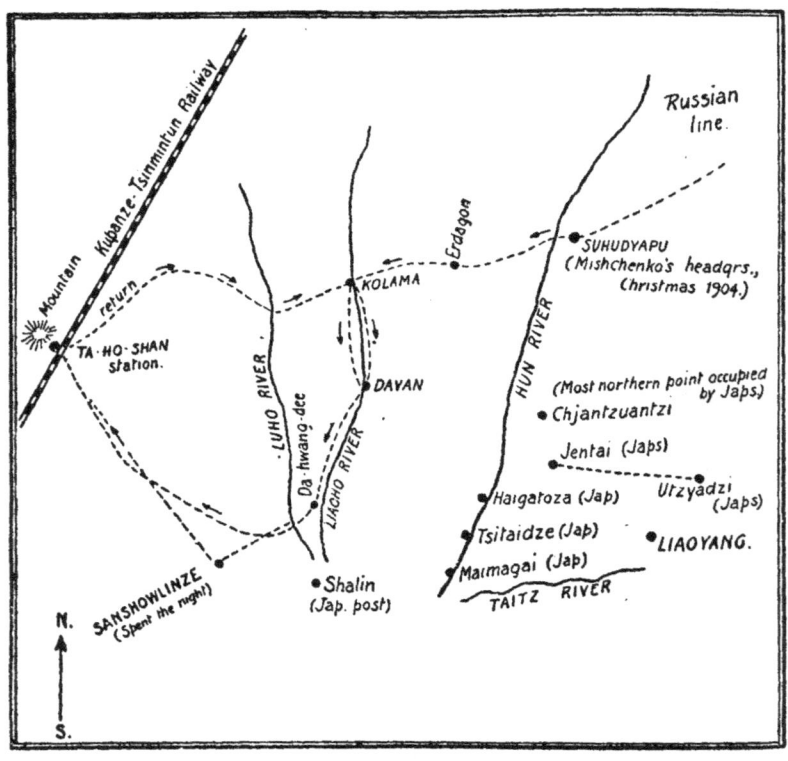

level plain, and being only a few hundred yards across. The ice was very firm, and would evidently have supported, without a groan, a railway train in addition to our two "sotnia."

We crossed in the teeth of an icy wind that filled me with a perpetual fear lest my ears, or nose, or feet, or some other part of my anatomy should get frost-bitten without my knowing about it, and I was continually putting my hands to these different sections of my body in order to ascertain if they were still there. The beards and moustaches of those who had got such appendages were thick with icicles, while horns of ice several inches long formed on the noses of the horses.

We rested for the night in a little village near the Liao, and on the next day set out towards Davan, one "sotnia" going down the left bank of the river, the other down the right. On the way we captured twenty armed Chinamen, who wore the uniform of soldiers, but most of whose rifles did not bear the Russian mark, and were therefore broken in pieces by the Cossacks.

I saved one of them, however—a German Mauser —for myself, and a large quantity of ammunition with it, and carried it until the end of the expedition. The colonel warned me that if the Japanese took me prisoner with this rifle in my possession, they would certainly shoot me; but, in spite of this, I continued to bear it. I did not mean to use it against the Japanese, but I did mean to use it against the Hunghuze in case I was left behind, wounded and dismounted. The prospect of being by some chance abandoned, unarmed, to a people who have reduced cruelty to a fine art, was one that did not appeal to me.

This bit of business done, we proceeded on our way: to our left a fringe of trees bordering the banks of the Liao, to the right a vast plain to which we could see no end. As we rode along, I noticed that something struck the ground sharply within a dozen yards of my horse, which, alarmed at the little puff of dust raised by the missile, whatever it was, swerved suddenly. I did not hear the report of firearms, but I was nevertheless under the impression that this was a bullet, fired from a great distance, probably by the Hunghuze, who caused us trouble later on, and the officers around me were of the same opinion. A few yards further on, a second bullet struck the ground, raising another handful of dust, but there was nothing further just then.

After crossing the Hun river we passed the night at Erdagow, and crossed the Liao-ho into Chinese territory at Kolama. At a place called Asin, near Kolama, we learned that a number of Japanese soldiers and Chinese ex-bandits had been there the day before, conveying grain to the Japanese army. We met several caravans of Chinese carts carrying grain and goods from Yinkow to Tsinmintun, so that it was evident that the Japanese were not interfering with the traffic along the road.

At Kolama we divided, and went down both sides of the Liao-ho as far as Davan, whence we proceeded to Da-hwang-dee, a great business centre, where, in summer, bean cake is shipped in large quantities down the river. We then went still further south to a point about thirty miles distant from Newchwang and twenty miles from the sea, and then, turning north-west, struck the Chinese railway at Ta-ho-shan, returning to Kolama by the more northerly route indicated in the map.

West of the Liao river, almost as far as the railway, there extended at that time a No-man's Land, with which I had previously been acquainted in works of

A CHRISTMAS WITH THE COSSACKS 141

fiction alone. My trip was like a plunge into the Scottish border of the sixteenth century. Instead of riding behind the Orange banner of the Cossacks, I seemed to be moving in the train of Shane O'Neil or Wallenstein. Instead of chasing Manchurian "Razboyneeke," I was chasing Irish Rapparees.

In this No-man's Land the villages were all fortified, in a humble way of course, but still fortified, with mounds and trenches. There was as a rule no drawbridge, only a very narrow path running through a gap in the ditch which surrounded the village. Inside the wall at this point there was always a little hut in which Chinese soldiers, with red-trimmed garments and an enormous Chinese character embroidered in crimson on the breast of each man's coat, kept watch and ward. On the eastern bank of the Liao-ho, the sole defensive weapons which the Chinese soldiers were allowed by the Russians to carry were long poles which for purposes of offence or defence were as pathetically and ridiculously useless as tooth-picks. On the western bank they were permitted to have rifles, so long as these rifles bore the Russian mark. The Russians were exceedingly apt to mistake them for Hunghuze and to shoot them on sight; while the Hunghuze always regarded them of course as natural enemies, so that, taking one consideration with another, the life of the almond-eyed guardian of the peace on the banks of the Liao-ho was at this time one of considerable anxiety. The same must be said of the unfortunate villagers whom these policemen were supposed to protect, for, though solitary bandits might be driven off, there was no chance of any village holding out against regular troops or even against the well-organised and well-armed bands of robbers who at that time patrolled the Liao valley.

Nevertheless, they seemed to have then collected inside their enclosures great quantities of "kiaoliang" stalks (for fuel) and of grain, and they used to keep their cattle there all winter, exactly as people did in troubled districts in Europe during the Middle Ages, as the names of many villages there still attest.

I used often, as I saw children staring at me, open-mouthed, from the mud-walls of the villages, to exclaim to myself: "What a training this is for a child!" And certainly, to live in a fortified village and frequently to see men killed is a unique if not a pleasant experience. But it was an experience our own fathers had.

Every village seemed to be a little republic. The elders ruled. Their married and unmarried children alike looked up to them for guidance. China seemed to have no representatives, civil or military, among them.

Lieutenant Burtin was astonished at this defencelessness of the Chinese.

"Why," he cried more than once, "this people deserve all they get. They have voluntarily disarmed themselves."

Nevertheless, his sensitive conscience was sometimes troubled about these poor Celestials. He did not like the way in which his Cossack orderly—who did not seem to have any conscience worth mentioning—commandeered Chinese forage, or crossed himself and said an elaborate grace over a chicken which he had not paid for; and although I once assured him that a lump sum was always given by our colonel to

A CHRISTMAS WITH THE COSSACKS 143

the village headman, I feel sure that he privately paid something on his own account so as to avoid any infraction of the Seventh Commandment. I may here mention that this young Frenchman was a very earnest Roman Catholic.

Owing to the severity of the winter the villagers had not much to do beyond gazing helplessly from their mud-walls on the different armed bands that rode within their ken. They crowded these walls as we approached, but wisely refrained from making any hostile demonstration. They always took the greatest possible pains, however, to induce us to go elsewhere. They invariably knew of a place a few "li" further on, where there were absolutely perfect houses—large, commodious, warm, overflowing with food and drink, and inhabited by kindly hearted people who simply doted on the Russians and had been waiting in vain for years an opportunity of entertaining them. We never managed, however, to find these people, or, if we did, they concealed their pro-Russian proclivities with remarkable success.

As we moved further west of the Liao river, we noticed a shade of difference in the character and even in the language of the people. There was also a slight change in the style of architecture. The houses were like this—

on the east side of the Liao; on the west they were often like this—

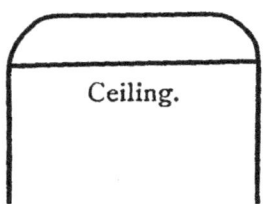

Many of the villages were very snug and prosperous, and some of the Chinese farmhouses were very fine, being (although I am an Irishman who says it) superior to the average Connaught cabin. In some places I saw attached to a single house a clean courtyard, large enough to hold a regiment; spacious underground cellars for garden produce in winter, symmetrical piles of "kiaoliang," strings of vegetables drying outside, great quantities of beans and sauces, and stores of beautiful silk dresses, for the members of the family of both sexes on festive occasions.

Whenever we came to a village no violence was used in turning the people out of the houses which we had decided to occupy. They were simply told to go, and they went,—to a neighbour's house, taking all their warm clothing and cooking utensils along with them. Some of the more respectable of these houses had, pasted on the walls of the rooms, the most indecent pictures, by native artists, that I have ever seen in my life. They were really so bad that we felt it would be almost criminal to allow even our polygamous Buriat Cossacks to soil their minds by gazing on them. In others there were strange and unexpected tokens of Western civilisation. One such token was a number of rude pictures, representing a railway train, a factory,

A CHRISTMAS WITH THE COSSACKS

filled with pig-tailed Celestials, and something that looked like an overhead street railway. In every village we found mugs made in Japan, although genuinely Western in style, and bearing representations of Japanese warships with hundreds of Japanese flags flying from them, and of gigantic porcelain factories labelled " Kobe, Japan."

In entering the larger towns we created somewhat of a sensation. At Da-hwang-dee, which is only about a day's march from Newchwang, the people did not know whether to laugh at us as missionaries or to run away from us as outlaws. I remember that we entered one largish town while a market was being held in it, and the effect which our sudden appearance had was magical. From the far end of the town we could see people hurrying from the scene with mules and donkeys laden with grain and provisions; those who remained behind stood in crowds on each side of the street, gazing at us with the appearance of people that had been suddenly petrified.

When we reached the centre of this town I gave the owner of a little street stall a Chinese twenty-cent piece for some of the small native cakes which he sold, whereupon he hastily offered me nearly his whole stock, while the bystanders audibly commented on the magnanimity of a person who, with twice a hundred armed men at his back, would consent to pay for anything.

I think that we could easily have got recruits if we wanted them, for at Shanlinze, not far from the railway, a young Chinese policeman, speaking about three words of Russian, came to offer his services as "boy" to any of us who wanted to employ him. None of us wanted him, but nevertheless he discarded his uniform and accompanied us for the next two days with his horse and rifle. The rifle was soon rendered useless, however, by one of the Cossacks, who extracted the lock; and this soldier of fortune was, later on, dropped unceremoniously *en route*, a suspicion that he was a spy having suddenly crossed our leader's mind. I believe myself that he was simply attracted by the blaze of martial glory which he saw pass through his native village in the shape of our humble selves, and I am afraid that he must have had a hard time of it afterwards, for if he escaped the Hunghuze, whom he professed to fear, he must have fallen into the hands of the Chinese authorities, who were doubtless aware of his desertion.

On December 23 I went to sleep as usual with all my clothes on, even to my cap and " polshubok," and at two o'clock next morning I was awakened and told that we were now about to set out on our march to Ta-ho-shan station on the Chinese railway. As we rode along, Colonel Plaoutine told me that the Chinese policeman who had enrolled himself in our band had brought him the cheerful information that this station was guarded by English soldiers. About the exact number of these soldiers he was uncertain. First he had said that there were one thousand men. Then he had considerately reduced the number to six. There was a delightful vagueness about this which prepared us for almost anything; but if there was only one English soldier there, I felt sure that he might fire a shot that would be " heard round the world."

Our colonel asked me somewhat nervously if it were possible that British soldiers occupied this station, and I answered that I did not know where they could have

A CHRISTMAS WITH THE COSSACKS 147

come from, unless some tremendous scheme of army reform had been suddenly put into operation since last I had had news from England. This grain of comfort was, however, modified by the lurid description which I gave of the *personnel* of the railway we were just going to tackle. At the head of it was Mr. Kinder, a violent Russophobe, married to a Japanese lady; while all the leading *employés*, down to the station-masters and conductors, were also Englishmen, and generally ex-soldiers. "Naturally," I added, "they all take their cue from Mr. Kinder," and I assured the colonel that if he asked one of these English ex-soldier station-masters to hand over his books to him for inspection, the Englishman would undoubtedly refuse and there would probably be bloodshed. On hearing this, the colonel became very grave, but said that he had been ordered to see the books and must see them, bloodshed or no bloodshed.

The rumour that the British were awaiting them had a very enlivening effect on the Cossacks. At last, then, they were to meet face to face this powerful, hostile people who had, from their sea-girt fastnesses, directed all the anti-Russian movements that had taken place in European and Asiatic politics for the last hundred years. I must say that the Cossacks never rode with such spirit to encounter the Japanese, against whom they never seemed to have any grudge.

It was an ideal Christmas Eve. The moon was very bright. The cold was intense. The cloudless sky was studded with stars, and deep silence reigned over the vast plain which we were traversing, a silence which was broken only by the creak of leather, the jingle of steel, and the steady, rhythmic ring of twice two hundred pair of horses' hoofs on the ground, which was frozen hard as iron.

Save for the furious barking of the village dogs, there was a deathlike stillness in the sombre and sleeping villages through which we passed, and, of course, not a light showed.

The village wells looked like the empty sockets of gigantic candlesticks, the broad sheets of ice spread all round them, and the rows of frozen drops hanging from the slabs of stone looking, in the white moonlight, like melted candle-wax.

Alternately trotting and walking, and dismounting for about five minutes every hour in order to ease our horses, we at length drew near to Ta-ho-shan. The mountain which gives its name to the railway station rose above the horizon, and as it rose there was first one faint flash of light from its summit, then another; and several voices in our party exclaimed simultaneously: "They are signalling!"

In one of his novels, Sir Walter Scott makes some Highlanders whisper to one another in a tone almost of awe the name of one of the great rivers of Scotland which they are approaching by night during war-time.

In approaching this Anglo-Chinese railway we experienced the same superstitious feelings. I say "we," for, owing to the danger that now threatened all of us in common, we had become one gigantic argus-eyed monster with two hundred pairs of arms and one soul, in which mine was, for the time being, merged,— a monster that was rushing forward, perhaps to destruction. To-night we could understand how those Highlanders felt, for, under certain conditions, a railway becomes almost as romantic and as awe-inspiring as a great river.

We felt that we were rushing into the lair of an alien civilisation. We had jumped at one bound from the tenth century into the twentieth, but it was not quite certain yet how the twentieth would receive us, for armed foreigners travelling in time of war are sometimes received unceremoniously when they attempt, during the night, to enter places that do not belong to them.

In the distance a railway engine whistled. It seemed an alarm, a tocsin, and we all broke into a "riceyou" (trot). Then the railway lights came into view over the brow of the hill, and a high column of grey smoke shifting spasmodically hither and thither indicated the whereabouts of a railway locomotive. After my plunge into the Dark Ages, I watched that moving column of grey smoke with as much interest as I had, when a child, gazed on a railway locomotive for the first time.

In another moment we had reached the track. The Cossacks were left several hundred yards behind, and only the Russian officers and myself crossed the line and mounted the platform.

There was no resistance. There were no English soldiers, and only a few Chinese sentries, who fled at our approach. It was dark, so we produced lights and went into the station-master's room. The station-master, a small, putty-faced young Chinaman, clad in that long robe which a Celestial seems to wear day and night, came towards us rubbing his almond eyes vigorously and repeatedly, and seeming to be considerably confused. He gazed in astonishment at his armed visitors, whose huge woolly busbies, superabundance of clothing, and icicle-laden beards and furs gave them on that Christmas morning the appearance of a number of Santas Claus.

Colonel Plaoutine at once asked if there was an English station-master, or any foreigners in the place. No, there were no foreigners there just then. Our leader, who seemed to be relieved on hearing this, then asked if he could see the books, at the same time picking them up in a casual sort of way and opening them. These books did not indicate, however, that the railway was carrying any contraband of war to the Japanese at Newchwang.

"Are there any Japanese here?" the colonel then asked abruptly.

"Oh, no!" returned the Chinaman, in a sad, reproachful voice, as if rebutting a charge of gross personal misconduct preferred against him by a friend, the last person in the world from whom he had expected such a stab.

When the ordeal was over, the colonel shook hands with the station-master and bade him good-bye, and the station-master said, "Please come again." He seemed to be uncertain whether he was dealing with Russian or English officers, or whether he was awake or dreaming.

It was still night when we left the station, but, by the time that we had found ourselves quarters in the neighbouring village, day was dawning. On this occasion, and on the following morning, the Cossacks' eyes were wide open with astonishment. "This is the English railway," they said, "but where are the English?" They had heard all their lives long about these Englishmen, and for them the great attraction of this trip was that it would bring them into close personal contact with these fabled beings; but, lo and behold! there were no Englishmen to be seen! It could not have been fear that had driven the English away, for the visit had been a surprise. No! the fact was that, just as those Englishmen had got the Japanese to fight Russia for them, so they were getting the Chinese to work their railway for them. Evidently they kept, as a rule, far in the mysterious background and pulled the strings.

The surprise of the Cossacks was all the greater owing to the contrast this railway presented to their own. The Russian line was alive with Russians—passengers, waiters, railway officials, clerks, peddlers, and functionaries of all descriptions. But here there was not a single white man to be seen. Engine-drivers, conductors, station officials were all Chinese; yet everything seemed to work smoothly.

"Where, then, are the English?" asked the Cossacks in chorus.

In the grey light of the early dawn a goods train came along from the south. It was chock-full of goods. What a contrast to the Russian line, which had for twelve months previous been carrying nothing to the front except soldiers and instruments of destruction, and nothing to the rear but wounded!

"It's a fine railway," remarked one of the officers briefly, as this long train slid slowly in and then came to a stop.

"Search the carriages for Japanese," said the colonel; but there were evidently no Japanese about. So, at least, I thought at the time; but I have since come to think differently. Seeing a Chinaman seated on a pile of corn bags in an open truck, I asked, not because I wanted particularly to know, but because I had nothing else to say, "Yeebin yo mayo?" ("Are there any Japanese about?"); and he replied by pointing to a depression in the pile of bags, on the edge of which depression stood, outlined against the eastern sky, one of those small, frayed, brown leather hand-bags which Japanese will, for some reason or other, persist in carrying with them wherever they go.

"By Jove! there's a Jap here, sure enough," I said to myself, as I clambered up on the truck so as to have a better view of the inside of the aforesaid depression. I was disappointed, however; for inside there peacefully slept a young Chinese, pigtail and all complete. Subsequent reflection has led me to entertain doubts, however, about the genuineness of that pigtail; but even had a Japanese soldier been there in full uniform, I should not, of course, have felt myself justified, under the circumstances, in making his presence known. It was not my business.

The passenger train from Tsinmintun was due at 9.30 A.M., and Colonel Plaoutine sent an officer and a Cossack guard to the station to have a look at it. They did no more. The Cossacks stared for all they were worth at the Chinese passengers with which the train was laden, and the Chinese passengers stared blankly at the weapons and the wolfish busbies of the Russians.

The station-master then appeared on the scene, and told us about some Russian deserters who had passed that way some days before. Having said this, he paused to see if we would confess that it was these

A CHRISTMAS WITH THE COSSACKS 153

deserters that we were looking after. He also told me in a confidential manner that he knew from the way I spoke that I was an Englishman, and then he tried to extract information out of me. In a flash I saw that he had become a different man since I had seen him last. Somebody had been galvanising this Oriental. He had had a wire from Peking, and it was no longer a Chinaman that I was dealing with, but the wizard Morrison or the astute Kinder.

"Philipoff," said I, turning to my Cossack, "you ask me where the English are. Well, the English are here."

At about two o'clock in the afternoon we started on our homeward march. On the way we picked up a flock of fine sheep, which we paid for. Soon after, when at a distance of about twelve versts from Ta-ho-shan, we selected a number of cattle, but the Chinese owners refused, in what seemed to me to be an obstinate and exasperating manner, to let us have them. We said that we would pay for them, but they said they did not want to take money. They would not sell their cattle; they wanted them back instantly. That was all. Amid the hubbub caused by this unexpected obstinacy, an incident that took place at the front escaped attention. A Cossack soon dashed in, however, at full speed to report it. One of the two men who always ride at some distance in front of the vanguard had been shot by a Hunghuze. Immediately, the cattle were relinquished and the sheep also, and we all started forward at the gallop.

"The Hunghuze! The Hunghuze!" was the word hat ran down along the line.

We seemed to think that it was merely a matter of

riding into a group of indifferently-armed robbers and slashing them to pieces, and were consequently as full of innocent glee as children who have been just released from school. Not one of us seemed to foresee at this moment the dreariness and the horror of the night which followed. We soon passed a poor Cossack lying on the ground with a broken arm. The "feldsher" was giving him first aid; his horse was standing beside him, and some of his comrades were helping him.

There was a village close by, and in front of it two parties of Cossacks dismounted and prepared to fire. In another instant the unfortunate hamlet would have been raked with bullets—for we did not know but that it might be filled with Hunghuze—but luckily our leader changed his mind and ordered his men only to advance and search the houses. Each party that advanced was headed by an officer, sword in hand; and the search which they made was remarkably thorough.

I accompanied the Cossacks into the village and was struck by the contrast between the set faces and resolute demeanour of the soldiers and the stupid countenances of the Chinese, who seemed unable to realise the danger in which they stood, and who kept feebly wailing in chorus "Hunghuze mayo .... Hunghuze mayo. ... Hunghuze dalyōko dalyōko." ("There are no robbers here. There are no robbers here. They are far away.")

One old man who was driving a little donkey which was attached to a big cylindrical stone under which corn was being ground, told us this over his shoulder and continued at his work. He did not seem to know how near he was to death.

While this search was going on, and while other parties of Cossacks were scouring the neighbourhood in all directions, the robber had met his doom. One of our vanguard had noticed him a few versts further on, riding in the plain, a most suspicious-looking object, mounted on a Chinese pony and armed with a rifle, and had charged down on him at once. The robber made no attempt to escape. Reining in his pony and unslinging his rifle, he calmly awaited the on-coming horseman, and, taking deliberate aim, had shot him at close quarters in the stomach. But the wound, though it finally proved mortal, failed to stop the career of the Russian, who had just time to give the Hunghuze a sword-cut that severed his jugular vein. Then the Cossack fell from the saddle that he never sat in again.

Before dying, the "razboyneek" made some remarkable statements. He said that he was one of Tulensan's men (Tulensan was the most formidable robber chieftain in Manchuria), and that there were a Japanese general (!) and ten Japanese officers among the Hunghuze all of whom were now paid by the Japanese. What interested us more was his statement that, in the village which we had occupied the previous night, there was a band of his brethren, a thousand strong, anxiously awaiting us, and that he was one of their scouts. A letter was found on his body and afterwards translated. It was addressed to his "fifth brother," also apparently in the Hunghuze business, but contained little of interest, being full of the obscure allusions to domestic details and pre-arranged plans which—with abrupt gaps between—are to be found in the letters of the uneducated all over the world.

In this letter he also asked his brother to buy rifles and ammunition for the band, these, as well as money, being scarce.

In no way did this document resemble any of the remarkable epistles found on the Japanese Hunghuze who were killed in Kobe and Tokio before the revolution of 1868, there being no patriotic allusions in it and no denunciation of foreigners. The writer never once seemed to rise above the level of the ordinary workaday highwayman, which was surprising, considering the manly way in which he had met his death.

I photographed him as he lay dead on the ground, which was ruddy with his blood. He was a strongly formed Chinese, somewhat above the middle height and between thirty and forty years of age. His dress was the blue dress of the ordinary native, the only thing distinctive about him being his new shoes, which resembled those worn by Chinese policemen. Either he had himself served in the police force, or else he had killed a policeman for his foot-gear. I am sure that the body was soon stripped by the local villagers for the sake of the clothes; but, if the dogs did not devour it, it must have lain there naked in a perfect state of preservation owing to the cold, for the next three months. We took the Hunghuze's pony and rifle. The latter was a Russian service rifle.

Darkness was now closing in, and the prospects in front of us were anything but cheerful. If we had come across that band of Hunghuze I am afraid that it would have fared but ill with us, had they all been as cool and as well armed as the gentleman we had just killed, for the two wounded men whom we had now on our hands greatly hampered our retreat. I could never have believed, had I not seen it, that two men could so impede the march of two hundred. They were both carried on stretchers, one by his comrades and the other by villagers who had been impressed for the purpose, and who were frequently replaced by fresh men from other villages that we passed through, and, as these bearers went on foot, we were all reduced to a very slow walking pace, which was as irritating to our horses as it was to us. If, at this stage, a few hundred Hunghuze had begun sniping us—and, even by night, it would not have been difficult for them to hit somebody in such a large body of men—there would have been nothing for us to do but to run for it, leaving such of our wounded as could not ride, to the tender mercies of the Celestials. If we did not do so, we should have been all cut off.

Needless to say, we kept a sharp look-out, for we expected an attack every moment. At seven o'clock we noticed a fire that looked like a signal, at a great distance to the right, and at the same time a powerful, steady, blood-red glow appeared on the horizon to our left. The peculiar appearance of the latter puzzled us until we found that it was the rising moon!

It was now out of the question for us to put up at any village in this dangerous neighbourhood, and our only hope lay in gaining, by a circuitous night march, comparative safety and the banks of the Liao.

For hour after hour I saw nothing but the same distant, dim horizon fringed with trees. The frozen ground sparkled in the moonlight with diamond-like points of frost. Every strip of white snow that gleamed in the distance seemed to me to be the longed-for Liao-ho, but, after being disappointed a hundred times, I began to think that we should never reach that friendly stream. Becoming impatient at the slowness of our progress I once rode on until I had almost reached the two horsemen who formed our extreme van. Then I looked back and, for a fraction of a second, a spasm of fear seized me. I was alone on this blasted heath between God and the world, and slowly towards me, with resounding jingle as of chains, crawled a long, dark dragon, an articulated monster, on whose bristles of steel the starlight flashed.

My horse was dead tired after the great work that he had done for the previous week, so that I walked a good deal on foot. I was probably more tired than he was, but then he was absolutely necessary for my safety. It is extraordinary what a lot of interest one takes in his horse during war-time. It becomes a part of one's own body, and is looked after with corresponding care. You are more alarmed at your horse's appetite falling off than at your own. You take a far keener interest in its hoofs than you do in your own corns. You frequently examine its back to see that it is not getting saddle-sores. You arrange the blanket under the saddle, with the same care as you would arrange a shawl on the shoulders of a fair lady. I can now understand why statues to great warriors always represent them on horseback. Another reason why I walked on foot was because that, in spite of my heavy furs, I felt freezing cold on horseback.

Owing to my fatigued condition and to the weight of my carbine and cartridges, I often lagged behind, whereupon the Cossacks would call out on Philipoff to wait for his master, "the gospodeen korrespondent"

(Monsieur le correspondant). When, finally, we did reach the Liao-ho, I was too tired to look at it. My only desire was to find a vacant " kang " in the village at which we stopped, and I must confess with shame that on this Christmas night I heard without an atom of sympathy—in fact only with irritation—the wail of women and children who were turned out of their beds and houses at that hour of the night to make room for the tired and desperate soldiery.

In the one unoccupied house which I and some officers at length discovered, we encountered unexpected opposition. The gate was barricaded, and when we climbed over the barricade we were met by three tall figures, all dressed from head to foot in white, who raised their arms and solemnly warned us not to enter. On finding that these people were Mahommedan Chinese and were in mourning for their father, whose dead body lay inside, we desisted in something like a panic and went elsewhere.

Late next night, when we were sleeping in another village on the east bank of the Liao, we were awakened by a scout, who came to tell us in a somewhat scared tone of voice that he heard a drum ("barabàn") beating in the village where we had slept the night before. Whether this eerie performance had anything to do with our attempt to enter the house of death I cannot say. We did not stop to see. But, trifling as it may seem, the faint roll of that Chinese drum, beating in the night on the frozen banks of the Liao-ho, impressed my imagination as strongly as anything that I saw or heard throughout the war.

CHAPTER IV

MISHCHENKO'S RAID

THE advance of Mishchenko's three columns was the best thing from the spectacular point of view which I saw during the war, and, if not very successful, it was, at any rate, the most daring enterprise which the Russians essayed.

On December 26, the day after the Russian Christmas, or January 8 with us, General Mishchenko crossed the Hun River, near Suhudyapu, at the head of twelve regiments, that is seventy-two squadrons of cavalry, with the object of destroying nine million roubles' worth of stores which the Japanese had accumulated at Yinkow for the use of their army, and which they had only left three hundred men to guard. The Russians had, of course, agents in Yinkow, who made them acquainted with these facts, and the expedition of Colonel Plaoutine, as well as various expeditions of other detachments of Mishchenko's command—one of which, carried out by the Tersko-Kubansky regiment, a force of Caucasian volunteers, went as far south as the Taitsze River—disclosed the fact that, with the exception of a few small and isolated Japanese posts at Shalin, east of Liaoyang, at old Newchwang, and in one or two other places, the road from Mukden to Yinkow, along the eastern bank of the Liao-ho, was practically open. Mishchenko would not, of course, refrain from destroying any force of Japanese or Hunghuze, or from burning any of the enemy's transports that he came across, but his main object was Yinkow.

Naturally this was kept secret, and in spite of all that has been said about the excellent, not to say miraculous, manner in which their Chinese agents served them, the Japanese did not seem to have suspected, until we had almost reached Yinkow, that our raid was anything more than one of the usual small Cossack forays against the Hunghuze. The cutting of the railway between Liaoyang and Yinkow in order to prevent the despatch of troops southwards, was a necessary part of Mishchenko's plan. I must say, however, that at first I did not know where Mishchenko was going to, and this secrecy made the expedition extremely attractive to my imagination. The Cossack officers said that we were about to march against China, and my profound ignorance of what was happening at that time in the outside world led me to believe it. There is a charm sometimes in being out of the world, in a place where you don't get your morning newspaper; news from the outside then becomes so beautifully vague! I had not seen any papers for months before, and I was not at all surprised, in consequence, to learn that this expedition would cross the Liao-ho and that it might be followed by trouble with England and the dismemberment of the Middle Kingdom. Why, this day week we might be stabling our horses in the Imperial Palace at Peking! "What's the game now?" I asked myself a thousand times as I walked along the frozen street of our village. " I would give anything to know. Is Russia going purposely to fasten a quarrel on China in order to extend the area of the war and to give an excuse for the seizure of Turkestan, Mongolia and even, perhaps, Peking?" There was nothing unlikely in this. England would cheerfully have done it in the grand old days before she had got tired of land-grabbing. But what an international sin! The stupendous nature of the crime appalled and fascinated me. It brought back memories of the Tsar Peter and of Frederick the Great. "I am now," said I to myself, "about to see the initiation of a movement compared to which the Russo-Japanese war is as nothing. I must therefore move heaven and earth for permission to accompany this raid."

The day before we started was the Russian Christmas Day, which, like good Christians, we observed by eating "kootia" and "varenookha" and by holding high revel. Strangely enough, it was in the midst of this revel that I first heard of the fall of Port Arthur. Colonel Orloff had ridden in, late at night, and his first words, uttered in a low tone to a brother officer, were "Port Arthur is fallen, is fallen." But few of the officers and none of the men knew it until weeks had elapsed.

Mishchenko had with him, in addition to his twelve regiments of dragoons and Cossacks, twenty-two cannon, that is almost three batteries. Two of these batteries fired melanite, the rest shrapnel. All of them were, of course, horse batteries, six horses pulling each gun. There were, besides, four Maxims with the Daghestan regiment, but these useful little guns were never, I think, used during the advance southward. We marched in three columns. The right column, which

MISHCHENKO'S RAID

THE COSSACKS CROSSING THE FROZEN HUN RIVER IN THE REAR OF THE JAPANESE

consisted of the Primorsky, Nerjinsky and Chernigovsky Dragoons and the Frontier Guards, was commanded by General Samsonoff, and until the main force reached the Taitsze it traversed the west bank of the Liao-ho.

The central column consisted of the Zaibaïkal Cossacks, that is, of the Verkhnyudinsky and Chitinsky regiments, and of the Ural Cossacks. It was commanded by General Abramoff, the leader of the Ural Cossacks, and General Mishchenko accompanied it.

The left column consisted of the Don Cossacks and of the Caucasian brigade. It was under the command of General Tyeleschoff and was followed by the Zaibaïkal battery, the soldiers of which bear in front of their black busbies a metallic scroll commemorating their bravery during the Boxer troubles. Besides, there was the mounted infantry, a fine body of men who should alone have carried Yinkow station on January 12. As is pretty well known, each Russian regiment of foot has attached to it about one hundred cavalrymen. As, under the conditions which then prevailed at the front, these horsemen were unnecessary there, they were all drafted for the time being into Mishchenko's detachment, which therefore amounted in all to some 7500 men. From this force different parties were from time to time detached for the purpose of cutting the railway, but of this hereafter. The four Maxims went with the Daghestan regiment of the Caucasian brigade, but it was not the Caucasians who were supposed to work these guns. Trained men had been brought from St. Petersburg for that purpose. They were under the command of Captain Chaplin, a promising young officer who had served in the artillery at Warsaw, but who was unfortunately the first man to fall on the occasion of this expedition.

On the afternoon of the first day all our different columns met at a village called Sifontai, east of the Hun river, and what a picturesque gathering that was! When I attempt to catalogue the different forces which composed it I feel inclined, like Homer, to call upon the daughters of Jove to assist me, for of myself I am not able to do justice to so vast a subject. It was one of the most composite forces that ever met together in Asia, a force worthy of "the mighty behemoth of Muscovy, the potentate who counts three hundred languages around the footsteps of his throne." It comprised Buriats, Tunguses, Baskirs, Kirghises, mountaineers from Daghestan, Tartars, Cossacks of Orenburg, Cossacks from the Don, children of the men who had won such victories in Italy under Suwaroff, who had captured Napoleon at Malo-Yaroslavetz, who had chased Jerome Bonaparte from his throne, who had pitched their tents in the Champs-Elysées, Buriats, whose race has produced "the most terrible phenomena by which humanity has ever been scourged . . . the Mongol Genghis Khan," descendants of the men who had followed the Scourge of God, flat-nosed Kalmuks whose very name recalls that great flight to China which De Quincey has immortalised, descendants of the Zaporogian Cossacks, that semi-religious order of bloodthirsty celibates who made their lair in the islands of the lower Dneiper. Mishchenko's force seemed to contain within it all the elements of a Yellow Peril, combined with a faint hint of a Moslem Peril.

Their green banners embroidered with red inscriptions in Arabic—all texts from the Koran—the Caucasians rode past on their graceful Arab steeds. Among them was a representative of every race and language in the Caucasus. They were those Mohammedan mountaineers who held Russia at bay for a century. All of them were splendid at single combat, and bore swords of the best tempered steel. The young men were often singularly handsome, with figures like Greek statues, oval heads, bold noble profiles, large dark eyes, delicately chiselled lips, and most murderous dispositions. It is impossible for me to give an idea of the proud dignity of their bearing, the grace of their movements and the fire of their look. They had got amongst them an extraordinary and valuable collection of fine Circassian swords and daggers, with damascened blades, often inlaid with gold, and always channelled so as to let the blood spurt out. Latin invocations to the Blessed Virgin inlaid in some of the blades seemed to indicate that they had changed hands as often as the poniard to which Lermontov devotes one of his poems. The sheaths of their numerous daggers terminated in a metal drop suggestive of blood. Their carabines they carried in covers of sheepskin with the hair outside, and they had also on their stirrups sheepskin covers, which are admirable protections against the cold. Later on I regretted exceedingly not having got such stirrup-covers myself.

The same thing always happened when a Caucasian mounted his horse. One caught sight of him poised for a moment on one stirrup while the horse reared and pranced; then there was a flop of variegated petticoats, a jingle of spurs, a rattle of weapons, and the rider had tumbled into the saddle and was telling his still prancing steed, in tones with more of admiration in them than of anger, that he was naughty, very naughty.

None of those Caucasians spoke any Russian, a fact which detracted seriously from their value as scouts. To make matters worse, there were in our little force of Caucasians about fifteen completely different languages, and it was very seldom that a man spoke more than two or three of those languages at most. The Russians explained this diversity of tongues by saying that every invader of Europe had passed through the Caucasus, leaving amid these mountains a handful of his people who immediately proceeded to form a new community, until, finally, that country became the ethnological museum it is to-day.

However they may rank as regular soldiers, there can be no doubt that in private life these Mohammedans are fierce. The first day I spent with them I saw one man draw his sword on another over some dispute about fodder. An officer, who was standing by, wearily told him to put up his weapon. " Reserve it for the Japanese," he said, and then he resumed an interrupted conversation about the latest opera at Bayreuth.

I do not know if Russia did a wise thing in sending these men out to Manchuria at all, for if there is any truth in the accusations of barbarity the Japanese have made, these Caucasians must—although nearly all of them are princes—have been the guilty parties. They are decidedly picturesque, it is true, but they are not much good against plain unimpressive foot soldiers. Then again, they came to Manchuria under a misapprehension. They thought the war with Japan would be run on exactly the same lines as the war with China ; and they cannot be blamed for falling into this mistake, since their officers also thought so. As soon as they had ascertained that the Japanese were not naked savages, armed with bows and arrows, they got discontented and wanted to go home, but were refused permission to do so, whereupon many deserted and were immediately caught and shot.

The Russian non-commissioned officers amongst these Caucasians belong to the Cossacks of Kuban and Terek, the " line of the Caucasus," names of rivers which recall bloody battles and the memory of the unhappy Lermontov. Up till a short time ago they fought continuously against these fierce Tcherkesses, whose arms and equipment they have adopted, and whose very features they seem to have borrowed—a fact which is explained by a venerable custom these Cossacks still have of massacring all the men in an *aoul* and conveying the best looking women to their " Stanitzi " in order to marry them.

Like the Transbaïkal and unlike the Ural or Don or Black Sea Cossacks, these Caucasians have no lances, but depend altogether on their good sabres. Among them rode the grandson of Imum Schamyl, who within the memory of living men troubled Russia with a guerilla warfare, which he conducted with a genius and energy scarcely paralleled in history. The St. George's Cross, which the aged standard-bearer of the Daghistan regiment wore, was won on the day that Schamyl surrendered.

At the head of the Caucasian brigade was Prince Orbelliani, of an ancient Georgian family, which claims to be descended from two Chinese princes who obtained in 240 A.D. the protection of Artaxerxes, whose son Sapor transferred them with their followers to Armenia. Prince Orbelliani did not, however, take part in the raid, being sick at Harbin, but his place was taken by an equally picturesque figure, Prince (Han) Nahitchivansky, a Mohammedan nobleman. The adjutant of Prince Nahitchivansky bore the name of Hadji Murat, a name which speaks for itself.

The names of the officers with whom I rode were all historical. Some of them are borne by the oldest Cossack families—Grekoff, Plaoutine, Platoff, Kaznetzoff, Krasnoff. One young colonel from the General Staff, who accompanied us bore the name of that gigantic barbarian who loved Catherine the Great and who strangled her Imperial husband. He is a polished diplomatist, a great linguist, a landowner, a courtier, an influential man at headquarters. He rode on this occasion a horse which was almost worth its weight in gold, and, according to his invariable custom on such occasions, carried in his pocket a copy of one of Shakespeare's plays. His knowledge of English literature and of every *nuance* of expression in the English language is extraordinarily extensive.

The colonel of the regiment to which I was attached was called Bunting, and was of English descent. One of the officers, a polite and well-educated young man from the Guards, was of Tartar descent, as his name, Turbin, indicates. Another was young Burtin, at one and the same time lieutenant in the Arab cavalry of France and centurion in the Mongol Cossacks of Mishchenko.

To make our crowd still more variegated, there was a

MISHCHENKO'S RAID

full-blooded negro in it. He had been born in the Caucasus, spoke only Russian, and seemed to be exactly on an equality with his white comrades-in-arms. With the exception of Burtin, I was the only non-Russian at this memorable trysting-place in the valley of the Liao-ho.

However much I might try to persuade myself that the Cossack is a thing of the past, I could not fail to be impressed by this great gathering of the men who guard the Russian frontier from the shores of the Pacific to the shores of the ebony and amber sea, and whose very designation, recalling the names of great rebels like Mazeppa, Stenka Razin, Pugatcheff, the false Dimitri, made me see, dimly, gigantic upheavals more Asiatic than European, and made me hear faintly, as at a great distance, the hoof-beats of innumerable hordes of horsemen galloping over the steppes. The Cossacks cannot fail to be interesting, for they are the only reminder we have left of the time when the population of Europe was fluid and nomad.

How many shades of Christianity, Mohammedism, Lamaïsm, and Buddhism there were amongst us I dared not inquire. When at set of sun I saw the Mohammedan pray with face turned towards Mecca, I felt as if I were in a Turkish army. When I saw the Russian kiss the collection of ikons and crucifixes that he wore around his neck, I felt as if I were among Crusaders. When the indolent Mongol laughed at both Mohammedan and Christian, I felt that I was back in my own century.

Thus we marched along in peace, each praying to God in his own way, some not praying at all. We were an overflow from the great Muscovite crucible, in which all sorts of strange undigested elements boil and bubble without ever uniting; and behind us came a helter-skelter of little cows trampling in a cloud of dust, beef still on the hoof, driven with blows of whip by a warlike people in migration.

I have already said that I was with the left column, but I could make out distinctly with the naked eye the long line of horsemen composing the central column. These horsemen were generally on the very verge of the horizon, and owing, I suppose, to the clearness and dryness of the air, their figures were frequently silhouetted with marvellous distinctness against the void of heaven, so that they looked like the little bronze Cossacks of Lanceray or Gratchoff, and that, in spite of the distance, I could see white atoms of dazzling sky between the horses' legs as they moved. To our left rode a strong flanking party, and, in all, the length of front swept by the three columns could not have been less than five miles.

It must not be imagined, of course, that there were five solid miles of soldiers. We only moved four or five abreast, so that each column resembled a long snake crawling slowly southward. The central column was connected with the right and left columns respectively by a network of scouts, who passed continuously between them.

As the scouts in front and rear and on the flanks were regularly relieved, there was no chance whatever for a strange horseman to accompany us without being observed. It would go hard, I am afraid, with any Japanese scout who attempted to get a view of us, even a long-distance view, for without doubt he would have been immediately "spotted." Once, in the rolling dust, Colonel Bunting became doubtful about the character of a solitary horseman who was riding on our left, and at a word from him a Caucasian sped off like an arrow to investigate. So well did we sweep the country with our scouts that game and domestic animals fled before us for miles. A hare ran in front of us all the way to Yinkow, and though again and again the Cossacks tried to overtake and kill it with their "nagaïké," it invariably escaped them.

This the Russians seemed to regard as a serious matter, but they laughed very much at the way in which all along our line of march young horses, mules and donkeys broke away from their Celestial proprietors and enlisted under our banners. These innocent beasts had never before seen such a collection of their species, and were probably under the impression that it was a great equine rebellion against mankind. If so, they were quickly disillusioned, for we soon caught and saddled them.

It must be admitted that the country was not the very best for horsemen, the land being all cultivated with the usual terrible thoroughness of the Chinese agriculturist, and traversed by interminable little ridges, which are bad enough for horses in any case, but which were rendered worse on this occasion by the countless millions of sharp kiaoliang stalks with which they were covered.

On the first night after crossing the Hun river we halted at Sifontai, and next day we faced south, and continued marching south until we reached Yinkow.

On the very day on which we reached Sifontai our scouts reported a conflagration in a village towards the south-east, but I should have concluded that it had no significance and was probably an accidental fire had it not been for what happened next evening.

On the second day we reached a village called Yowdyeze, near the confluence of the Hun and the Liao rivers, and it was here that we came for the first time into contact with the Japanese. Towards evening our foremost scouts overtook a small party of the enemy, who were conveying a transport train consisting of twenty Chinese carts filled with hay and kiaoliang.

The main body of our column—that is, the right column—had no sooner reached these carts than we noticed an enormous cloud of black smoke rise from an adjoining village and hang suspended in the still air, a portentous omen to us and a warning to all the Japanese for scores of miles around. I had been previously disposed to scoff when I heard the Russians declare that every flash of light or column of smoke which they saw in the distance was a "signal;" but there could be no doubt about the nature of this conflagration, for an officer of the Tersko-Kubansky regiment who entered the village found that the burning house was surrounded by empty tins of kerosene, the contents of which had evidently been poured over the building.

It was on this day that I saw the last of my friend Burtin, the French officer, who was killed the next day. He had ridden over from the central column to my column, that is, the left column, along with a young sotnik of the name of Turbin, who was accompanied by about a dozen Verkhnyudinsky Cossacks, and I can still see him bent forward, Arab-like, on his Cossack saddle, the refined, eager face of the enthusiast scanning the horizon, and oblivious to everything in the near vicinity.

When night came on we could see fire after fire being kindled in the east, one further away than the other, the remotest probably burning within easy distance of Yentai. They were certainly signals, and as from a hillock I watched the "ghastly war-flame" speed eastwards, I could not help recalling Clytemnestra's description of the watch-fires which brought to Argos the news of the fall of Troy, and at the same time thinking how much inferior after all is the vivid imagery of the most warlike poetry to the bald truth of the "real thing."

On the morning of December 28 (O.S.) we got ready before dawn—although, of course, there was not much to get ready, for we travelled as lightly as possible, and our horses were always kept saddled—and assembled to hear the order of the day in a vast sandy valley, one of those bits of the great Gobi desert that break out here and there like a rash on the smooth face of the interminable ploughed land.

The scene was peculiarly striking. The sandy waste and the dunes, red with the kindling fires of the east, on which the figures of horsemen stood motionless as Arabs at prayer, and sharply outlined against the glowing sky, reminded me of pictures I had seen of Morocco and the Sahara. The crimson light of dawn streamed over the bare hillsides, and if one ascended a cliff and looked down on the troops gathered in the glen below, he could not but be struck by the rich oriental colouring of the scene. Only Salvator Rosa could do justice to such a sight.

When I gazed on this interesting spectacle from a

hillside and with the rising sun at my back, the extraordinary mixture of colours came out very effectively; but when I descended the hill and looked at the Cossacks with my face turned towards the sun there was no colour, only one uniform dark grey, and no details of the figures before me, only silhouettes.

It was clear to us all this day that something big was afoot. The signals of the night before had probably prepared the men for something, and you could not fail to notice that they were prepared by the vigilant glances they threw around them and the care with which they scouted. I happened to be riding on this occasion with the advance guard, not because I wanted to see the first shot fired, but because I had mistakenly supposed when it started that it was the main body.

As our strong fresh horses bounded beneath us over the illimitable plain I began for the first time to understand the delight which the soldier takes in war. I had not been able to understand it previously, having been mostly occupied during battle in mournfully sitting on a bare hillside watching the Japanese shells creep closer and closer, and scribbling in my notebook instructions regarding the disposal of my horse and camera. That sort of warfare drives fear into the marrow of one's bones, but on horseback, his lungs filled with ozone, and his eyes bright with health, I think that even the coward gets an infusion of courage sufficient to make him laugh in the teeth of death, or at all events to bear himself like a man until the ordeal is past.

As a pastime pursued for its own sake, war—of the kind which old Mishchenko gave us on that occasion—

leaves fox-hunting far behind. In both cases you have the hard riding and the open air and the glorious sweep of country; but in war you have the piquant spice of danger, and even if you are a non-combatant the intoxicating sense of power, without which a ride across country will ever afterward seem to you like salad without vinegar, like an egg without salt. Little wonder, then, that when, on the day after the fight at Yinkow, I left my orderly, my Caucasian friends and Mishchenko in order to ride into a part of the country that had not yet been visited by the belligerents, I felt like Brigadier Gérard after Waterloo, and determined to get back to the army again as speedily as possible.

Nearly every Cossack engagement opens in the same way. A Cossack scout rushes back breathlessly to his leader, and somehow or other there is never any mistaking the news he brings. On two occasions, at all events, when I marked the agitation of the courier and the fleetness with which he rode, and noticed our leader bend forward in his saddle in an attitude of keen expectation, I said to myself, "Something serious has happened," and on both occasions I was right—a man had been shot. One of these occasions was the present, but when the man reached Colonel Bunting and saluted, he gasped and remained silent. It was not that he was wounded or breathless. The reason of his silence was that he was a Caucasian and unable to speak a word of Russian. A few moments before, the first rifle had cracked, and Staff-Captain Chaplin had fallen from his horse, shot through the heart.

An interpreter having been found, Colonel Bunting succeeded in ascertaining from the Caucasian scout that there was a band of Hunghuze in the vicinity of a village called Lee-quee-shou. He therefore gave the order to charge, and the Tersko-Kubansky and the Donsky Cossacks received at the same time a similar command. The Hunghuze were on the opposite bank of the Hun river—we were not far now from the point where the Hun joins the Liao —and had apparently fired at us from behind one of the earthen mounds which the Chinese have constructed for scores of miles along the banks of the river in order to protect their fields from inundations. The Cossacks, therefore, crossed the ice (*see* photo.) and swept like a whirlwind on the Hunghuze. The memory of that charge will remain with me the longest day I live.

The horses rushed across the plain at a speed which one could scarcely have believed possible considering the nature of the ground, and, amid the clouds of dust raised by their horses' hoofs, the swords of the Cossacks flashed. The Hunghuze scattered so rapidly that I could form no idea of their number, but some officers put it at five hundred. Many of them stood their ground bravely, firing on the Russians until their heads were cloven by the Caucasians, who did not, I must say, keep them waiting long. They did not fall in heaps, however, as you see in battle pictures, but were very widely scattered over an immense plain, so widely that I only saw two corpses, both corpses of Chinamen, dressed like the Hunghuze we had killed during Plaoutine's raid, and with nothing remarkable about them.

There can be no doubt but that this band of robbers was in the service of the Japanese, otherwise we should not have found them down there in the rear of the Japanese army. Besides, we captured from them a Japanese flag bearing a Chinese inscription meaning "the right camp of the left wing," a " camp " in the Chinese army consisting of five hundred soldiers. They were all hardy, well-formed men in the prime of life, and they rode good Chinese horses, but did not carry any swords or lances. Their Japanese instructors had evidently taken great pains to drill them, and on this occasion they were a credit to their teachers.

Somewhat further south our central column got into a far stiffer fight. Near the confluence of the Hun with the Liao there is a small walled village called Shoutoze, and in this village several hundred Japanese infantry-men held out with characteristic obstinacy for all the rest of the afternoon, thus delaying us by half a day, and incidentally saving Yinkow.

The Verkhnyudinsky Cossacks were ordered to dismount and advance against them, and they did so with great courage, their officers going in front. The first report we got was that the Cossacks were driven back and two of their officers wounded, one of these wounded officers being afterwards carried inside the village by the Japanese. But next morning we saw the leathern-coated men from Verkhnyudinsky advancing with the rest of us, and heard that they had taken the village on the previous evening, all the Japanese being killed or dispersed. Unfortunately, two brave young officers of the Verkhnyudinsky Regiment lost their lives on this occasion, one Nekrasoff, a "sotnik" or centurion of great bravery, who had previously been wounded twice during the present war, and the other Ferdinand Burtin, the French officer of whom I have already spoken.

Burtin had gone forward on foot to attack a village with the "sotnia" to which he was attached, but was shot in the leg and fell to the ground, when he had come within a hundred yards of the enemy. If he had remained quite still he would have been safe, but he raised himself to a sitting posture and waved his sword as a sign for his men to come in, whereupon he immediately got one bullet through the head and another through the chest, and died soon afterwards, without saying anything. The official paper of the army afterwards came out with a long eulogistic account of him. Lieutenant Burtin was not a personage, he was only an ordinary French officer, but he fully maintained the French officer's high reputation for bravery, skill and courtesy, and deeply the Cossacks of the Transbaïkal "voisko" mourn the loss of the gallant foreigner who could not tell them how he sympathised with them, but whose actions spoke louder than words. He was buried before dawn next morning, January 11, General Mishchenko and all his staff being present, and the same day we crossed the Taitze and advanced on old Newchwang. Not all of us went that way, however. The Primorsky Dragoons cantered off toward Ta-shih-chiao in order to blow up some of the railway, and thus prevent the Japanese from bringing troops into Yinkow by rail. To hear these officers talking lightly of riding over to Haicheng and Yinkow made us almost inclined to imagine that we were back in January 1904, and that the fall of Port Arthur and the defeats at Vafangow, at Liaoyang and on the Shaho were merely dreams. I, for one, was inclined to rub my eyes when I saw again in the distance the familiar hills of Ta-shih-chiao.

On the previous day a mixed detachment, composed of half a "sotnia" of the Chitinsky Cossacks, half a "sotnia" of the Verkhnyudinsky Cossacks, and half a "sotnia" of the Uralsky Cossacks, had been despatched eastwards with a good supply of nitroglycerine in order to cut the railway north of Haicheng. They accomplished this task with the greatest ease and expedition, but in such a way that the line could be repaired again in a few hours. When they reached the railway there were only a few of the enemy there, and these retired without firing a shot, whereupon the Cossacks proceeded to look for a bridge underneath which they might plant their explosives. Unfortunately they could not find any bridge, so they had to content themselves with blowing up part of the line—damage which the Japanese probably made good in a very short time.

A detachment of the Tersko-Kubansky regiment reported that it had destroyed five hundred mètres of the railway at another point, and at four o'clock next morning an explosion from the direction of Tah-shih-chiao led us to conclude that a bridge on the Tah-shih-chiao-Yinkow line had been blown up. But this could not have been the case; for just before our attack on Yinkow two trains came through, probably from the south.

At old Newchwang we had another tussle with the Japanese. Fifty of them occupied a house there, and as we could not afford to waste time taking it, we contented ourselves with making prisoners of two or three wounded officers—who, by the way, spoke Russian tolerably well—and then we pushed further south.

At old Newchwang there was the usual litter of

Japanese telegraph and telephone poles and wires, and more than the usual capture of transports. In fact, too much time was spent, I think, in burning these transports, which included clothing, kerosene, provisions and ammunition. Hundreds of cattle and sheep were also taken and driven before us. Every Cossack had a small bag of flour at his saddle-bow, and the Japanese must have found the tracking of him closely to resemble a paper chase, for his route was marked by empty boxes of "Peacock" and other brands of cigarettes which the Japanese soldier loves, and which the Cossack had now got hold of.

On the night of the 11th there were no less than two huge conflagrations reddening the horizon. They were Japanese transports on fire. We spent that night in the village of Hundyatun, twenty miles from Yinkow, and in the morning we set out with the determination of reaching our destination before sunset. We passed on our way still another flaming transport. On this last day the extraordinarily mild weather that had favoured us thus far, still continued, but unfortunately the warm sunshine thawed the surface of the cultivated earth, so that whenever there was a breeze blowing from any point of the compass we rode amid dense clouds of dust. Of the Cossacks a few yards in front of me I could only see a faint grey outline, like figures of men on an over-exposed photographic plate, and I could hardly recognise the officers who rode beside me, so powdered were their beards and faces with the grey dust.

The country became richer as we approached nearer to Yinkow, the villages far more prosperous, and the land even better cultivated. I was under the impression that we were still at a considerable distance from our destination when, at about 4 P.M., boom! went a gun on the right, and a little cloud of shrapnel burst over a village, which was situated, as I afterwards discovered, a short distance in front of the Niuchatun Railway station. Boom! boom! boom! went other guns, and then came the rattle of a heavy musketry fire, and we knew that the fight had begun.

Early on the morning of this day a Chinaman whom we met at Hundyatun had told us that there were only three hundred Japanese soldiers at the Yinkow railway station, and that there were no soldiers at all in the town. Our officers had been of the opinion that a party of Cossacks would be sent to smash up the Japanese administration buildings while the rest of us were burning the stores at the station, but, just before the fight began, General Mishchenko communicated to his officers his plan of action, which was as follows:

The Japanese, who were found to be strongly intrenched in front of the station, would be shelled and then attacked by a mixed force composed of detachments from the Tersko-Kubansky and other regiments, amounting in all to about one thousand men. If this attack were successful the Japanese stores would be set on fire, and then the Russians would fall back as fast as they could. Fearing that indiscriminate looting and subsequent complications with foreign Powers would take place if the Cossacks entered the town, the general forbade them to enter in any case.

Just as we approached Yinkow a train filled with soldiers rushed in from Ta-shih-chiao. It was made up of sixteen trucks, and, calculating that each truck could accommodate forty men, it must have brought the strength of the garrison up to about a thousand; that is, it made them equal in strength to the attacking party, which had, therefore, of course, no chance, especially as the Cossacks were without bayonets and had no skill whatever in attacking intrenched infantry. It is a truism to say that cavalry can do nothing against an equal force of infantry calmly lying behind earthworks, with their eyes on the sights of their rifles. Our Cossacks dismounted, of course, and advanced to the attack sword in hand, but they suffered seriously from the Japanese fire, and could make no progress. The courage of the Cossacks seems to be outside of themselves (to apply to them what Tacitus said of the Sarmates), for once dismounted they are lost.

Among those killed in our brigade was Captain Koulibakine, a wealthy and fashionable officer of the Horse Guards, who had volunteered for the war.

Meanwhile the bulk of Mishchenko's force was held in reserve. I was with the Caucasian brigade on the left flank, that is, on the railway, where for some reason or other it was suspected that an attempt would be made to flank us. These suspicions were increased by the fact that a few shots were fired on this part of our line, but these shots were probably fired by isolated Japanese volunteers, or perhaps by our own scouts, who mistook one another for the enemy. Luckily, however, no harm was done, only two horses wounded, I think. But the fear of an enemy who was not there kept us close to the railway line until five o'clock, when the fight ceased.

About half-past four, a Chinese building in front of the station and another on the railway line burst simultaneously into flames, and many of us thought that the former building was the station itself, or, at least, some of the buildings in which the Japanese stores were kept. But the murderous fire of the enemy still continued, and it was easy to see that we were making no progress. Just then an imperative order from General Mishchenko reached us. It was to the effect that we must at once retreat as quickly as we could to a village seventeen versts north of Yinkow, and we lost no time in doing so. There was not the slightest panic or disorder in our retreat, and I do not think that there was the slightest panic or disorder in any of the other detachments. The general had evidently given himself an hour to do the work he had got to do at Yinkow, and had decided beforehand to leave, directly that hour was up.

It was too dangerous to remain, especially with such a composite force. If a night attack had been carried out, these different races in our brigade might very probably have come into collision, each under the impression that the other party was the enemy. With the stores at Yinkow station left uncaptured, the success of the raid was, however, incomplete. It was a pity we did not destroy these stores. A little more would have done it.

I have just said that we got orders to fall back on a village seventeen miles north of Mukden. We did so in good order, and reached our destination in two hours. It was a smart piece of work all round, for all the other regiments were there before us, all except the Verkhnyudinsky and the others that were guarding our rear. Unfortunately the village in question was too small to hold us all, so that most of us—including the present writer—had to sleep out in the open, by no means a pleasant experience in Manchuria at that time of the year.

We heard next morning that 20,000 Japanese had assembled at Haicheng and were going to cut us off by establishing a network of infantry posts from that city right across to the Liao River; but neither this information nor the more startling news that a Japanese infantry force was advancing towards us from the east of Yinkow caused us to hurry in the least.

By eleven in the morning we still occupied that village, or, rather, the surrounding country, for the village was just large enough to contain General Mishchenko's staff and no more, and were looking after our wounded and making preparations for our journey north. Before noon, however, the Caucasians advanced to the south-east, covering the artillery, which had been ordered to shell the approaching infantry. The infantry did not approach, however, so that in the afternoon Mishchenko marched due north with great rapidity, as if he intended to retreat the way he came. The Japanese probably expected that, and had made every preparation to give him a warm reception as he crossed the Taitsze and Hun Rivers. But just when it seemed certain that he was heading direct for the trap that had been prepared for him, the wily old Cossack swung suddenly to the left, and was on the west bank of the Liao before the Japanese could properly realise what had happened. Next morning the enemy had also crossed to the other side of the Liao, but Mishchenko made it hot for them from eight o'clock to nine with his artillery. Then he moved on until he reached the main Russian army.

CHAPTER V

HOW I LEFT MISHCHENKO

WHEN Mishchenko made his attack on Yinkow I determined that if it was successful I would cross the river and, from the neutral territory on the other side, send off a telegram to my paper describing our success. I was told that there was a censor at the telegraph office on the right bank, so I offered to take him back alive if they sent a Cossack with me, explaining that the gratification I would thus confer on the correspondents with the Japanese would be almost beyond human conception. The detachment with which I was connected made its attack on the Japanese left wing, however, so that I was a long way from the river, on whose frozen surface I could nevertheless see reflected the light from the blazing house near the railway station.

Seldom in my life did I experience keener vexation than when the Cossacks galloped north without having done anything, and I went with them.

"Here," I said to myself, "is a magnificent opportunity lost! I could have struck west towards that burning building and crossed the river in its glare. But now, alas! it is too late."

So angry with myself did I feel that I kept a continual look-out on our left for the Liao-ho, and if we had come within sight of it again, I should certainly have crossed it, although I now realise that under the circumstances it would have been an excessively dangerous and foolish thing to do. Not to mention the risk I should run from Chinese, Japanese, and Russians, I should almost certainly be drowned if I attempted to cross the river on horseback at this point; for, near Yinkow, it had not been quite frozen over that year, and even where I did cross it much higher up, next day, I had to take the advice of a local resident and to travel under his direction in a very zig-zag manner, otherwise I should have infallibly gone through the ice in several places.

At last I caught the glitter of the moonlight on a great sheet of ice, and without further ado I informed Colonel Bunting that I was going to cross the river.

"But that's not the river," said he, "that's a lake You're a long way from the river now."

These words convinced me that it was hopeless to try to get away that night, but I made up my mind to get off next morning; and, when next morning came, I took advantage of our delay in setting out to tell Colonel Bunting that I was determined to leave him, to cross the Liao-ho, and to send off my telegram from the town of Tenshwantai above Newchwang, but on the Chinese side of the river.

He told me that Mishchenko would cross the Liao-ho himself a little further north, and that I might as well accompany him for some distance; but, having studied the map, I thought it would be better for me to strike due west at once. Besides, the further north I went the greater danger I ran from the Hunghuze, whom I feared very much more than I feared the Japanese.

Accordingly I induced Colonel Bunting to write me a statement to the effect that I had left the regiment with his permission in order to cross the Liao river, send off a telegram from neutral territory, and afterwards return to the Russian army by way of Tsinmintun. This document proved useful later on, when I did return to the Russians and found them labouring under the delusion that I was a traitor.

I next engaged the Manchurian who had guided us to Yinkow to guide me across the Liao-ho. He was a young dare-devil of nineteen or twenty, probably a bandit, and if the Japanese had caught him I am afraid that he would have had a short shrift, for in his purse were the rouble notes which he had received from his Russian employers. I might also mention the fact that I carried some telegrams which the commander of our brigade had casually asked me to send for him; and though they were apparently private messages, the Japanese might have made short work of me too if they had found them on me. Worst of all, however, I carried on my person rouble notes to the value of about one thousand pounds sterling. At this time it was necessary for a correspondent on the Russian side to carry these large sums of money with him, as he never knew when he might have to send off a telegram which would require every kopeck he had got, for the Russian telegraph officials would not adopt the "receiver-to-pay" system that obtains elsewhere. And if a Japanese or Russian scout had caught me, searched me, and found all this money on me, I am extremely afraid that he would not have spared my life.

At first our young Manchurian guide was very reluctant to go with me, but when our regular regimental Chinese interpreter had told him that I was Yingwa (English), and therefore a great favourite with the Japanese, his hesitation was at once overcome.

In order to get past the lake which lay to our west, I had to ride some distance to the south—that is, in the direction in which a body of Japanese infantry was said to be advancing to attack us; and I felt excessively uneasy, therefore, until I was able to ride due west.

As soon as I got clear of the Russian scouts I took off the Cossack jacket which I wore; but my Astrakan cap, my high boots, and a number of other things gave everybody I met the impression that I was a Russian soldier. Besides, it is nothing less than mysterious how closely one comes to resemble, even in face and manner, a foreign people among whom one has lived for any length of time.

On approaching the first village on my line of march my heart beat rapidly, for the heads of all the inhabitants thereof were visible above the earthen wall which surrounded the hamlet, and it was as likely as not that somebody would have a pot-shot at me. I passed through in safety, however, and, in four or five hours, was near the Liao-ho.

These four or five hours were not, however, among the most agreeable which I have spent in my lifetime, for the eyes were ready to start out of my head with the strain of keeping a look-out for Japanese. At one place I saw ten or twelve horsemen on the verge of the horizon, but my guide told me that they were Chinese peasants: and, anyhow, we did not encounter them. As a rule I made out distant objects myself, and I was surprised and gratified at the accuracy I had acquired; for I remembered that at the battle of Ta-shih-chiao I had been practically unable to see anything of the enemy, while the officers around me were able to see them easily.

Having at length come near to the Liao-ho, I was horrified to discover casually from my guide that there was a Japanese guard in Tenshwantai, and I made no secret of my alarm.

"But I thought you were a friend of the Japanese?" gasped my young Hunghuze.

I tried to explain that I was not fighting against them, and had nothing to fear from them except delay, which, considering the business I was on, would have been fatal; but all this failed to reassure the youth, who now came evidently to the conclusion that I was, like himself, a dangerous outlaw. I sometimes heard him discussing me in the villages through which we passed. He always referred to me as the "p'ing" (soldier), and did not, I think, give the inhabitants a very reassuring account of me. He took to lagging behind in a very sulky manner, and I began to wonder if his object was to shoot me from the rear—for he was armed—and then, in good old Celestial fashion, to carry my head to the Japanese as a peace offering. I induced him, however, to bring me to a crossing-place some four or five miles north of Tenshwantai; and when I finally did—albeit not without some difficulty—effect a crossing at this point, under the guidance of a middle-aged Celestial, who trembled with fear as he stared at my strange accoutrements, I felt as elated as if I had discovered the North Pole.

It was not quite a safe place, however, for it was about here that, after the battle of Ta-shih-chiao, the unfortunate Russian gunboat *Sivoutch* was so pestered by Hunghuze, who fired on her night after night from the bank, that the position of the crew became almost as horrible as that of the Master of Ballintrae when he was tracked in the woods of America by vengeful Indians.

The country through which I now passed was as flat as a billiard-table, but it was very well cultivated, and, I should say, very prosperous, for the war had never touched it. I felt it odd not to see shrapnel on the remote horizon, and to realise that there were no longer any of the enemy's horsemen to keep a look-out for on the edge of the distant plain. I thought it odder to see fat hens and chickens walking placidly about the village streets, as if there wasn't a Cossack within a thousand miles of them. Again and again I found myself directing covetous glances towards fine old Chinese houses, such as General Mishchenko would undoubtedly have made his headquarters if he had come that way. My horse seemed to be in an equally demoralised condition, for I sometimes had difficulty in getting him past some of the well-stocked farmyards.

Towards evening my Chinese guide said that his horse was lame, and wanted me to stop for the night in some of the native inns which we passed; but I did not believe him, and, besides, I was determined in any case to get my wire off that day. Furthermore, it would be safer to stop at a railway-station, where I might probably meet with a foreigner, or where, at any rate, I had a chance of getting off by train to a safe place, than in a no-man's land where the Japanese

HOW I LEFT MISHCHENKO 191

might still catch me themselves, or induce the Chinese authorities to detain me, as I had no passport and therefore no right to travel in the district. I had also to consider the safety of my guide, who seemed wholly unconscious, however, of the danger in which he stood.

Accordingly I pushed on at my topmost speed, inquiring at every village how far we were from the railway. Luckily I understood enough Chinese to ask this question and to understand the answers to it; otherwise my guide might have succeeded in persuading me, as he tried hard to persuade me, that the distance was twice as great as was actually the case. I noticed, by the way, that he unblushingly mistranslated the answers of the villagers on this point. The distance was great enough, however. That railway seemed to fly before me like the horizon. Village after village I passed, and I seemed to be making very little progress. At last, long after the sun had sunk below the horizon, but while there was still some light in the sky, I descried at an immense distance a little square house standing out against the last faint flicker of red on the western clouds. From its foreign shape I knew at once that it was the railway-station that I was looking for, the station of Dava. As I came nearer I saw an embankment, then a railway bridge, then ten of the Viceroy Yuan Shikai's Chinese soldiers—the usual railway guard—strolling about on the line. On observing me they rapidly retreated towards the station, and I feared I was going to get one of their dum-dum bullets in my body just as I was on the brink of safety.

I got safely into the station, however, had my horse

attended to, sent off my telegram, and slept that night in a crowded Chinese "hotel" of the dirtiest description.

A few days after, I went to Tientsin by train. The conductor of the train, a young Englishman, an ex-Tommy, who had been in South Africa, and who had naturally a keen relish for adventure, took an extraordinary but embarrassing interest in me, owing, I suppose, to my Russian attire and to the romantic circumstances under which I had made my appearance, and insisted on hiding me in the kitchen of the dining car.

"Impossible," he said, "to go into the car. *There are two Japs there!* One is the chief of police at Shan-hai-kwan. If you show yourself, they'll try to take you off the train at Kupanze. They've often done it with Chinese. Why, they dragged a Chinaman out of this train only a few weeks back, and shot him behind my house in Kupanze. He was probably a Russian emissary of some sort, or had betrayed them or something. No, the Japanese were not in uniform, of course. In fact, they were disguised as Chinamen, but we all know that they are Japanese. This is their great centre for the organisation of the Hunghuze, you know. Yes, they've often dragged people out of this train. But let them try it this time! I'll fix them. Now, keep quiet. Your revolver's loaded? Good! Have another whiskey and soda! I'll be back in a minute to report."

A few moments after he had left, however, and while I was sitting on my saddle and rugs trying to control my laughter, the little slide through which the dishes are passed from the kitchen into the dining-car was suddenly opened, and the aperture filled with a stern, beardless, yellow face, with ugly, determined mouth and slanting eyes, which pierced me unrelentingly like gimlets for fully a minute. It was the face of a Japanese; and, though I was conscious of no crime, I felt as uneasy under its stare as if it had been the face of a judge drawing on the black cap to condemn me to death.

A few stations further on, I found a Japanese horseman—undoubtedly a soldier, although he wore civilian dress—staring at me with equal intentness through the carriage window; but, luckily, I passed Kupanze without being interfered with.

Immediately after we left Kupanze, the slide which I have already spoken of was again drawn aside, and the aperture filled with a face very different to the last one. It was a fat, rubicund, Semitic visage, and at the same time a cheerful voice began speaking to me in bad Russian, offering vague, incoherent and respectful promises of help. The owner of the voice, a prosperous Greek or Jewish sutler who had just come down from Mukden and Tsinmintun, after having successfully sold a large consignment of liquor to the Russians, was divided between awe of me, who might turn out to be a general, and intense curiosity to know what I was up to.

I disappointed him keenly, however, by telling him coldly that I was an Englishman, and not a Russian.

"Well, I only heard the people in the carriage talking about you," he mumbled in an apologetic tone, "saying that you had been with that party which attacked Newchwang yesterday, that you came on at a wayside station where by right this train should not stop, and that you were hiding here. I don't want to know anything about you, but "—mysteriously—" I may tell you that I'm working for the Russians myself. See here "—and he handed me a Russian paper which I at once saw to be merely a sutler's pass allowing him to convey goods inside the Russian lines at Tsinmintun.

He then went on to speak of his intimacy with Colonel Agorodinkoff, the Russian military agent at Tientsin, and of the confidence reposed in him by Kuropatkin himself, until, to get rid of him, I left my hiding-place, and, to the unutterable horror of my English Tommy, walked right into the dining-car. Here I found several Greek sutlers, also on their way from Mukden for more liquor, a few Japanese, and a few Chinese, who were, no doubt, disguised Japanese officers.

At Shan-hai-kwan, where we arrived after nightfall, my English friend insisted on enveloping me in a greatcoat, giving me a bowler hat in place of my Russian cap, and bringing me with the utmost secrecy to his own lodgings, which I quitted next morning in a suit of my friend's clothes, and, to all appearances, quite a different man. My friend had even insisted on giving me the name of Brown; but, of course, the Japanese intelligence officers in Shan-hai-kwan recognised me at once. One of them was within earshot when I asked for my ticket, and another never took his eyes off me all the way to Tientsin.

I might here mention a trifling but characteristic circumstance, that afterwards occurred to me at Kupanze station, on my way back to the Russians. A Chinaman, whom I did not know, walked up to me and handed me a letter addressed to me by my real name—which, by the way, I had not used once during this trip. Forgetting for the moment that I was Mr. Brown, I accepted the letter mechanically; but its contents were not in keeping with the mysterious manner in which it had been delivered to me, for it was simply a last demand from the tax-collecting bureau of Tokio (in which city I had lived for a long time) for the payment of income-tax. Meanwhile the Chinaman had disappeared, but how he had got to know my name was a mystery.

All the way down to Tientsin the Greek sutler and his friends spoke loudly and disrespectfully about Japan, drank expensive wines, and freely displayed bundles of five-hundred rouble notes which they had got up in Mukden. I went down horribly in their estimation by suggesting that they might bring cameras and books into Mukden next trip. "What we makes money on, young man," said one of them, turning his back on me contemptuously, " is—booze ! "

My object in coming to Tientsin was to purchase photographic supplies, a new suit of clothes, books, a fountain pen, and a number of other things which could not be had in Mukden; but, as I intended to return immediately to the army, and as I wanted to keep myself above all suspicion of having dealings with the enemy, I went to the house of Colonel Agorodinkoff, the Russian secret service agent in Tientsin, and, at his request, took up my abode with him.

A few days in Tientsin showed me how it was that the Japanese were getting so much better information than the Russians. The latter had to depend on a set of most unreliable Greek, Armenian, Polish and

Jewish sutlers. The news these ignorant and bumptious men picked up in their sober moments was unreliable and inaccurate. Besides, they blabbed it to everybody who wished to "draw" them, and I am sure they would have cheerfully sold it to the Japanese if the latter had been foolish enough to bid for it. They used to come round after dark every day to the Russian agent's quarters, but the Japanese knew them all perfectly, for a Japanese agent had a room commanding the entrance to the colonel's house, and in this room there was always a watcher, day and night. Besides this, Japanese, got up as Chinese "jinrickshaw" men, were always stationed at our door, and nobody passed in or out without the head of the Japanese secret service organisation knowing of it at once. In fact, the Japanese system of espionage was absolutely perfect, and that because of the zeal with which every one of the Mikado's subjects in Tientsin worked for it. I shall give one example.

Going into a Japanese barber's on one occasion to get my hair cut, I talked to the barber while the operation was being performed about his native town, which I knew thoroughly, and I think he got the impression that I had just been in Japan. On going away, I found I had only got Russian money to pay him with. Now in Tientsin at that time, Russian money marked the owner of it as having been in Mukden, and I am told that, in Haicheng and Liaoyang, the Japanese used to imprison, and even put to death, Chinese whom they found in possession of rouble notes which they could not give a satisfactory account of. Therefore, the fact that I had Russian money and that I had evidently just come from Japan

HOW I LEFT MISHCHENKO

at once aroused the suspicions of the barber, and he very cleverly managed to detain me while he sent for a soldierly-looking fellow countryman who was probably in the secret service, and who came almost instantaneously to have a look at me.

It was their infinite capacity for taking pains that made the Japanese win in this war, and that made their intelligence service far superior to that of the Russians; but, by saying this, I do not mean to throw any discredit on Colonel Agorodinkoff. In fact, I was surprised that he could have done as much as he did, considering the unreliable tools he had to work with. Unfortunately, any European nation that gets into trouble with Japan will have similarly unreliable tools to depend on. It will be a question of money against patriotic fanaticism.

A Russian secret service agent in Mukden—I must explain that the censors were all secret service agents—once confessed to me that he found it absolutely impossible to get information from Japan.

"It's amazing!" he said. "It's as if the country were hermetically sealed. We can make no connections. We can get no news of military movements."

This was about the time that a persecuted Polish patriot, who had fled to Tokio, cursing the Tsar and all his works, had been coldly received by the Japanese, who had lost no time in seeing him on board the first outgoing steamer.

Of course the Russians got some information. Like the Japanese, and like every political or Press agent who cared to spend the money, they got all the telegrams that passed along the Chinese wires. A Russian newspaper correspondent, acting, I presume, for the

Russian agent at Shan-hai-kwan, with whom he lived, had bought my telegram about the Mishchenko raid over the counter of the railway telegraph office at Shan-hai-kwan, just as you would buy a box of cigars at a tobacconist's, and, when I came down to Tientsin, the Russians knew all about my despatch. This is not fancy on my part, for I afterwards met the correspondent in question in Shanghai, and he unblushingly acknowledged what he had done.

A peculiar thing about the Russians in Tientsin was that, when introduced to them for the first time, they always asked me, with a certain odd intonation in their voice: "What brings you here?"—and I soon saw that this was a pass-word exchanged among their secret agents. I never tried to find out what the answer was, but, although I always remained outside the charmed circle, I felt that the Russians trusted me implicitly.

Before leaving for the north, I paid a visit to Mr. Lessar, the Russian Minister at Peking, now, alas! dead. When I called on him, he was sitting before his desk with his legs extended on another chair. He wore the uniform of a general, and was looking very worn. He told me that he had been in Central Asia and had known Skoboleff; but most of his conversation was devoted to a heated exposition of the dangers to which European and American interests in the Far East were exposed through the Japanese propaganda in China. He told me in the most earnest manner (and I must say that, owing to his ghastly appearance, for he was then dying, his words had a great effect on me) that the Japanese were working, through Yuan-shih-kai and the Yangtsze Viceroys, towards the

HOW I LEFT MISHCHENKO 199

overthrow of the Manchu dynasty. They were exciting a revolutionary spirit in the country. They were at the back of some of the powerful secret societies, and they were even using their Buddhist monks down in the south to scatter the seeds of revolt. The Japanese wanted in China a strong new Government, which would be able to unite with them against Europe ; and England would be the first to suffer when Japan had attained this end.

Mr. Lessar protested against the enormous quantity of ammunition and supplies that the Japanese were bringing into Newchwang through Chinese territory and against Admiral Togo's seizure of the Elliott Islands, a breach of neutrality of which the Powers had taken no notice. He would not, however, allow me to publish his name in connection with these remarks, so that I made no use of them at the time.

I returned to Tsinmintun with a number of Russian Legation officials who were going home that way to Europe, and I again met my Tommy Atkins friend at Shan-hai-kwan, and heard from him a lot of strange stories about the prosperous Anglo-Chinese railway, for which he worked. It seems that since the war began, and especially before the fall of Port Arthur, the Russians had spent enormous sums in bribing the *employés* of this railway to convey food, ammunition, etc., from Tsinmintun to Shan-hai-kwan, or some other port, whence it was shipped to Port Arthur by captains who had also received enormous bribes, and who would each of them have been rich beyond the dreams of avarice if they had succeeded in bringing their precious freight of explosives into the beleaguered fortress. In spite of this outlay of money, which must have come to millions of pounds sterling, Japanese agents—not one of whom received, I suppose, more than a pound a week—nipped nearly every scheme in the bud. Most of those they did not nip were nipped by Togo's blockading squadron.

I left Tientsin for my Cossack camp with the greatest delight, for, after such a long absence from cities, the life of Tientsin disgusted me. To be separated from my horse, to sleep within four walls, to eat my meals in a restaurant, was intolerable. I could not understand how the people of Tientsin lived the unnatural life they led. I failed to comprehend how a clerk could sit all day at a desk, and great was my pity for the shop-boys who had to wear immaculate linen, and whose only exercise consisted in vaulting over the counter. I felt that I knew immeasurably more of life than they did, for I had seen wholesale death. I was accordingly delighted when, on reaching Tsin-mintun at nightfall one day, I found there a force of about twenty Cossacks awaiting to convey my friends from the Legation, inside the Russian lines.

Assuming again my Russian top-boots, leathern jacket, belt, "polshubok," and cap, I went along with them on my faithful horse, which an English railway *employé* had kindly taken care of all this time, and for which I had now brought, by way of New Year's gift, a beautiful new English bridle that I had purchased in Tientsin. Three or four hours' headlong gallop in the dark brought us across the Liao-ho and to the first *étape*, a very clean one, where we had a rousing reception.

At last, after wandering long amid narrow streets and unsightly houses—at last I had come home!

CHAPTER VI

THE BATTLE OF SANDYPU

On my return to Mukden I found the wildest tales in circulation regarding my departure from Mishchenko's force. Cossack officers said that they had seen me with their own eyes ride into Newchwang, a general at the "état-major" had declared that he would have ordered the Cossacks to fire on me as I went off, if I had dared to leave *him* under the same circumstances. Kuropatkin had complained to Mishchenko about me. Mishchenko (who had not heard my version of the story) had casually told his men to hang me if I ever fell into their hands.

I found that I was as one excommunicated. The censor had wept at my treachery, and declared that his belief in human nature was shattered. Brother correspondents shook their heads dolorously, and said that it was all up with me.

The Russian diplomatists with whom I had travelled from Peking, and who were now my guests in Mukden, solemnly advised me, after seeing some prominent Russian officials, not, as I valued my life, to go back to the front. The soldiers might do something violent.

I went back, however, that very day. It was snowing and cold (20° below freezing-point at the time I started, but in a day or so it seemed to have gone down to 50° below freezing-point). I had now no Cossack with me, for Philipoff was with Mishchenko, but I thought it imperatively necessary to explain matters to the general at once ; so I set out alone, with but a very vague idea of where I was going to, for I knew that Mishchenko had left his old quarters, and was far away somewhere down along the Liao-ho.

Towards nightfall I reached the village of Sahudyapu from which Mishchenko had started on his famous raid ; but as it was now the headquarters of General Grippenberg, a very severe disciplinarian, who had been maddest of all about my escapade, and who would have at once sent me back to Mukden if I had dared to call on him, I rode past as quickly as I could. The cold was now rendered intense owing to a cutting wind which blew from the north, and which seemed to penetrate to the marrow of my bones although it had to pass through no less than three thick coats each lined with sheepskin. It also blew snow in my eyes so that I could hardly see, and, anyhow, there was nothing to see—nothing but a vast snowy plain of infinite desolation. It was impossible for me to distinguish on the horizon where sky began and earth ended. I seemed to be caught in an immense sphere of snowy crystal. No words can express the bleakness of these polar wastes.

At last I knew what a northern winter meant, and realised the force of Nekrassov's description of that terrible monarch :

> In the sepulchres, King Winter said,
> With flowers of ice I deck the dead ;
> I freeze the blood in living veins,
> And in living heads I freeze the brains.

THE BATTLE OF SANDYPU

Under these circumstances I was delighted to meet with a red-bearded Donsky Cossack, who told me that he was riding to rejoin the detachment of General Mishchenko. We managed to converse, after a fashion, on quite a variety of subjects, and finally became fast friends.

By-and-by we met signs of life in this desert. The first signs of life consisted of a young Chinese woman and an old man who seemed to be her father, both of whom were being conveyed to the rear by a Cossack. Then came some more Chinese. An aged man was carrying on his back an old door! One young couple had with them an ass and a baby boy. I thought of the Flight into Egypt; but, alas! this child is more likely to be a Genghis Khan than a Christ. Then we met signs of battle, wounded officers and men being carried on stretchers, and a score or so of Japanese prisoners. I talked with the latter, and noticed that, far from being downcast, they spoke up cheerfully, asking me to give them cigarettes. One of them, however, looked very sad. He was a handsome youth, and, in contrast with the jeering Cossacks, he had the calm, unexpected, foreign face of an Egyptian statue, of a Rameses II. or a Queen Tai. Late that night my friend met other Cossacks from the Don, who had established themselves snugly in a Chinese hut, which they had managed to make as hot as an oven. The Cossacks welcomed me, and asked me to share their simple meal of soup, beef and black bread, which I very gladly did, although the beef was handed to me in hands which were none too clean. I gained their hearts by repeating snatches of Russian songs that I had picked up, but grieved them, I think, by going to bed, apparently without saying my prayers. "And thou, dost thou not say thy prayers, Little Hawk (sokólik)?" As for them, they prayed long and fervently, standing up facing the east most of the time, but very frequently dropping to the ground with startling suddenness and touching the floor with their foreheads.

Next morning I found favour with them again by photographing them all in a row in front of the hut where we had passed the night. It took a long time before they had arranged themselves to their own satisfaction with drawn swords in front of the camera, but at last they were satisfied, albeit a trifle hurt at first because I could not give them the "sneemki" (photographs) there and then.

After drinking some tea I and my companions set out again, and late that night we reached the house of an old general of the Don Cossacks, who delighted my heart by telling me that I was now at the extreme front—a fact which I had already discovered, however, from the continual rumble of cannon and the crackling of musketry—and that a big fight was going on a few miles off. Even while he was talking, a young Japanese cavalryman was led in prisoner, and in order to give the Donsky general a high idea of my utility, I forthwith attempted to converse with him. His name was Sakimoto, he came from Marga-Uchi, Inaga, and had been captured in a neighbouring village, which he and about a dozen other scouts had entered. The Cossacks had rushed the village, but all the Japanese had escaped save our friend, who told me to ask the "seokwan" (general) not to cut his head off. When the general heard this, he swelled visibly with benignity,

A JAPANESE PRISONER
TAKEN AT PEN-SHI-HU, OCT. 1904

THE BATTLE OF SANDYPU

and, beaming on the prisoner like a father, he declared that Russians never put prisoners to death, etc. etc. Hearing some of the Russian officers using the word *geisha*, the prisoner told me that if they did not kill him he would bring back from Japan any number of *geisha* they wanted—very beautiful *geisha* too. In spite of this he was evidently convinced that he was going to be put to death, for nothing could be sadder than the look in his dark eyes as he gave me the military salute before being taken away. His last words were a request to feed his horse, which had been captured with him, and which had not had anything to eat since morning. The old Cossack leader was much affected when he heard this, and issued immediate directions for the horse to be fed.

As soon as we had had a hasty meal of preserves, I wrapt myself in my warm overcoat, without of course removing my clothes or boots or hat, or cameras even, and laid down on the "kang," but at about three next morning, before I had been more than twenty minutes asleep, one of the officers awoke me, saying that we were all leaving immediately. When I went out into the courtyard I thought I should have dropped dead, for the cold was something beyond all description. I had never before experienced such a temperature. I had never imagined that human life could exist in such intense cold. The Kirghiz desert, the Antarctic table-land, cannot, I said to myself, be half as bad as this. Owing to the snow which had fallen during the night-time, and to the freezing of the natural vapour arising from my horse, that animal had the appearance of a pre-historic monster embedded in an Arctic snowdrift. Its breath had frozen on leaving its nostrils so that there was a horn of ice a foot long projecting from its nose, and lumps of the hardest ice of unequal sizes had become attached to its hoofs. I think that at that moment I would have sacrificed all my prospects in this world and the next for a warm bed and safety. But, unfortunately, I had to go, and, in a few moments after I had been awakened, I had saddled my horse, although the bit burned my benumbed hands like frozen mercury, and was riding along with the Donsky Cossacks. The earth was all a white blank, the stars were of extraordinary brilliancy, the cold prevented me from noticing more. I wore the thickest woollen socks that Tientsin could furnish, and over them I wore high felt-lined boots that would have been intolerably hot in the coldest English winter; but, in spite of all this, the cold stirrups burned through the soles of my boots like red-hot irons, and, to save myself from the loss of my legs by frost-bite, I jumped off my horse and walked on foot. How long I walked I don't know, but I noticed that the hardy Cossacks were also on foot. At dawn we entered a deserted Chinese village at one end, while in at the other end came my friends the Verkhnyudinsky Cossacks and the men of the Caucasian brigade. I very soon explained to their satisfaction my ride across the Liao-ho, and they told me of the bloody battle of Sandypu and of how Mishchenko had been wounded during a desperate attack on the village of Wukiatsz, which a handful of Japanese had stuck to with their usual bull-dog tenacity.

Now, for the retreat from Sandypu. I had just

made myself comfortable in a Chinese house, with my friends of the Daghestansky Polk, when the usual news came—instant retreat. It was now evening, and the snow was falling heavily. Displacing a fleecy pile of it from my saddle, I mounted and rode north through a country ensanguined, despite the thick white mantle which enshrouded it, by a blood-red glow extending all over the western heavens, in which the sun was now sinking.

Long after darkness had fallen, we reached a village in which there were lights and crowds of soldiers and officers, and stopped in the outskirts of it for some time, trying to locate ourselves. Under the impression that we were going to put up here for the night. I dismounted and entered a house, but soon discovered that my party had gone on elsewhere. Where to find them on such a dark night was now the question. Fortunately I encountered a soldier from the Daghestansky regiment, and followed him. It was very difficult to do so, however, for he rode a fine horse, and went at a break-neck pace, threading his way through crowds of other horsemen from whom it was difficult to distinguish him. In fact the only way I could distinguish him in the darkness was by the fact that the rump of his horse was grey and that a weapon by his side glinted at a certain angle.

So much ice had become attached to the hoofs of my horse, that the unfortunate animal seemed to be walking on four stilts, no two of which were of the same length, and, to make matters worse, I almost lost all feeling in my own extremities owing to the intense cold. I should have liked to walk on foot in order to restore my circulation, but I could not now do so, as I had got to keep up with this horseman.

Some time before daybreak my guide and I blundered into a large body of cavalry standing compact and almost invisible on the outskirts of a village, and, in spite of the darkness, I could see at once from the multiplicity of strange banners which they carried folded up, that they were the Caucasians I was in search of. There seemed to be some difficulty about getting quarters in this village, for we had to remain on the outskirts for half an hour while our leaders held a heated discussion with some soldiers who were already in possession.

Finally we crowded into two or 'three houses, at least the officers did so. The men lighted huge fires in the spacious courtyards of these houses and slept beside them.

Prince Nahitchivansky and the Caucasian officers insisted on my coming into the house which they occupied and taking my place on the warm "kang" where, after an hour or so, I slowly began to thaw.

Our next tribulation came in the shape of a frozen general and his men, all of them Donsky Cossacks, who insisted most emphatically that this village had been assigned to them. A long and heated debate on this subject raged between our adjutant and the adjutant of the Donsky general, the latter gentleman being apparently too frozen to speak for himself, and, while it lasted, our hearts almost ceased beating, for the prospect of having to leave our cosy quarters to face the biting cold outside was too terrible. It was like the prospect of being dragged from one's warm bed on a winter's day and thrown naked into a hole in an icy river, and the reader may therefore imagine the agonising interest with which I followed the contest between the prince from the frosty Caucasus and the general from the quiet Don.

Luckily it ended in an amicable compromise, the general being given a place on the "kang" and his followers being allowed to sleep outside. My companions did not sleep, however. They played cards, and the words "clubs," "trumps," "hearts," and "ya eegrayu; ya panemayu" ("I play : I understand"),—the strange rhyme which one hoarse-voiced player kept repeating every few minutes,—were the last sounds I heard as I dropped off. On such occasions the congestion was terrible and was made worse, in the morning, by every one insisting on washing his face inside the hut. As a Russian officer, when he washes, requires the attendance of his orderly, who first pours water on his hands out of a cup and then pours it on his head, neck and face, it was generally impossible to cross the floor of a room without upsetting somebody or something.

Under these circumstances it might be expected that rows would take place, but the Russians were invariably good-natured and forbearing. For my own part I always washed outside, but as I could never pluck up sufficient courage to take off any of my three overcoats, I am afraid that my ablutions were of rather a perfunctory character.

CHAPTER VII

MUKDEN BEFORE THE BATTLE

JUST before the battle, which will for ever make its name celebrated, the city of Mukden was at its best.

In order to find that ancient capital presenting as picturesque and animated a picture as it did then, one must go back to the early days of the Manchus, to the days when Mukden was a real capital.

For several reigns it has not received an imperial visit. The palace is in decay, and it is hard to discover what the Tartar-general does with the thousands of pounds sterling which he annually receives from the Court at Pekin for its upkeep. Probably he pockets them. Anyhow the continual neglect of the Court had doubtless a good deal to do with Mukden's loneliness two years ago.

When I came to Mukden, in April 1904, I found the city very dull, contrasting strongly in this respect with Liao-yang. Filled with temples and with Buddhist monks, it seemed to be a sort of faded ecclesiastical capital, like Kandy in Ceylon, Ayuthia in Siam, or Kyoto in Japan. When travellers landed at the bleak little shanty which serves as the railway-station, they found the place almost deserted. The station-master, a Greek barber, and a few officers and soldiers, were the sole inhabitants of this sequestered spot. There was no

MUKDEN BEFORE THE BATTLE

buffet, and no "jinrikshas" or other means of conveyance waited outside. As the city is miles distant from the station, this lack of transport facilities was a serious matter; and travellers had to walk toward that part of the horizon where they believed Mukden to lie, much in the same way as Red Indians out in the prairies of the Far West stalk stolidly homewards after leaving the train at some point where, barring the railway-station, there is not a house in sight.

In the city itself there were only two or three houses where European commodities could be purchased. The streets were almost deserted, and the citizens had not yet got over their habit of staring at European customers as if the latter wore more than the regulation number of heads.

February 1905.—What a change has now taken place!

The station is provided with a buffet, into which I have only been able to penetrate] once or twice, owing to the throngs of officers, doctors, and Red Cross nurses that always fill it.

The crowd of "jinrikshas" that wait outside reminds one of Shimbashi station at Tokio. There is a big detachment of soldiers going north, for a body of Japanese cavalry has just blown up a railway bridge at Changchun, 160 miles north of Mukden, and a brigade of the 41st Division has been sent to intercept them. Two regiments of Cossacks have also marched into Mongolia on the same fruitless mission, and, when they return, they will find that the battle of Mukden has been fought and lost.

The streets of the city are as crowded as the streets of a flourishing market town in England during the

Christmas season. Sometimes, indeed, the congestion of traffic would do credit to the Strand.

Interminable lines of transport-carts and horses get locked together at the gates and block the street traffic for hours together.

"Jinrikshas," pedestrians, horsemen, and Chinese carters try to make their way through the swaying mass of cursing men and rearing horses with the result that they only render the confusion worse confounded. What a mixture of races and variety of types one now meets in the streets! Here a Buriat Cossack sits in an "arba" (cart) on the side of the street, bargaining with a placid Chinese shopkeeper, who, patiently, smilingly, insistently demands five hundred per cent. above the market price. This Buriat has to take supplies to his "sotnia," which is fifty miles off to the south-east, and to-night he will sleep in his cart outside the walls, wrapped in his capacious but dirty "shuba," or sheepskin coat, with his purchases under him and his horse tethered to the shafts of the vehicle.

Alas! here comes a melancholy crowd of Chinese refugees—the inhabitants of some once prosperous village. Clad in rags and scarcely able to walk from hunger, they present a pitiable sight, and, strange to say, it is not the Russians but their own countrymen and countrywomen who jeer at them as they stagger past.

Half a dozen magnificent horses, half of them Arab horses, half English, are held by orderlies outside a small place which calls itself an hotel. These horses belong to officers who had volunteered from the Guards at the beginning of the war. They—the officers—had heard of the parade into Pekin in 1900 and thought

THE SOUTH GATE OF MUKDEN

MUKDEN BEFORE THE BATTLE

that there was going to be a similar parade into Seoul and Tokio in 1904. They had therefore promised their friends souvenirs from the Mikado's capital, and had all been careful to provide themselves beforehand with handy little Russo-Japanese phrase-books.

One of the greatest surprises in Mukden is the cosy little "interior" belonging to Dr. and Mrs. Ross, of the Scotch Presbyterian Church. It is a perfect British home, with library, drawing-room, clock ticking in the hall, warm blazing fire, everything complete. A supper with Dr. Ross after one has come in from some Cossack raid is enough to make one imagine that he has never left the English shore, and that all his recent experiences are only unpleasant dreams.

Throughout the meal, the doctor, whose medical work among the Chinese poor has made him respected by every one in Mukden, speaks about China—on which country he has written several valuable books; after supper is over and grace has been said, young Miss Ross plays the piano; but it remains for the baby to add by its artless prattling the last touch needed in order to make one imagine oneself back in the old country. There are not many English folk in Mukden, but, nevertheless, English influence is strong there. The Chinese postal and telegraph officials are under Sir Robert Hart, and therefore pro-English. This is useful in many ways to the correspondents. For instance, we not only pick our own mail out of the mail-bags at the post office, but pick out all the newspapers addressed to the censor as well. As these newspapers sometimes contain uncensored articles their seizure saves trouble, but some correspondents go too far. One of them, for instance, an American, has had the audacity to intercept for a year or so all the English papers and periodicals that come to Admiral Alexeieff, the Viceroy of the Far East! The censor, who has arranged to get two copies of each of our papers, is amazed sometimes at their non-arrival. He always manages to get hold of the *New York Herald*, however, and I was very proud of this fact until I discovered that it was not my articles which attracted him, but a series of coloured cartoons in the Sunday edition representing the career of an American *enfant terrible* called Buster Brown.

Outside the west gate, the Dai-Lama's Temple, Quan-si-howlo, in which I lived for a time after coming to Mukden, has greatly changed. It has lost its pristine calm, and is full of Russian officers and soldiers. The young Lamas are rapidly acquiring Russian, but losing, I am afraid, their vocation. Luckily, however, monastic life in Lama monasteries is not too strict.

Members of the Caucasian brigade are strolling down the street with their hands on the hilts of their swords and their brains—such as they are—busy with the solution of the perplexing problem, "Why is this place not delivered over to loot?"

These bold Mohammedan mountaineers have stout hearts and fine swords, and horses and a picturesque costume, but as soldiers they have, as I tell elsewhere, their shortcomings. Their discipline is anything but perfect, and no two of them speak the same language, so that when their colonel gives the order to charge, hours elapse before the numerous translators have made a fair proportion of them understand what is required of them.

MUKDEN BEFORE THE BATTLE

It is surprising how well the Russian privates and the Chinese fraternise. They shake hands, they play with one another like children. They are on terms of perfect equality. I have seen officers shake hands with Chinese interpreters. Just imagine what would happen if a choleric old Indian colonel stepped out on to the verandah of his bungalow one morning, and observed any of his men making as free with Ramasamy, as the Russian soldier does with " John Chinaman." He would immediately conclude that the man was intoxicated. But whatever trouble he may give his superiors in other directions, Tommy Atkins is not likely to distress them by over-familiarity with the natives. Drunk or sober, he will stroll about in gloomy and magnificent isolation, so far as his dusky Aryan brothers are concerned, and be more likely to kill one of them with a kick than with kindness.

At every step you see soldiers bargaining with inflexible Chinese for a bottle of vodka or a handful of nuts or a pair of socks. Sometimes you see a soldier eating an apple at a fruitseller's stall. This soldier is supposed to discharge the duties of a policeman, and the apple represents bribery and corruption.

A Manchu woman walks down the street with a free stride, which contrasts with the mincing gait of the small-footed Chinese woman. This and the arrangement of the hair are the only tokens by which you can distinguish the Manchu woman from the Chinese woman. As for the men, the Manchu is practically undistinguishable from the Chinese. Yet, once upon a time, the Manchu came down on the Celestial Empire like a wolf on the fold, even as the Russians have done. He has given a dynasty to China, but that dynasty is now more Chinese than the Chinese dynasties that preceded it. The Manchu bannermen have become more cowardly and worthless than the Chinese soldiers whom they conquered ; and Manchuria, the mother country of the Manchu, is now overrun by Chinese. Has not Japan, therefore, been too hasty? Whether Russia remains master of Manchuria or not, the Chinese will, in a few thousand years, be all over the Primosk, Ussouri, Transbaïkal. A few thousand years are nothing to the Empire which has seen Assyria, Egypt and Rome flourish and decay.

A Chinese "perevodcheek," or regimental translator, rides by in all the glory of high boots, spurs, striped trousers, a fur cloak, a sword, a revolver and a busby. Beneath his gaudy headgear there is no pigtail ; he has cut it off, or some soldier has done so for him. He is a handsome boy of some sixteen summers, and I happen to know something of his history. He went originally from Chefoo to Port Arthur, where he learned Russian in a small Chinese shop, over the counter of which he many a time and oft handed me boxes of cigarettes and parcels of humble groceries in exchange for Russian roubles. On the outbreak of the war he first returned to Chefoo, then went to Yinkow, and was finally engaged as interpreter by a Russian colonel of Cossacks, then stationed in Liaoyang. He stops his pony in the street in order to question an old Chinaman who happens to be passing by, and a curious crowd quickly collects around him. The old man gazes sadly at the well-favoured youth, and answers his questions with the same melancholy sarcasm as an aged Tipperary man would employ in answering the questions of a fellow Irishman who had

MUKDEN BEFORE THE BATTLE

forsworn the wearing of the green and was bursting with importance in a suit of " England's cruel red."

Since the retreat from Liao-yang the streets of Mukden have all blossomed out into Russian signs, more or less grammatical. Some of them may possibly have been brought from Liao-yang, for I remember that on the day that General Stackelberg abandoned Shu-shan all of the Russian signboards over Chinese shops were hastily withdrawn. All of them are easily detachable, so that at a moment's notice they can be thrown into a cart and sent on to Tie-ling or Kharbin.

Every second shop in Mukden is now selling European goods. It may have been a pawnshop before or a Chinese drug-store, but it is now selling Armour's beef, St. Charles' cream, Wright's health underwear and a variety of other European and American articles—all of them made in Japan, although the manufacturers refrain from stating that fact on the labels.

Mukden's great original line is furs, of which there is an imposing display in the streets; in fact, the whole city is one vast fur market. Sheepskins are especially plentiful—sheepskin gloves, sheepskin stockings and sheepskin overcoats. Most of the sheepskin in the gloves and stockings was originally worn by Chinese dogs, in the ridiculous belief that it was dog-skin, or by goats labouring under a delusion that it was goatskin. Nevertheless, there is enough good fur in Mukden to make me regret that the wise old custom of our ancestors, according to which a pagan city held by Christian troops was periodically looted so as to inspire the presumptuous burghers with the fear of God, has been allowed to fall into disuse. If that custom is revived there are one or two shops in Mukden that I should like to pay a visit to.

There are crowds of horsemen, mounted and dismounted, vociferating outside the numerous saddlers' shops that line the street and dazzle the unwary rider with a display of imitation Cossack saddles that come to pieces at the end of a day's ride.

A Chinese showman with a performing sheep is gladdening the hearts of the simple Russian soldiers; while close by there passes, unobserved, a farmer carrying on his shoulders two trampled bundles of kiaoliang, or Chinese corn, representing the harvest yielded perhaps by a dozen acres of land. This harvest he had tended with unwearied care until the storm of shrapnel burst, and men, horses, carriages and guns rolled like an avalanche over his crops.

At this time a strange trade has sprung up in Mukden —the collection, at the front, of cart-loads of the little leaden tops of shells, and their sale to Chinese lead merchants in the city. I may mention that during a battle I often found these little caps useful as drinking cups, when nothing else was available.

A long side street is entirely devoted to tinkers, who turn out the best work that is produced in Mukden to-day. They make those fine strong copper household utensils which are so largely used in China and which look so much better than our tin articles. Day by day they work in their little open shops, surprised and delighted if a foreigner manifests any interest in their humble labour, careless about wars and rumours of wars, and sure to be safe, no matter who wins or loses. Akin to the tinker is the old cobbler at the street corner, the man who makes small dough pies, the ragman, and all that honest humble brotherhood which is not interested in politics and has nothing to fear from the destruction of armies and the fall of thrones.

A Mongol lama, with vestments of green and gold and shaven head, is slowly picking his way across the crowded street, fingering his beads all the time and feverishly muttering: "Om mane padme hun, om mane padme hun," for, owing to his lack of a pigtail, he has been already arrested six times to-day on suspicion of being a Japanese. Majestic mules move along, their upper lips curled as if in disdain, but really because a slender steel chain passes across the upper gum, and is used for guiding them. Mandarins go past in faded sedan chairs.

Suddenly there is a commotion, and two long lines of Chinese dressed in red and carrying staves in their hands come along at a brisk trot. One can at once see by their bearing that they are the retainers of some great man; and so they are, for behind them comes the famous Jan-June or Tartar-general, carried in a curtained palanquin. He is on his way to the temple, where he will return thanks to the gods, for to-day is the Empress Dowager's birthday; and, as he is borne hurriedly past, one catches just a fleeting glimpse of his gorgeous robes, enveloping a tall, bent, meagre form, his worn parchment-like face of the Li-Hung-Chang type, with deeply marked semicircles underneath the eyes, his head crowned by a Chinese cap with the peacock feather, and his scanty beard and moustache.

Are we in the China of the twentieth century or in the Jerusalem or Antioch of the Cæsars? It was under this mild old gentleman's *régime* that the Christians, were martyred four years ago in this very city. Just outside the south gate stands the wreck of the cathedral where the massacre was carried out.

Poor Père —— has to say Mass now in a little shanty hung around with tawdry Chinese decorations, but I think I can say that I generally hear Mass there with more devotion than I ever experienced in any of the historic churches of the Continent. The strange, nasal, strident chanting of the Chinese congregation is not, it is true, conducive to devotion, but many of these men bear scars that they received at the sack of the cathedral; and, though they wear pigtails, I fail to see the difference between them and the Georges and Andrews whose emblems are embroidered on royal standards. Some Polish soldiers also turn up every Sunday and thumb their way religiously through greasy prayer-books, and, on one occasion, I met there the late General Gerard, the British *attaché*, who probably never expected at that time that in a few months more he would be dead at Irkutsk.

Meanwhile the Jan-June continues his march—but, hark! Clear and unmistakable above the roar of the busy street comes the boom of distant cannon. If his triumphal progress through the city has lulled the hoary persecutor of the Christians into a sense of false security that ominous sound will quickly awaken him.

The Japanese are thundering at the gates of Mukden!

CHAPTER VIII

THE BATTLE OF MUKDEN

IN the beginning of March 1905, three great Russian armies lay in a line south of Mukden. On the extreme left of this line, in fact away over near the Yalu river, was Colonel Madridoff, with a small force of Cossacks and Russified Hunghuze. On the left was Linievitch with the first army. On the extreme right, that is, near the Liao river, were the Cossacks of Mishchenko and Tolmatcheff. On the right was General Kaulbars, who commanded the Second Army, composed of the 8th and 10th corps and of a mixed command made up of three rifle brigades, and whose headquarters were at Meturan. The headquarters of General Tserpitsky, who commanded the 8th corps, and to whom I was attached during the battle, were in a village a little east of Meturan.

The space between Kaulbars and Linievitch was occupied by General Bilderling, whose headquarters were at Suiatun or Suchiatun station on the railway.

Against Kaulbars came Oku with the 2nd Japanese army. Against Bilderling came Nodzu with the 4th army. Against Linievitch came Kuroki with the 1st army. I need hardly say that Nogi with the 3rd army turned our right flank, and that on our right therefore the fighting was hotter and more desperate than at any other point in the battle-field.

On Friday, February 24, I happened to be in a village called Ubanyula, some ten or fifteen versts south-west of Sifontai, and, therefore, near the Liao River, and on the extreme right of the Russians. In this village, Rennenkampf temporarily commanded Mishchenko's Cossacks, Mishchenko being, as I have already intimated, in a hospital at Mukden, wounded in the knee. On this day a typical Cossack banquet was given by the colonel and officers of the Verkhny-udinsky regiment to commemorate the departure next day of Rennenkampf's whole detachment for the south. Orders had been received to march next morning as far as Davan, a place on the Liao-ho, some dozen miles further south. Nobody knew what was to be done after they had reached Davan, but the general impression was that they were then to march on Yinkow, or east on the Japanese railway. Next day however, this order was countermanded, and, shortly after, Rennenkampf was sent east to replace Alexeieff, who seemed to be handling his corps very badly. Mishchenko's cavalry force was then broken up to some extent, and Grekoff took what remained of it.

Grekoff is a short, stout, red-faced man with Dundreary whiskers, very fond of the pleasures of the table, and formerly notorious in Mukden for hanging round the provision waggon of the Ekonomitchesky Obchestvo in the hope of buying some new delicacy for his kitchen, so that he was hardly the man to leave in command at this important point; and, as a matter of fact, some Russians attribute the loss of the battle to the inefficient way in which at the outset this cavalry

THE BATTLE OF MUKDEN

leader handled his Cossacks. In the opinion of these critics—of whose qualifications to judge I must, however, say that I know nothing—Grekoff should have been able, by means of his scouts, to hear of Nogi's approach; but probably the Cossacks, who were taking things easy after the withdrawal of the iron-minded Rennenkampf, whom they hated for the way in which he made them work, were somewhat to blame themselves. However that may be, Grekoff was quite surprised to learn, on February 26, just as he was sitting down to dinner, that a strong Japanese column was approaching from the north—of all places in the world!—while another was coming from the south. The Cossacks had just time to escape, and, save for their subsequent repulse of an attack on the railway north of Mukden, I did not hear of anything done by them on the right flank at this battle. After all, Charles XII. was right when he said that the Cossacks are only good for cutting up a defeated army.

I was not with the Cossacks on the occasion of this interrupted banquet, as I had left them the day before in order to return to Mukden. After passing through Sifontai, I came to the district occupied by the 1st Siberian Corps, and was astonished to find that it had been evacuated. All the villages were deserted, and sundry indications pointed to the fact that the soldiers had left only a few hours before. The names of regiments were still chalked up on the walls, but there was not a soul about, not even a solitary specimen of the aboriginal inhabitants, the Chinese. In the high wind that blew, doors swung violently on their hinges, and nobody cried to the soldiers to shut them. No smoke issued from the chimneys. There was no sign of life save a few hungry dogs. The landscape was to the last degree sad. It was noonday, and the sun was making some attempt to shine, but a graveyard by moonlight would be a cheerful spectacle in comparison with the scene which lay spread out before me on that occasion. The surface of the illimitable, bare, brown plain had thawed, apparently to the depth of a few inches, and the dust flew from it in whirling clouds and pillars. Whenever one raised a foot, a huge puff of dust rushed out tumultuously from under it, like genii out of a magic bottle which had accidentally been uncorked; and it was like being overwhelmed by an avalanche to find oneself on the windward side of a passing patrol of horsemen, or of a train of transports. There was a thick coating of dust on every face, so that the passing soldiers looked like corpses. A ghastly grey mask covered their features and their beards. The wrinkles around their mouths and eyes looked like deep scars. The eyes themselves were distant and sunken.

I overtook a company of Siberian foot soldiers trudging along the road, and learned from them that the 1st Corps had been suddenly ordered to the extreme left flank. The soldiers and officers were so dead tired, so utterly done up, that they could hardly speak. They had not even enough energy left to arrest me for not having the password. They found it hard even to drag one leg after the other, and had to throw themselves flat on the ground every twenty minutes or so in order to get a short rest. A little further, however, they were able, I dare say, to take the branch railway to the main line, whence they could go by train to Fushun, but they had so far to walk after they got to Fushun that they must have had no great desire for fighting when they reached their destination. A few days after, when Kuropatkin discovered that the Port Arthur army was on his right flank, instead of on his left, he brought the 1st Siberians back again to the extreme right, and, in spite of the fatigue and demoralisation all this aimless wandering meant, they resisted Nogi's terrible onslaught with conspicuous bravery and stubbornness.

I put up this evening at the head-quarters of the Second Army, that is, at the village of Meturan. This village is on the south bank of the Hun, and at the end of the branch railway running east along that river. It was a clean, whitewashed village, in which every house was numbered, and bore on its exterior a list of the people staying inside. In spite of its being a Chinese village, there was an air of severity, cleanliness and order about it which reminded one partly of a barracks and partly of a convent, so that when I saw the flames licking it up a few days after, I felt almost like a man who sees a dignified person knocked down and trampled on.

I might, however, have early seen the seeds of decay beneath this fair exterior. The private soldiers I spoke to told me about an advance that was to take place that night on the left flank. Unaware of the true state of affairs, they thought that the Russians were taking the initiative, but they spoke of the matter without enthusiasm. They were melancholy and dispirited in this strange disagreeable land, which they did not want in the least to fight for. "I'm getting thirty-five kopecks a month," said one unwashed, melancholy young man. "I don't mind getting killed, but if I lose a leg or arm I cannot work afterward, and I shall only get a pension of three roubles a month for the rest of my life."

Nearly all the soldiers I came across in Meturan were depressed, sad-toned men, who frequently sighed as if they were suffering from some fatal internal malady. Even the songs that I heard the orderlies crooning to themselves were very mournful. One of the saddest of them, which described a conscript's leave-taking of his home, made me think, by way of contrast, of the gay processions I had often seen escort Japanese conscripts to barracks. An oldish-looking man, who looked after my horse, astonished me by saying that he was only thirty-five years of age. He was a reservist, and wanted to go home. They all wanted to go home. Among the few who were cheerful was a little lark of a fellow who had been a waiter in an hotel at Nijni Novgorod. He once whispered to me in a very confidential manner the news that he belonged to some very heterodox sect, of which I have forgotten the name. Another, a boy of seventeen or eighteen, with the gentle manner and the smooth face of a girl, told me that he was a Pole and a Roman Catholic, and that there were two Roman Catholic priests in the whole Russian army.

After telling me a tale of woe that made me feel quite sad, one of the melancholy men said to me: "I suppose, sir, your lot here is also very hard." He looked surprised and incredulous when I told him that I could go home whenever I liked, and that to be sent home in a luxurious train, *via* St. Petersburg, was one of the direst threats held over the heads of the correspondents by the censor at Mukden.

I must say that I honestly tried to cheer up that young man, and to make him see the romance of war, but I did not succeed. On the contrary, he succeeded in making me very doubtful of the Russian chances of success in the battle which had just begun; for I now remembered that the Cossacks, and every other branch of the army, were just as homesick and discouraged. Many of the officers had no better name for their generals than "prokhvost," while in medical circles the freedom and latitude of the criticisms indulged in shocked me—me, whom a year's stay in the army had led to regard a general as something peculiarly sacred. On one occasion, I remember, I was lamenting, in very guarded language, the comparative inefficiency of the Cossacks during the present campaign, whereupon a doctor remarked, with a dryness of manner that would do credit to a Scotchman: "The Cossacks are only good in the streets of St. Petersburg."

The officers seemed to be almost as dispirited as the men. I found one of them reading a most gloomy religious book on "How to Prepare for Death," and another deep in the perusal of that unhinged genius Dostoievski. A third officer was reading Nekrassov, whose funereal verses are the best antidote to martial enthusiasm that can be found in the whole range of Russian literature.

Meanwhile Kuroki and Kawamura were rolling back the Russian left with such rapidity and violence that General Kuropatkin could be excused for believing that the principal Japanese attack was to come from that quarter.

CHAPTER IX

MARCH 1 AND MARCH 2

ON March 1 I rode out with General Tserpitsky to his "positions." The scene was not one that would look well in a photograph. If a landscape painter were to paint it, people would think that his intention was to picture immensity, not to represent a battlefield. There were bright sunlight and warm spring weather, but it was not so warm that one could dispense with an overcoat while riding. There was no sign of life save a distant scattered line of soldiers advancing over the vast expanse. The silence and the great distances suggested to me, somehow or other, Sunday, the great sea, eternity. The shrapnel was bursting far away to the right, where Miloff was losing village after village, and falling back step after step and verst after verst before the terrible men who had taken Port Arthur. Against old Tserpitsky, however, with his twenty-four batteries of field-pieces and four batteries of heavy guns, Oku did nothing, and I went home that night thinking that the Japanese had put their hand to a work they could not carry through. My home was in the very exiguous Chinese house of a Red Cross doctor, and, just before we turned in, the doctor received orders to hold himself in readiness at four o'clock next morning to accompany two divisions which were to leave for Tsinmintun, which a large force of Japanese had, it was reported, seized. This news cast a gloom over all of us; for, if the Japanese had a large force on the west of the Liao, they might easily succeed in turning our right flank and in cutting the railway in our rear.

We lit our cigars and went out into the night to discuss this new development of the situation. The stars were clouded, the earth was dark, but, far away on the edge of the plain, search-lights were swinging their long arms backwards and forwards, unweariedly, in an acute angle, and, despite the darkness, shells were still bursting. Occasionally the heavy boom of a single cannon, followed at a short interval by its echo, reached our ears. Later on there came from the south-west a continuous crackling rifle-fire, which lasted, with few interruptions, all night. We afterwards learned that this rifle-fire marked several unsuccessful but desperate night attacks which the Japanese had essayed against Wangkiawopeng and Likiawopeng, and one unsuccessful counter-attack made by the Russians.

When I awoke in the morning, my kind host, Dr. Pusep, had vanished, and with him all his assistants and furniture. There remained to me, however, a small but very valuable friend in the person of Andrew Mikhaïlovitch Rikacheff, the correspondent of the St. Petersburg paper *Nasha Jeezn*. Andrew occupied a somewhat anomalous position in the Russian camp, for his paper, which had been imprudent enough to declare that the war should be brought to an end, had been suspended for three months, so that he did not quite know whether to regard himself as a correspondent or not. In spite of this discouragement, however, he worked with extraordinary zeal, while his patriotism and singular fearlessness endeared him to the soldiers.

As soon as we had succeeded in getting a cup of tea, Andrew Mikhaïlovitch and I rode out to Davanganpu, the terminus of the branch railway. It was filled with wounded and with dusty, broken, and dispirited troops, who freely confessed—in Russian—that they had retreated because they could not keep back the Japanese. According to one soldier, the enemy kept coming on, coming on, like ants, four or five times in succession. At last the officer said, "Children, we cannot stay here any longer. We must go back."

The Decauxville railway that ran south-west from Davanganpu was overtaxed owing to the multitudes of wounded. In one hospital alone, a hospital which normally could only accommodate a few hundred men, there were more than a thousand patients.

We then rode over to Meturan, the headquarters of General Kaulbars. Here we found everything packed up, and everybody ready to move. Rikacheff and I got transferred to the 8th Corps, as that corps seemed to have most of the fun, but the trouble was where to find its headquarters. There was no difficulty, however, about locating the Japs, for their shells were bursting in showers at Dzeurpo, a few miles to the west. At last, by dint of diligent questioning, we got the name of the village in which Miloff would probably be found, and galloped towards it, passing, on the way, great bodies of troops slowly advancing in loose formation. We found the village all right, but we did not find Miloff, for he had gone away some hours before, no one knew in what direction. The village looked like the Roman catacombs, for most of it was underground, and its underground houses— I mean of course the Russian trenches and dug-outs— were all deserted, as were also, indeed, its overground houses, in some of which large quantities of stores seemed to have been left behind. A regiment, the Volinsky regiment, lined the walls and houses at the back of this village, which the Russians called Towtaidze, but the place was not under fire. In fact the Japanese shells were bursting a few versts in front of us, on a fringe of trees which marked the horizon of the usual naked plain. Just in front of this ultimate fringe we saw the Russian firing line. Some of the men who composed it were lying down, some were advancing by short rushes, some were getting jammed behind hillocks, farmhouses, the river bank, some were swinging with great caution to the right or to the left. While we were watching this scene, a score of soldiers were busy plundering the stores which had been left behind in Towtaidze by the staff, and which comprised many different kinds of provisions. In doing so they exposed themselves freely, but where was the harm in that? The Japanese were not firing at them—probably could not fire on account of the range. The sky was clear, but the atmosphere was ominous and threatening, as if a thunderstorm were about to burst.

Suddenly, like the first big drops of rain heralding a tropical downpour, a few shimose shells dropped casually in different parts of the village. At this time Rikacheff and I were following the colonel of the Volinsky regiment to a place further back, where there were some officers that he wanted to introduce us to. Before we had gone many steps, however, hell was let loose around us. Common shell tore up the ground. Showers of shrapnel bullets hopped on the road like hailstones. One projectile burst less than six feet in front of the colonel, who was leading the way, covering us all with dirt and clay. Our ears were filled with explosions like claps of thunder. The rear of the village was, if anything, more dangerous than the front. A big trench that ran behind the usual mud wall was filled with anxious-faced soldiers. The ground behind them was strewn so thick with shrapnel that I soon filled my pockets with these sinister curios.

The Volinsky colonel impressed me as one of the best soldiers I had ever met, simple, suspicious, calm, brave, uncommunicative. "We've got to hold this village to-day, and we'll hold it," he said. At any other time I would have thought that he was boasting, but not at such a time as this. He explained to me that the Russian line north of Sandypu and south of Changtang had fallen back, but that two divisions of Russians had gone to turn the Japanese left flank.

The scene in Towtaidze at this moment is deeply engraved on my memory. The colonel is drawing a map in the ground with the end of his scabbard, and is talking, although the appalling visitations of shimose prevent me occasionally from catching what he says. Projectiles throw up dun clouds of earth. Shells burst among us with reverberating roar. It is an inferno. Two dead men are lying on the roadside and two living men are working hard to scoop out a grave for them in that frozen ground. There is a wild, frankly frightened look in the eyes of the soldiers who are hidden in the trenches. The sky is overcast. The officers are remarkably affable, but nobody cares to look any one else straight in the eye lest his secret be revealed, lest it be found that his own eye is rolling unsteadily in its socket, that his cheeks are flushed and that his manner is slightly unstable and exaggerated. Our horses are feeding peaceably, as if there was no such thing as war. On such occasions one can always get them plenty of fodder which has been left behind in the confusion. Things are lying about—typical Russian things. Here is a long folded grey overcoat shaped like a yoke for a horse's neck, both ends meeting and clinched together by means of a very black and sooty tin porringer. It was evidently intended to be worn athwart the shoulder. There are also many blood-stained, nondescript rags, sad reminders of the wounded. A patriarchal soldier hobbles past, all hunched up as if broken in two. He is only wounded in the hand. Another man comes, reverentially carrying the overcoat belonging to the wounded man. A third brings his rifle and cartridges. The colonel is easy on these men. He does not curse at them and send them scurrying back to the front, as an English or American officer would have done. He talks to them affably for several minutes and then lets them go on. Shrapnel bursts among the trees on the other side of the road, sending the sparrows flying with sharp chirpings of discontent to every point of the compass and making the tethered horses jump. Bullets kick up the dust on the road. Evening is coming on, and Rikacheff and I are anxious to know where we can find the 8th Corps. We are told that their headquarters is at Davanganpu. The leaden storm of shrapnel and shimose continues. I often discover myself muttering, " What terrible fellows these Japs are! What superhuman perseverance! What incredible bravery! How little did I think that the awkward, smooth-faced lads in uniform whom I used so often to meet walking hand-in hand in Uyeno Park like Dresden shepherdesses, would prove to be such demons for warfare! What can we, any of us—Englishmen, Germans, Frenchmen, Russians—what can any of us do against a race which fears no more the supreme dolour of death than we fear a shower of rain? And these, if you please, are a people 'ayant une nature d'oiseau ou de papillon, plutôt que d'hommes ordinaires.'" Amidst the obstinate, incessant, exasperating uproar the words of that silly Frenchman ring in my ears like the mocking laughter of a fiend.

Meanwhile the distant boom of the valiant Tserpitsky's four-and-twenty batteries added to the nearer roar of Miloff's great guns and of the Japanese cannon, the unceasing crackle of infantry fire, the continuous rattle, rattle, rattle of the machine guns. At some point in front—I am afraid to raise my head to see where—some vital issue is in arbitrament, some point of ultimate importance is being discussed. Towards that point the troops are now rushing like water above a cataract. I quickly raise my head and glance in the direction in which they are going. What a scene! The fighting line is marked by a pall of shrapnel smoke and dust, hanging in mid air like the mists of Niagara. The Japanese are coming on like the whirlwind from out of the North which Ezekiel saw in his terrible vision.

A colonel of the 1st Rifles (European) rides up to our little group. He is a stout, tired, flabby man, the ghastly pallor of whose face is rather heightened than otherwise by a thick coating of dust. He speaks French, has had severe contusion, sits down heavily near us on the roadside. The talk runs on contusions until something shrieks past and bursts with a bang somewhere close by but out of sight. Then the Volinsky colonel observes cheerfully that you never hear the whizz of the shell that kills you. As if to contradict his theory, a shell whose augmenting whizz we had been listening to not without anxiety for a second or two, bursts in the immediate neighbourhood. It does no damage to anything except to the colonel's theory, for it might just as well have alighted on top of us. And here, let me remark, parenthetically, that there is something peculiarly angry, vicious, abrupt, vehement and impolite about a shell that bursts close to you. It annoys and displeases. If it were human you would cut it dead ever after for giving you such a devil of a start. The angry bark of an unexpected dog within a few feet of your calves is like a maiden's sigh in comparison.

Rikacheff tries, in his ingenuous way, to get some information about the troops, but the colonel is very cautious and reticent. The conversation flags, and we turn our attention to the landscape. It is the same brown bare country, with the same long melancholy lines of men advancing over it. Sometimes they run. Dozens of little fleecy clouds of shrapnel hang over the distant villages.

Suddenly a small excited man rides towards us. When he dismounts, we see that he is a lieutenant, a plump man on the shady side of thirty, with a weak, babyish face, and round protruding eyes. His clothes are very good, his trousers fit tightly on plump legs, he is provided with brandy-flask, binoculars, compass, all complete. He is also in a state of awful, undisguised "funk." Terror is writ large on his face, and in every movement of his body. His unfortunate condition is in great contrast to his warlike and fashionable equipment. He points to little clouds of shrapnel north and north-east.

"They're getting round us," he blubbers, his fat face working like the face of a baby that is going to cry, "and the Cossacks tell me they have gone along the west bank of the Hun and are now near Mukden."

The Volinsky colonel is very reasonable and calm. It seems so odd to find him so, for one generally associates personal uncleanness and disorder with drink and incoherence.

"Impossible!" he says. "I know the exact position. . . ." (I could only catch fragments of the conversation; the Volinsky colonel is very cautious). "The 10th Corps and 16th Corps are on the other side of the Hun River south of Sifontai. . . . Japanese will be caught between two fires . . . heard to-day seven attacks Baitapu . . . three days fight . . . demonstration left, right, centre, but real attack from direction of Tsinmintun . . . yes, Kaulbars has got command of the army between Tsinmintun and Mukden. The Japs wanted to cut the Mukden-Tsinmintun road. Rifles? General Staff sent the Rifles to strengthen the centre . . . the 17th and 19th Rifles are with Kaulbars. . . . What? Over there? Yes, the 14th Division is over there on the west bank of the Hun, the 15th is on this side. Yes, Jentan was taken this morning, but we're going to retake it to-night." *

A very calm courteous young officer rides up, dismounts, salutes—bad story to tell—" Japs awfully close, sir." Projectile whizzes viciously overhead, but young officer remains quite unmoved, his hand still to the salute. Colonel says things cannot be quite so bad. Still, to my unpractised eye, the outlook is black enough. A circle of fire, a thunder-striking girdle of artillery seems to be slowly closing in around us. A ring of shrapnel looking clearer and more dreadful in the gathering night is bursting round ninety degrees of a circle; the little gap, the tenth degree, may be closed at any moment. If I were in command of the Volinsky regiment I am afraid that I would lose no time in making a bee-line for that gap. A young Polish officer, who has been looking at this awful scene for some time, quotes some of Mickiewicz's terrible verses describing Napoleon's advance into Russia, and immediately after gets into a violent argument with the Volinsky colonel. Rikacheff and I make another effort to get news of staffs and armies, but the colonel leaves us absolutely in the dark. He is kind enough, however, to remark that if we don't like to go away, we may remain with him in Towtaidze for the night. It is like an invitation to remain on the top storey of a burning house. All indications point to the likelihood of the Japanese making five or six bayonet attacks on Towtaidze under cover of the darkness, so we hastily excuse ourselves and

* This is not an imaginary conversation.

mount our horses, which, having fed, are now standing sleepily by, with sad, pendulous under-lips which occasionally move as if in prayer. The colonel gives each of us a feeling handshake, and says that we both deserve a St. George, but he refuses to give us the password. "You may be challenged by Japanese, and give it to them involuntarily," he argues, "and, anyhow, you don't need it. If our people arrest you, they'll bring you direct to the staff, and isn't that exactly where you want to go?"

Thus we parted with this brave, unsympathetic man, and lucky it was for us that we did so, for, perhaps, on that very night the terrible circle of steel and fire closed in around Towtaidze. I cannot say for certain, however; for in those troubled days it was as hard for me to get any information of what was happening at a distance as it would be to get news about friends in England in case primeval chaos had returned to earth and upset all the postal arrangements of the nations.

Just then, however, we are too much concerned about ourselves to mourn for the doom impending over this shell-battered hamlet. We hurry off like men pursued by a tidal wave. On right of us, on left of us we hear the roar of the Japanese advance grow louder and louder. It is like the deep rumbling of a sea that has burst its bounds. High above the plain on right of us, on left of us, far as the eye can reach, are long lines of fleecy shrapnel cloudlets, the foam and the spray of that on-rushing ocean. Two projectiles burst with an appalling crash right in front of us. We go forth, feeling like men going out on a torpedo-boat which stands a thousand chances to one of being sunk. It is a beautiful evening; the sky is lovely; I count six villages burning on the horizon. Miltonic images arise in my mind as I contemplate this terrific battle-field. Can the pen of poet, can the brush of painter ever convey an adequate idea of the horror of such a night as this? Never! Never!

I have not the least notion where we are heading for. I soon became aware, however, that we are in a hot place, for the whizz of the bullets is unceasing; and ominous, unseen things strike the ground in several places close to us, raising little puffs of dust. Shells hurtle overhead with long shrieks. The r-r-r-rip, r-r-r-rip, r-r-r-rip of the musketry is getting louder. The furnace roar of the battle now becomes deafening, We are going the wrong way! We are approaching the enemy! Panic-stricken, I persuade my companion to come back. Back! Whither? To Towtaidze? Impossible! Towtaidze is nought now but one of half a score of burning villages, which flame like red torches in the immense black night above innumerable multitudes of men trampling by. Even if it still exists it will be impossible to find it. Whipped by the mad wind of panic, we gallop—I don't know in what direction. At last we meet several military waggons advancing, and join ourselves on to them. The drivers of these waggons are visibly perspiring. Vapour rises from their faces like steam, and they are crossing themselves briskly with large, unsteady hands. We notice that one of the flaming villages is Meturan, the former headquarters of Kaulbars. Alone and unprovided with the password, there is a great chance of our being taken for Japanese. But what information could a Japanese scout get on such a night?

He would lose the points of the compass. He would only run up in the darkness against large bodies of men standing he knew not where or marching he knew not whither. Of what use would such information be to him unless perchance he had, combined in his single person, the technical knowledge of a Moltke, the coolness of a Wellington, the bravery of a Skobeleff, and the topographical certainty of a local Chinese peasant?

The night has come suddenly, but the darkness is rendered more confusing by reason of the tremendous glare from the burning villages—vast sacrificial fires roaring up from gigantic altars to bloodthirsty, pagan gods. There is a red glow in the sky overhead. Sharp, continuous explosions, sounding like rifle-shots, proceed from the burning houses, but whether these explosions are due to ammunition left behind or to the crackling and falling of the wooden beams, I cannot say. During lulls in this storm of noise there comes to us a faint ripple of sound like the washing of the waves on a shingly beach. It comes from away beyond Shahepu and the railway, where the stern Nodzu is vainly hurling his brave Kumamoto men against the bristling rifles of the Putiloff Asobke. Vainly, O children of Kato Kiyamasu! Spartans of Japan! throwing yourselves with a very fury of courage on that fatal hillside? No! not vainly! You were never meant to take that hill. Man born of woman could not take it by frontal assault. You were merely meant to die there by thousands until trench and fosse and *trou-de-loup* were choked with your dead, until the Russian soldiers saw with horror the living carrying forward the frozen corpses of the fallen in order to use them as a screen against that hail of bullets. You were merely meant to do all this so that the enemy would get the impression that the Japanese centre was overwhelmingly strong, and that it could not be cut. That centre was composed of two frail divisions!

At Chukwanpo on the east, and at Wanghsiutai on the west, the Japanese are making the last desperate bayonet charge which won them those places. At Changtien, some miles to the north of the river, five battalions of Russian infantry are madly, bravely, vainly, rushing on the veterans of Nogi.

For Rikacheff and me things begin to look serious, in fact they have been looking serious for some time past. There is firing going on north, south, east, and west, and we do not know where is friend and where is foe. The Russians with whom we are travelling are as puzzled as we. As a matter of fact, they had thought we knew the way, and had been following us. At last, emerging from a swirl of smoke, we come suddenly on a big body of men, tense, waiting, with weapons levelled at us. It is like coming face to face with a tiger prepared to spring. As they prove, however, to be Russians, Rikacheff rides up to an officer and questions him with engaging and child-like frankness about things that should only be spoken of in a whisper at secret councils of war. And, wonderful to relate, he is answered. The answers come slowly and sullenly, however, like drops out of a withered orange. Then there is a pause, and the officer says, contemplatively half to himself, "Many Japanese spies around here. One cannot be too careful. One of them came here the other day, representing himself to be from the General Staff and speaking Russian perfectly."

Rikacheff laughs and says, "Well, if you're afraid that we are spies, we'll go along with you to the General Staff and we shall show you our papers."

But the officer, who is very young and simple-minded, will not hear of this.

"No, no," he hastily returns. "I don't mean *you*. But just now, just this very moment, a soldier came up to me and said: 'Vashe Blagarodie,' says he, 'perhaps these are *not* Russians.'"

And sure enough, I had noticed one or two soldiers peering in the darkness at my face and strange saddle. My silence and Rikacheff's very small size are both sufficient to excite their suspicions.

Finally, we come to Miloff's headquarters, a pillaged cabin in a half-burned village. The place is cold, uncomfortable, upside-down, and filled with high officers in furs and spurs, discussing things in a heated manner over maps, by the light of one dim candle. Miloff receives us in a kindly but distracted manner, but says that as there is no accommodation, and as he is leaving in a few minutes himself, he will send us on to Davangangpu with his adjutant, who is leaving directly. I wait for almost three hours listening to a discussion that I cannot understand, and trying to read fragments of the *Novoe Vremya* which are pasted over cracks in the walls and holes in the windows, and which, taken in connection with other signs, indicate that the place has at one time been the snug quarters of some officers.

Finally, the adjutant, a young, handsome, voluble man, tells us he is ready to start. When we go out into the courtyard we find that it has been snowing, and that our horses and saddles are all white and fleecy. It can easily be seen, however, that the fierce cold which marked the first battle of Sandypu has passed. Lucky as ever, the Japanese have begun the battle at the right moment. A week earlier it would have been too cold; a week later the ice on the rivers would have been too thin to bear artillery. Alas! The stars in their courses have fought against us!

A few days before, I saw Davangangpu for the first time, and was powerfully impressed by the aspect of the place. It was like a busy railway terminus in Western America. A dozen sidings were filled with trains. Veritable mountains of provisions were piled along the railway and guarded by soldiers. Close by was a long row of hospital tents, whose inner shell was made of earth, and from the gables of which smoking stove-pipes projected. A dozen enormous siege-guns lay alongside the tents, and imparted an air of finality to the scene.

Davangangpu now wears a different appearance. The tents, guns, and railway trains are gone, and the mountains of provisions are going—going up in flames and smoke. The whole place is lit up by a furnace glare. The windows vomit great red flames. It is like the mouth of the Great Pit. In the lurid glare there rushes past a frightened flood of men, horses and cannon. There remains, however, one good house, the house set apart for the use of General Miloff's staff. In this house I am asked to eat and to sleep, for death and defeat have failed to make the Russian officers forget their traditional hospitality. I lie down in my boots, after midnight, and am lulled to sleep by the tremendous roar of the flames, which sound as if it were London that was burning, and am awakened at 3.30 A.M., though we do not leave the village till daybreak. I put in the interval looking after my horse, for which I had previously been unable to get a handful of oats for love or money, but which I am now in a position to present gratis with whole bags of corn—bags snatched from the burning. The great conflagration is still going on within a few hundred yards of me; and I now discern, as the light of dawn slowly filters through the eastern clouds, that what I at first took to be a low crenellated wall standing between me and the flames, is in reality an enormous swarm of humanity, the innumerable hosts of the Tsar, warming themselves, countless as a hive of ants, in front of the fire, against whose genial but expensive glow their heads show like crenellations.

Two groups of prisoners are now brought into our courtyard. One is a group of Japanese, all of them wounded, the slightly wounded ones supporting the badly wounded ones with fraternal arms. The other is a group of Chinese, who are accused of having been caught signalling to the enemy. The two groups are kept separate, are looked upon with different eyes, will be treated in a very different fashion. It is now nearly dawn, but not one of these Chinamen shall see the sun rise.

CHAPTER X

A VAST VODKA DEBAUCH

MARCH the 3rd dawned beautifully. The stars faded away. The moon, which was the thinnest possible crescent, merely a geometrical line, also disappeared. The pale light of dawn was reflected from the snow, which lightly covered the ground.

Finally the sun rose, promising a bright day. With the rising of the sun the retreat commenced.

We pushed on towards Suhudyapu, along the branch railway, forming three columns of enormous length.

At the beginning of the year I had been living in Suhudyapu, or Suhupu, with Mishchenko's Cossacks, and my feelings on returning to it were like those of a man who returns to his native village after a long absence. Suhudyapu had been quiet, sequestered, roomy; now a railway ran past it, and it was dreadfully busy, overcrowded, and forgetful of me. General Mishchenko's former residence was choke-full of stores; and the former "Sobranie" (club) of the Verkhnyudinsky Cossacks had been converted into a Red Cross Hospital. Rikacheff and I managed to discover a Greek store, in which some tinned provisions still remained, and here we made the first decent meal that we had had for some days. While we were eating, a strange thing happened. I chanced to see at the door a venerable Manchu woman, with a fine face, almost Roman in the regularity of its outline, and with a striking dignity of manner which was sadly in contrast to the dry leaves and pieces of straw which, frozen to her dress, indicated that she had been sleeping out in the open. She was looking wistfully into the house, and, anxious to air the few words of Chinese that I know, I asked her what she wanted. She then came into the room, carrying a little child in her arms and leading another by the hand, and, pointing with a dramatic gesture to the "kang," she said in a whimpering voice and with tears in her eyes that her children had been born there. It was a striking way of saying that the house belonged to her, and the superstitious Greek became visibly uncomfortable. He became still more uncomfortable a few hours later, when a Japanese shell frightened him out of that house and almost out of his wits.

At Suhudyapu railway station I saw a sight that made a greater impression on me than anything that I had witnessed so far. A large quantity of "vodka," bread, conserves and other eatables and drinkables had been thrown to the soldiers, as it was impossible to save it; and, considering the thousands of men there were around who had not eaten a morsel for days, it is easy to imagine what occurred. Fierce currents of humanity set in simultaneously from north, south, east and west towards this loot. Many of the men immediately carried away loads of preserves, most of which they would undoubtedly have to drop before they had marched a mile. Nevertheless they snapped ferociously at any comrade who offered to relieve them of a tin or two. Some sat down on the ground and began to cut open tins with their swords and bayonets and to devour the contents on the spot. The veins stood out like whipcord on their temples, their eyes were bloodshot, and the perspiration streamed down their faces as they savagely attacked the food. Others cut open more preserves than they could eat in a week. Their hunger seemed to be appeased by the mere sight of the food, and their excitement was so great that they sometimes cut their fingers without noticing it. But the great scenes raged around the "vodka" casks. The barrels had been stabbed with bayonets and hacked open with knives, swords, and axes until they bled from scores of wounds. A frantic crowd of men struggled around these openings, seeking to apply their mouths to them or to catch the precious liquid in cups, cans, empty sardine tins, and even in the cases of the Japanese shells that were falling conveniently around. A huge red-capped Orenburg Cossack jumped on one of the barrels, wielding an axe, with which he soon stove in the head of another barrel amid wild cries of drunken triumph. The sight of that red-capped Cossack and the frenzied crowd that surged around him recalled ominous historical scenes from the pages of Carlyle.

" This is more dangerous for you than Towtaidze," whispered Rikacheff, white as a sheet; "for God's sake don't speak English."

This warning was necessary, for of late the soldiers had developed a distinct tinge of Anglophobia. They had all got the idea that the Japanese could not have carried on the war so long had it not been for the financial assistance given them by the British and the Americans, and this financial assistance they seemed to regard as a breach of neutrality, a *casus belli* almost.

A drunken infantryman rolled unsteadily towards me, his beard and the breast of his coat all wet with "vodka," and began to speak volubly and unintelligibly; but Rikacheff, who probably did not want to see my head smashed in with the butt of a rifle, as soon as the soldier had discovered that he was addressing a Britisher, edged in between us and took up the tangled thread of the discourse.

The "vodka" that overflowed from the burst casks had collected a foot deep in a depression of the ground. Men knelt down to drink the muddy liquor. Some scooped it up in the hollows of their hands, as you would scoop up water from a well. Some fell into it bodily. Many were wetted by the jets of liquor from the barrels squirting over them. Buriat Cossacks, Mahommedans from the Caucasus (forbidden by their religion to touch drink), riflemen, dragoons, all sorts and conditions of military people, joined in this mad spree; and, with the dust and the smoke from the burning stores eddying around them, they looked like alcoholic demons struggling in the reek of hell.

The liquor made some of them insane or good-natured, I don't know which. I saw men working like slaves at handing out tea, meat, etc. to their comrades, laughing hilariously all the time. One very unwashed soldier applied himself enthusiastically to the task of giving away bars of soap! Officers shouted to their men to stop, and, finding that their orders were disobeyed, turned to me and said: "All discipline is gone."

Then they themselves began to loot Government property from the train that stood close by.

Meanwhile I looked on awed and thunderstruck, as one who sees the small but unmistakable beginning of great events—the first miracle of Christ, the crossing of the Rubicon, the march on Versailles.

It is, I said to myself, the commencement of *la débacle russe*, and I am the only foreign spectator of it. It is the first fatal, unmistakable sign of disintegration and decay in a great military body that has awed Europe and Asia for fifty years.

There were little hillocks of "sukharee" (hard tack) and of fine, newly baked bread, but nobody touched them. They were not valuable enough. It was pleasanter far to destroy costly preserves and scatter them all over the ground than to eat black bread. The love of destruction for its own sake had seized upon the soldiers and threatened to become uncontrollable. Letting troops loot their own stores is like letting partially domesticated tigers taste blood. Unfortunately for the Russians, they had, from the beginning to the end of the war, no stores to loot save their own. And at Tah-si-chiao and Liaoyang they had not much to loot—only a few waggon-loads of preserves. In Mukden, and all around Mukden—at Fushan, Quanshan, Kandalusan, and Suhudyapu—they were turned loose on an enormous accumulation of provisions. The result was that many drunken soldiers fell into the hands of the Hunghuze over by Tsinmintun during the great retreat, and were put to death with horrid tortures; and that, after the Russian evacuation, the railway station at Mukden was strewn with the corpses of Russians who had been murdered and stripped by the Chinese while lying there drunk.

What lent a zest to this looting of the stores was, I think, the feeling among the soldiers that they were doing with impunity what they could not have done the day before without being shot. These stores were then guarded, and a private soldier hardly dared look at them. The sudden removal of all restraint caused them to lose all control of themselves. They felt as if God had suddenly repealed the Ten Commandments.

I don't know if it would not be better for retreating generals to let all the supplies they cannot carry off fall into the hands of the enemy. In that case only a few soldiers would be scandalised; whereas, when the soldier is let loose on his own stores, everybody in the army hears about it, everybody sees the columns of smoke, and shares the pilfered dainties, hitherto sacred to officers alone.

By the light of these burning stores, the ignorant mujik gets one awful, fleeting glimpse of a new world —a world without police, without rulers, without laws— and the sight is not good for him. There is something peculiarly demoralising in the wholesale, deliberate destruction of millions of roubles worth of valuable property, something calculated to make even a Carthusian giddy. The corner-stone of society is knocked away; all the copy-book maxims about thrift seem the veriest drivel; and it suddenly occurs to one, with all the force of a supernatural revelation, that he has been on the wrong tack all the time, that the "small profits, quick returns," system is absurd, and that for all who are not monarchs or millionaires the one sound political faith, the one true religion in this world, is—anarchism.

The fact that all these men were armed, and the accidental discharge of a rifle now and then in the middle of the throng, made this orgy tragical. Sometimes a dusty Cossack rode in with the news that the Japanese were coming. "They fired on us half a mile off—other side of the river." On such occasions there was a momentary commotion, bloodshot eyes and flushed faces were turned towards the frozen stream, fire-arms were clutched, preparations were made to fly, to advance; but, a few moments after, the panic had subsided, and the orgy had recommenced.

Being Irish, I can understand a crowd of men getting drunk in order to make themselves cheerful, but this was the most sombre crowd of drunkards I had ever seen. Instead of making them gay, the drink made them mad.

Meanwhile there were the usual contrasts in which war is so prolific. A short distance from the station I met three officers of the Zamostie regiment, who looked dirtier and more wretched than even their own soldiers. One was wounded; two were suffering from contusions, which were probably worse than wounds. Dazed and feeble, with arms around each other's necks, these unfortunate gentlemen staggered along—a tragical parody on Burns's famous drinking-song.

Still more neglected, of course, were the wounded privates. I met long strings of them in the streets of Suhudyapu. Several of them came to me on one occasion with their wounds bound up in dirty pocket handkerchiefs, and asked me "for Christ's sake" (radee Khrista) the way to the "Perevyazyochny

Punkt." Not being able to give them the necessary information, and knowing that my accent would at once betray me, I remained silent, whereupon one of the wounded men caught at the arm of a man worse wounded than himself, saying:

"Come along, little brother! Come along, golubchik tui moï (my little pigeon). You see nobody will answer. Nobody speaks."

His tone was charged with sorrowful resignation, not with anger. He was a typical Slav.

Some of the Cossacks excited my admiration by stealing bags of corn for their little ponies before they themselves tackled the "vodka," thus unconsciously carrying out the orders of their Cossack-poet Davidoff. Close by, a gang of soldiers were working hard, loading boxes of shell into a train. Why they did not throw all discipline to the winds and join in the mad revel that was going on beside them, I cannot imagine.

Other soldiers were carefully lifting the wounded into poseelkee (stretchers). Even in the midst of this indescribable uproar, some Red Cross sisters, all honour to them, remained at their posts not only self-possessed, but cheerful. I remember little Rikacheff significantly drawing the attention of one of them, a large, red-cheeked lassie, with the bearing of a Tsaritza, and the serene self-possession of one of Turgeneff's heroines, to his horse, which he was tying up in the yard of the hospital, the inference being that she would keep an eye on it, for at this time all the distinctions between "meum" and "tuum" had completely disappeared. After listening for a second, her dark eyes brimming over with merriment, she flew lightly backwards towards the door of the hospital,

A VAST VODKA DEBAUCH

clapping her hands together, and giving vent to a clear, ringing laugh, the memory of which did me good for weeks after. "So! so!" she said, "you want me, then, to mount guard ('vstupeet' v'karaool') over your precious horse. 'Spasibo' (thanks), I've got enough to do looking after my little boys"—and sure enough she had, poor girl, for the wounded were being carried in by scores.

The reports brought us from time to time by the Cossacks with regard to the advance of the enemy were not exaggerated. The Japanese were coming on with the force of an inundation. Their right wing rolled like a tidal wave into the villages of Sankiatsz, Hsiaofanghsin and Mentapu. Their centre drove the Russians out of Meturan, Davanganpu (which I had left only a few hours before), and Danjanhay, Tserpitsky's former headquarters. Their left wing swept along the west bank of the Hun, capturing Wokiapu, in the rear of Suhudyapu, the village in which I was standing. One could almost fancy that he heard the increasing roar of this fierce advance, that he could catch, like the deep rumbling of unchained waters, the sound of this oncoming ocean of armed men.

Meanwhile, in the north, Nogi and his outflanking army were literally carrying all before them. They even reached Tehshengyingtsz, due north of Suhudyapu, and almost in a straight line between that place and Mukden. Indeed, as I shall afterwards tell, Japanese horsemen rode as far as Madyapu or Mokiapu, the point where the road from Suhudyapu to Mukden crosses the Hun river, and fired on the retreating Russians there.

We watched this terrible advance as Arabs in the

desert might watch in the heavens the approach of the dreaded simoom. We could not see the enemy, but we could mark his progress by an awe-inspiring precursor, by a reverberating vanguard of shrapnel and shimose which scourged the earth for half a dozen miles ahead of him.

To-day we are conscious of defeat. We live in the shadow of a final cataclysmal disaster, the news of which has not yet been broken to us. What are these ominous whispers about Tsinmintun, Teihling, the road to Mukden. Oh, tell us, Vashe Blagarodie, one of noble birth! is the battle lost? Is our retreat cut off?

We feel like an unarmed man groping in a dark room, where he knows that a strong enemy awaits him, in silence, hidden, with uplifted sabre.

Let us eat and drink, for to-morrow we shall die. O source of hope! Orthodox Tsar! O Little Father! O Gosudar! You were once our God, but now God and you have alike failed us. Holy Russia, we shall never see you again! God we shall never see, for there is no God! Our popes have lied to us about Him. If God existed He would never allow His chosen people to be butchered like swine by the savage Hunghuze and the pagan Yapontszi.

I left Suhudyapu before the Japanese appeared on the scene and brought to a conclusion this Belshazzar revel. I afterwards asked the practical-minded conquerors what they had seen, but they did not remember anything beyond the exact number of the bags of corn which had been captured on this occasion.

CHAPTER XI

GENERAL KUROPATKIN'S TRAIN

ON the evening of March 3 I left Suhudyapu with a Finnish officer in order to join General Kaulbars west of Mukden. The road to Madyapu was crowded with retreating troops. At Madyapu itself some excitement was caused by a Japanese patrol firing on the Russians. The audacity of the Japanese in coming so far inside the enemy's lines was one of the most remarkable things in this battle, while the entire absence of Cossack patrols at that point was a piece of inexcusable neglect on the part of the Russians. In fact, the Cossacks were more useless during the battle of Mukden than they had ever been before in this war, and that is putting the case against them very strong indeed. It is true that the Japanese are bad riders and have bad horses, but their superior audacity and pluck more than counterbalance these defects.

Crossing the Hun we rode northward for some distance, thinking that we should find Kaulbars in that direction, but several circumstances induced us to retrace our steps. The first was that all the villages in front of us and to right and left of us were ablaze. I counted about a dozen different conflagrations on the horizon, and unless we expected to find Kaulbars' staff in the middle of a burning village it seemed that the only safe thing for us to do was to go west to Mukden. Then, again, we noticed a number of suspicious-looking horsemen riding about in the distance, and though it might be that they were Russians, there was a considerable probability they were the very Japanese who had been firing on us half an hour before.

We returned therefore to Madyapu just in time to witness an unpleasant incident. There was a big uproar in a Chinese farmer's house, and riding up to the kiaolang fence which surrounded it we looked over. Inside, a Russian officer, whose eyes were concealed by large black goggles and the rest of whose face was as effectively hidden under a thick coating of grey dust, was ordering, with violent gestures, the arrest of all the Chinese in the house. A handsome young Chinese woman, with a baby in her arms, threw herself at his feet, but he repulsed her violently. An old, palsied woman was dragged out of the house by a pair of soldiers. A young Chinaman, evidently the husband of the young woman, lay on the ground outside, almost unconscious and evidently unable to move, despite the blows and kicks that were rained on him. An old man was dragged out, then an elderly woman. The sight was enough to have melted the heart of a stone, but in the faces of all these thousands of soldiers there was not the faintest gleam of pity. I do not know the rights and wrongs of the case, but the general cry of "signalizieravat!" seemed to indicate that these people had some connection with the arrival of Japanese scouts in the near vicinity. These poor people may have been spies, but this cry and the blows by which it was accompanied reminded me more than anything else of another cry: " He is a blasphemer! Crucify him! Crucify him!"

Such things may be necessary for the prosecution of war, and they may be done on the Japanese side as well as on the Russian, but, if so, I hold that victory gained at such a price is too dearly gained.

North of Madyapu we made another attempt to reach Kaulbars on the west, and, in fact, if we had gone north we should undoubtedly have reached him, for, as we afterwards learned, the Japanese had not yet come so far. But again we were intimidated and checked by the number of the burning villages. In some cases the horizon was lighted up for miles by an unbroken line of red, leaping, wavering flames, from which rose enormous columns of smoke. We rode up to the nearest of these conflagrations and found it to be the bakery of the Eighth Corps. Here we remained for a moment discussing our plans. The Finnish officer met a compatriot, also an officer, and it was strange to hear them talking in their own proscribed tongue, while Russian soldiers, tired to death, lay all around on the bare ground, fast asleep. I asked for an explanation of the arrests at Madyapu, and was told that the Chinese had set their house on fire in order to give notice to the Japanese that it was a good time to attack.

Another suspicious circumstance was that a Chinese boy was found bringing to this house the latest issue of the *Vyestneek Manjchurskoi Armee*, the official Russian newspaper of Mukden, the inference being that this paper was to be passed on to the Japanese, though, as it only chronicled Russian victories, I do not see how it could have contained much news just

R

then or have been of much assistance to the enemy. But if these Chinese were really spies, they were certainly in good position to supply their employers with news, for all the troops that went to the Russian right had to pass through or near Madyapu.

The Russians also pointed out to me that, on the night before, big conflagrations, started by the Chinese, had revealed to the enemy the headquarters of General Kaulbars and those of Generals Miloff and Tserpitsky respectively; but I am still unconvinced by these arguments, feeling sure that these fires were lighted by the Russians themselves. At the same time I am also convinced that the Japanese got a vast amount of valuable information from their Chinese spies during the course of the battle.

There was at this stage a lot of the usual flapdoodle among the Russian officers about Kuropatkin being "very angry with Kaulbars for burning all these stores," and, again, about Miloff being perfectly able to hold out if "that idiot, Kuropatkin," had not ordered him to retire.

Finally we got lost in the swollen torrent of men, horses, guns, Red Cross waggons, transport carts and commandeered Chinese vehicles that was rushing toward Mukden. The dust, combined with the darkness, was such that for half an hour after I reached the Russian settlement I could not find the railway station. Lights shone all around me, but they were merely pin-points of varying degrees of brightness in the dense, dark grey haze. They threw no more radiance on the buildings around them than did the Great Bear. We seemed to pass dozens of lines of railway, from which I conjecture that we passed and repassed the numerous sidings about the station. In one of these sidings was Kuropatkin's train. Kaulbars' train was near it. Although the compartment of the commander-in-chief was lighted by electricity, there was also on the table, inside, a neatly shaded lamp, which suggested studious ease and literary seclusion. One window of the brilliantly lighted dining-saloon was blocked by the back of a typical waiter standing in faultless evening dress behind his master's chair, his spine bent at an angle of well-bred attention.

On the steps of the carriage stood Kuropatkin's adjutant, bold, smiling, suave, exceedingly well groomed, every brass button and gold tag on his uniform shining like a mirror. He was chatting pleasantly with somebody and seemed as serenely oblivious of the hordes of beaten men who were tramping past as if he were standing in one of the most exclusive drawing-rooms in St. Petersburg.

At last we found the station and made our way to the restaurant. It was packed with officers, so closely packed that the waiters could not circulate outside the counter, and dishes had to be passed to the people at the tables over the heads of the dense crowd in the centre of the room. Every one save Rikacheff and myself and the waiters was in uniform, and every one was talking loudly and excitedly. It seemed from what they said that all the Japanese attacks on the Russian left and centre had been repulsed with great loss, and this was perfectly true. It was only on the right that we were beaten back this day; and this was due to the absence of the First Siberian Corps, which was now, however, on its way back to the west.

It was everywhere expected that next day—that is, March 4—Kaulbars would deliver a decisive battle west of Mukden, with the object of isolating and destroying General Nogi, whose presence in that part of the field was now known, and I made an appointment with an officer on Kaulbars' staff, who was to leave Mukden with the commander of the second army at five o'clock the next morning.

Kaulbars did not start, however, at five o'clock the next morning. In fact, he did not start at all. I think he remained in his railway carriage at Mukden station for the next few days—that is, until the battle was decided. And no one can blame him for this, as the Japanese had now come so close to Mukden on the west, and from Mukden better than from any other point Kaulbars could direct the operations of his subordinates against Nogi.

On this day, March 4, the excitement at the railway station reached fever-point. From morning till night troops poured in—Cossacks, artillerymen, dragoons, infantry. What became of them afterward I do not know. I suppose some were sent west and some north. Great numbers of wounded were also brought along. Long rows of tents were run up alongside the railway line for the reception of these wounded. Outside these tents were piles of blood-stained first-aid bandages as high as your armpits. The great square in front of the station was black, or rather grey, with troops. There was a large Cossack escort waiting outside Kaulbars' railway train on a siding. There was another escort near Kuropatkin's carriage, which nobody was allowed to approach. There was a third escort outside the carriage of General Tserpitsky.

GENERAL KUROPATKIN'S TRAIN 261

Crowds of officers were also standing outside these carriages awaiting the behests of these and other generals. Inside heated discussions were going on. Through the window-panes you could see that some of the officers were standing up, gesticulating and pointing to maps. Messengers were arriving every few moments. Once an excited Cossack rode up shouting that the Japanese were only three versts off. The restaurant at the railway station was as crowded as ever. There was hardly standing-room on the platform.

The number of trains that were in would have been no discredit to a big depôt in America. Most of them, however, were Red Cross trains, white, and bearing the name and coat of arms of some princess or other.

There was a crowd of *czvoscheeks* in front of the station. Private soldiers who seemed to have nothing else to do turned many a decent penny by holding horses. The collection of fine horses there reminded one of a horse show. The little village of Greek stores near the station did a roaring trade, and, strange to say, the prices were not exorbitant.

In the censor's office, No. 15, sat Colonel Pestitch, the head censor, displaying a gold molar in an unceasing smile, the result of the good news he hourly received. This news he generally communicated to the correspondents. Colonel Pestitch was a personification of optimism.

In an open space on the road leading to the city there was to be seen on the 4th a sight which would, even in the days of miracles, have been considered striking. Four or five hundred of the former Hunghuzes which Russia had for some years past kept in her pay were there marshalled. They were all young men, well armed, well mounted, dressed in flaring silk, yellow cummerbunds tied around their waists, golden ornaments hanging from their necks. One could hardly believe that these men belonged to the peaceful Chinese race, so firm were their handsome faces, so fiercely did they return through their oblique eyelids the stare of inquisitive foreigners. On Russians whom curiosity led to finger those very unusual specimens of Celestial manhood they promptly drew their swords, and it was easy to see that when they did so they were not showing off, as Russian officers sometimes show off with naked sabres in the *cafés chantants*.

These interesting gentlemen had evidently attained that enviable state of mind (which, with the exception of Japanese soldiers, few people in the modern world can be said to have attained) in which, every morning that they open their eyes, they are perfectly prepared to regard their own violent death as one of the most probable occurrences of the coming day, and when men reach that stage their conduct is not always distinguished by an excess of caution and self-restraint.

From afar off, the good citizens of Nurhachu's ancient capital watched, in awe and wonder, this band of freebooters. Village legends and tales and old nurses' rhymes had often spoken of them, but never a single specimen had the good burghers of Mukden seen before, save, disarmed and bound, on the execution ground outside the west gate of Mukden.

Where these desperadoes came from I do not know. Where they were sent to I do not know. I can only say that they all disappeared mysteriously next day. But on this day of troubles and rumours, their apparition excited no great attention, and, with the exception of a local photographer, I think that I was the only foreigner to notice them or to snapshot them. They seemed to me like one of those mysterious but necessary signs which are, according to the Apocalypse, to precede the end of the world. Their coming and their going were alike mysterious, but in that day of death and destruction and red ruin, of the imminent fall of Mukden and the tottering of the Muscovite throne in Manchuria, the dead would hardly have excited attention had they risen from their graves and walked the streets.

At 3 P.M. I set out with Tserpitsky for the west. With our Cossack escort we rode at great speed to the little village of Tapau, north of Madyapu and south-west of Mukden. Tserpitsky's new line ran from Kwanlinpu to Likwanpu. North of him was Gerngross and the brave First Siberian, or at least as much of it as had arrived. South of him was Gershelmann, with the Forty-first Artillery brigade, and Roussanoff. We had now, among others, the fourteenth division. Previously the Japanese had been able to hurl against the numerically inferior Russian right no less than eight divisions, equivalent to the whole Japanese army at the battle of Liao-Yang. Now the fight would be fairer, for, in addition to Gerngross, an independent corps, to operate north-west of Mukden, was formed under Von Launitz, but, alas, it was already too late.

After remaining at Tapau till the evening Tserpitsky started at nightfall for Yangshihtun. There were six huge conflagrations in front of us. As we drew close to them we discovered a long line of our infantry waiting in a field. Tserpitsky, short, red, puffy, but brave as a Paladin, rode impetuously among them. They surged around him with fixed bayonets like frightened children around a father. They pressed close to him, shaken, terror-stricken, as if the sound of his words could confer invincibility. "Men of Minsk!" he began, but this was too formal. "Rebyata!" he said, "children! Russia always conquers! We'll conquer now! Advance and sweep those pagan Japanese to hell! Now!" imploringly, almost tearfully. "There will be no retreat, no coming back!" (A loud cry of "Nyet! nyet! vashe prevoshoditelstvo!") For a moment the old general was overcome by emotion. Then he mastered himself by a strong effort and recommenced: "Rebyata! molodtzi!" but suddenly his voice broke, and, turning to his staff, he said huskily: "Give them vodka! Give them anything! Send them on! God bless you! God bless you!" and, shaking hands fervently, tearfully, with the colonel of the regiment, who had at the time been standing at attention beside his horse's head, he plunged his spurs into his steed and went off at his usual breakneck pace.

We now approached very near to one of the burning villages, trampling in the darkness over thousands of preserved meat tins, which had probably been carried off from Suhudyapu. On the walls of this burning village figures were outlined against the flames, figures of soldiers, small soldiers with round caps and overcoats of which the skin-lined collars swept upward round the face and ears after the manner of a lotus blossom. Crack! crack! crack! They were firing at us. We had come too near. Increasing our speed we soon left the dangerous village behind and came, in the densest darkness, to another where there was no conflagration, not even a gleam of light, and behind which thousands of Russians were massed in trenches. These men also Tserpitsky addressed, winding up by ordering the colonel to give them one yen each! On hearing this the poor, simple-minded, tow-headed Muscovites, going in hundreds to their death, nearly went mad with delight; but, good heavens! that very morning a Chinese jinriksha coolie had nearly stabbed me in the streets of Mukden for presuming to offer him only three yen for an hour's work!

The General and his staff entered the village, while Rikacheff and I got a soldier to hold our horses. We promised him twenty-five kopecks; and he was delighted. Taking us for Cossacks, he began to expatiate on how differently Cossack officers and infantry officers treated their men. " Why, one of our officers would never think of talking to us so friendly as that," he began, but without waiting to hear the rest of it, we left him hurriedly and joined the General in a Chinese house, where after sleeping somewhere in my boots, as usual, I was awakened toward daybreak by the loudest bombardment I had ever listened to. We were like insects living in a drum which was getting a tremendous whack on both sides every few minutes. The house shook as if from the shock of an earthquake. The paper window-panes bulged out like the sails of a ship in a typhoon and then relaxed with a shiver. We feared that with the next terrific bellow the flimsy structure would fall to pieces. Meanwhile, the rattle-rattle-rattle of the rifles was incessant, close and angry. Hearing that sort of uproar the first thing in the morning, when it is dark and one is only half awake, the average person is inclined to imagine that he has died during the night and is not waking up in heaven.

It was my good friend Rikacheff who aroused me, and I remember that he spent a considerable time trying to make me grasp the fact that, so far, I was alive, and that if I intended to remain alive I had better hustle and find my horse, as we were leaving instantly. Oh, those horses! the trouble they gave us! they had never been unsaddled day or night for weeks, so there was no trouble on that score; but they had such a habit of breaking loose, and it was so difficult, with our hands almost frozen, to put the bit into their unwilling mouths. On this occasion the man we had bribed with twenty-five kopecks to look after them had disappeared, and so, of course, had the horses. Before we had found them we had received several kicks from strange irascible animals, whose hindquarters we had unwittingly bumped against in the darkness, but bridling them was a task I should not like to undertake again. When I had got the bit under my horse's lip and all seemed to be well he would suddenly knock me down with a toss of his head, which seemed to say:

"No, no, no! By no manner of means! Why, I haven't finished breakfast yet," and I would have to begin all over again. His usual plan, however, was to keep his teeth tightly clenched, evidently with the idea of convincing me that there was no opening in that quarter and that I had been mistaken in thinking that there was. Finally, however, I succeeded in getting the bit into his mouth, and, having done so, I had to wait full three hours before the General left!

It was, of course, our own artillery that made most

GENERAL KUROPATKIN'S TRAIN 267

of the noise, and not the Japanese artillery, but, nevertheless, our danger was considerable, and I did not quite know whether to admire or to blame Tserpitsky for running such risks. When he sent me a message to come and have breakfast with him I decided, however, only to admire him.

It seemed to me that the Japanese knew we were in this village—perhaps we had been followed thither by some of the soldiers who had fired at us from the walls of the burning village—at any rate, two shells exploded in the front yard of our house, and one shrapnel made a hole in the roof of the room where General Tserpitsky and his adjutant were sitting, filling the room with dust, but doing no further damage. Many bullets also struck the walls of the house, and many more whistled harmlessly overhead.

I spent only about an hour in this house after daybreak, but I could write a book about it owing to the marvellous clearness with which at this period of excessive strain every little detail impressed itself on my mind. I went into the street to wash myself at a frozen horse-trough, and I shall never forgot how deserted that street looked. It was not the desertion of early morning—it was the desertion of death. London town must have looked like that during the Great Plague. At the street corner a horse lay dead. Further off lay a dead man. By-and-by the Russian troops stole past me with the silence and cautiousness of thieves in a bedroom. I should not have been so particular about washing myself at this particular time had it not been for the fact that, not having washed for several days, my eyelashes had become clogged with dust. While I was washing myself three Shimose shells fell in quick succession at the back of the General's house, and as it now seemed certain that the Japanese really knew we were there Tserpitsky decided to leave, and accordingly we went eastward across the plain, galloping at a great rate, amid the billows of impenetrable dust, which sometimes permitted the heads and bodies of the Cossacks to be seen—sometimes the heads alone. We went as far back as Tapau or Dapu.

CHAPTER XII

MARCH 5, 6 AND 7

MARCH 5 fell on a Sunday, and, comparatively speaking, it had something of a Sabbath calm about it, as far at least as I was concerned. I remained all day at Dapu with Tserpitsky, watching a great semicircle of bursting shells at a safe distance. I soon began to feel bored, however. It was like watching a football match at such a distance that you could only see the dust raised by the players. It was a fine day, and the sun shone brightly on long lines of wounded being carried past and on numbers of unexploded Japanese shells scattered over the fields.

It is a mistake to suppose that a battle is a display of terrible energy all the time. Sometimes officers and even generals take tea and smoke, and on such occasions the irresponsible correspondent comes perilously near to loafing. Two Zabaïkal batteries and two sotnia of the Verkhnyudinsky Cossacks were this day attached to our force; and, in spite of his wounded leg, General Mishchenko came all the way from Mukden in his carriage in order to give his old chief, Tserpitsky, the benefit of his advice. They had been together during the Boxer troubles in China, but, alas! to use an expressive American colloquialism, they were now, "up against a different proposition."

How strange, pathetic almost, it was to read at this time in old newspapers of the great exploits of Russian generals against the Chinese in 1900, generals who were now unable to do anything against the Japanese! Sakharoff's march along the Sungari, Linievitch's capture of Newchwang and Mukden, Rennenkampf's storming of Aïgoun, Orloff's celebrated passage of the Khingan mountains, how great these feats would have looked if there had been no Russo-Japanese War! How small they now seemed! It was good for Pizarro and Cortes that they had never been called upon to fight some stubborn people like the English or the Dutch. Perhaps, too, it was good for us English that we never stirred up in India such a nest of hornets as the Japanese.

At five o'clock in the evening, four mortar batteries—thirty-two guns,—moved slowly round on our left towards Madyapu in a long and most imposing line, which greatly cheered our soldiers; but what we on the spot considered as the most important event of the day, although history may take a different view, was the fact that one of the fine kitchen waggons which the Russians made use of in their army, paid us a flying visit, which greatly improved our temper. Immediately after, however, a couple of ugly incidents rudely disturbed this happy state of mind. A party of one hundred and fifty Russians, who told a rather incredible story about having lost their regiment, were found wandering about near the Japanese lines in the direction of Madyapu, evidently with the intention of surrendering. Tserpitsky gave them a terrible scolding, and immediately marched them into the very hottest corner in the whole field, a place where they might easily get killed, but could not possibly surrender without being cut to pieces by their own men.

Then a Russian deserter was brought in with his hands tied behind his back, charged with having been among the Japanese, and having even fired on his own men. It was an extraordinary tale; but the dusty, bitter soldiers who led him in asserted that he did not belong to any regiment in that part of the field, and that they had seen him leave the Japanese lines and come crawling in among them, evidently in order to ascertain their strength and then to bring the information back to the enemy. The inference was that he had surrendered to the Japanese, perhaps months before, and that they had ever since employed him to go about in his Russian uniform and get them information which neither they themselves nor their Chinese spies could obtain. This unfortunate renegade met with little sympathy from his captors. On his observing with white lips that he had a wife and children at home, one of the soldiers told him not to worry about them, as "the Japanese will send them the money all right."

The chief of staff abused him fiercely, winding up by asking him if he belonged to the Orthodox Church and if he wore a cross. It would have been a great discovery if he had turned out to be a Jew; but, on the breast of his shirt being torn open, it was discovered that he did wear a cross—a Greek cross, too, not a Latin one.

About the same time several Chinese, accused of signalling, were brought in. Most of them were knocked all in a heap, so to speak, with fright; but one handsome, affable youth, who spoke two or three words of "pigin" Russian, used an amount of diplomacy which, considering the great disadvantages under which he laboured, was truly magnificent, although at times the awful fear clutching at his heart would show for a second through this veneer of self-confidence. Unable to make much use of his tongue, which must have been a very sugary one in his own language, he used his fine almond eyes and winning smile with all the skill of a coquette; but he might just as well have ogled a milestone. I did not go to see him killed, but employed myself more usefully in going around the village with Rikacheff, trying to find a vacant house, for it was rather crowded at the general's. We were astonished to discover one fine house quite empty, and on inquiring why it had not been occupied, we were told that it was because a Japanese bullet had come through the roof on the previous day and killed a soldier as he was eating his dinner. Flattering ourselves that we, at any rate, were free from superstitious fears, Rikacheff and I at once took up our abode here, but when darkness fell we suddenly discovered that it was a mistake after all to separate ourselves from the Staff.

On Monday, the 6th, things were again quiet, and even monotonous. This was all the better for us, as it showed that, in spite of their five or six general assaults daily, the Japanese had practically failed to move us from the positions we had taken up west and south-west of Mukden on the 4th. A day or so more and we would take root in those positions, as we had taken root in the positions south of the Hun after the battle of the Shaho. That day or so was not to be given us. On the 7th Nogi began one of the most terrible assaults in history.

On the morning of that day I was awakened about an hour before dawn by the roar of thirty Russian batteries, 240 cannon, and by the continuous explosion of Japanese shells.

I shall not soon forget the scene. It was the bare interior of a wretched Chinese hovel, which the staff had casually appropriated at a late hour the night before—I may here remark that, whether from chance or design, we slept in a different village every night—and I found myself lying on the "kang" wrapped in a Russian *pelisse* and with a brick for a pillow. There were several colonels on the same "kang," and the ground was strewn thick with orderlies, who were lying around in such a way as to suggest that they had all been killed by a shell. One, a Don Cossack, was even lying asleep in the doorway.

There was a light in the adjoining room, and an excited voice was calling into a telephone. There seemed to be some difficulty about getting the party at the other end to understand, for the same phrase was frequently repeated. It was to the effect that the Japanese were advancing against Fudyatun, and that this was the commencement of a grand general attack on the part of the enemy. In the subsequent conversation the names of General Churnin (the gallant defender of Yangshihtun), General Roussanoff, General Pavloff (the commander of the Transbaïkal brigade), and of other leaders were frequently mentioned. Sometimes it would be Tserpitsky himself that would shriek into that telephone. Sometimes it would be his adjutant, Yannoffsky. Now it was the General Staff at Mukden that was communicated with; now it was some of the subordinate leaders in the firing line.

Meanwhile the Transbaïkal and Stryelkovi cannon almost deafened us. Louder and louder became the roar; swifter, angrier, more insistent, more breathless. And the greater grew that iron-throated clamour, the less confident I felt. I fancied I could detect in this frightful bellowing a whine of terror, a distinct note of fear. All this uproar simply meant that those yellow demons were just at their best for offensive purposes, when they should, had they been human beings at all, have been tired to death by their innumerable onslaughts for more than a week past. How could we continue to withstand such a people?

While ruminating in this dismal manner I got a message from the general, asking me to have breakfast with him. I accepted the invitation with almost indecent alacrity, for Tserpitsky always brought an excellent Russian cook along with him. While I was eating, my host told me that he was going to Fudyatun that morning, and urged me to order his cook to make anything I wanted in case he himself was absent throughout the day. This was the last I saw of this brave and kind-hearted gentleman. I went out next day to see the fighting on the west, and was never able to return to the 10th Corps, which held on, however, to Tapau till ten o'clock on the morning of the fatal 10th. How Tserpitsky himself managed to escape is a mystery to me. He received several wounds, from the effects of which he died, and I am not surprised at it, for Skobeleff himself was not more indifferent to his life.

Before leaving the 10th Corps Rikacheff and I paid another visit to the hard-pressed village of Yangshihtun, against which Nogi was at that moment hurling his bravest. The sunlight now flooded the vast, grey plain, which, devoid of even a single blade of grass, seemed the very image of desolation. On the sky-line was a small Buddhist chapel, looking like a Catholic shrine in the Sabine Hills, and beyond it was the Chinese village which we wanted to reach.

Half-way across the plain we could see several long widely-spaced lines of Russian soldiers lying on the ground, with heads raised slightly above the level of their bodies, and rifles projecting in front of them. They were not firing, however, for the firing-line, which they were on their way to reinforce or replace, was beyond the distant village. Very frequently we saw, afar off, small groups of men advancing towards us, slowly, mournfully, and as fearlessly as if they knew themselves to be invulnerable. When they came nearer we saw that each group was carrying a wounded comrade to the rear on a stretcher.

Shells were falling at intervals all over the plain, raising volcanic columns of black smoke, which slowly dissipated as the wind whirled them lazily along. When not thus engaged, the wind amused itself by raising, on its own account, columns of dun-grey dust, almost exactly like the columns of shimose, and whirling them about in the same way.

A soldier gravely told me that there was a wizard inside each of these "dust-spouts," and it did not seem at all improbable, for sometimes these pillars of dust went spinning down the wind like phantoms with long, flying robes.

A semicircle of snow-white, fleecy, shrapnel cloudlets hung over the line of prostrate Russians, like the aureole of stars one sees in pictures of the Blessed Virgin ; and, like a youth in crimson garments, the sun now appeared in the east. On seeing that a regiment was slowly following us in extended formation, probably in order to stiffen the force already at the front, we reined in our horses and waited for it to come up. It was a beautiful sight so long as I watched it with my face to the east, for then the hard details of the ground before me were all obliterated, and the spaces between the soldiers were filled by a wondrous misty, golden haze, amid which, hooded and gowned like Franciscans, the men advanced solemnly, like silent files of the Beatified in some mediæval Italian painting.

But when they had gone by and I gazed after them with the sun at my back, all the hard lines on the brown earth, and all the sordid tokens of toil and stress on the men's persons, came out with ghastly clearness. The blaze of martial glory ceased all at once to dazzle. The golden mist of illusion and romance which surrounds the military profession passed suddenly away, and the hard, clear daylight of reason illuminated inexorably this reluctant march to a miserable death.

Rikacheff, however, was not disillusioned. He seemed on the contrary to become more enthusiastic than ever. Riding in amongst the men, he spoke to them of God and of Russia, coupling these two names together as if they were the names of the two great facts of the Universe. The men were visibly touched and impressed by the zeal of this young man, and many a rough voice was heard thanking him. Circumstances such as these make me see in Russia a latent fanaticism which bodes ill, some day, for the countries on her frontiers both in Europe and Asia.

On a level plain east of a frozen brook on whose western side lay Yangshihtun, we found two batteries pounding away at the Japanese, and as Rikacheff said that he knew an officer in one of them, we approached to make inquiries. The artillery officers were reposing on their backs in shallow pits, each man with a telephone at his ear, and some tattered novels and empty sardine tins lying on the straw beside him. They told Rikacheff that his friend was at that moment in the Kumernya or village temple on the other side of the brook. We accordingly visited this temple, which was being used as an observation station, and which was consequently the focus of a hot Japanese rifle and artillery fire. Once I got inside this temple enclosure, I discovered with a shock that I had never before known what a hot fire meant.

Every Chinese temple has got an elaborate gateway, with a covering like a roof. This particular temple had got a fine, large specimen of such a gateway when I came in; but there was not much of it left when I departed, somewhat precipitately, a few moments later. There was also an additional rent in the temple roof, while the ground outside was as full of holes as a pepper-pot. The courtyard of the temple would have been in the same condition had it not been for the fact that it was paved. Consequently shells did not go deep into it, but, whenever one struck it, showers of stone and iron flew about in all directions. A few moments before my arrival, part of the gable had been blown off the sanctuary, and in the new, white light from heaven that now streamed straight down on their faces—for the first time probably since the temple roof had been put on—the distorted idols inside glared diabolically against the sombre background. The light fell as in a painting by Correggio, but never did that joyful Italian make light fall on faces like those. My Celtic superstitiousness made my blood run cold at the prospect of meeting my last end in such an unholy spot, and my horror was increased by the presence of an insane Chinese bonze, whose sorceries and incantations, directed apparently against the unseen powers of the air that were smashing his temple to pieces, were demoniacal and uncanny.

The officer in charge of this post lived in a bomb-proof, from which he frequently emerged to take a hasty look through one of those telescopes, which, by means of a series of mirrors inside, enable a person to look over a wall without raising his head above the level of it—a hydroscope, I think, they call it. It was good that he was provided with such an instrument, for the sheet of bullets that flew over that massive temple wall could only be compared to a slanting hailstorm. I was able to get just one glimpse of the Japanese, or, rather, of one or two jet-black Japanese heads bobbing up and down behind a group of Chinese tombs a few hundred yards off; and of a single active little figure in a khaki-coloured overcoat that shot from one mound of earth to another. At this point the Japanese were overpoweringly superior in numbers, all that stood between them and us being a bleak grey line of Russian infantrymen lying, close-packed, behind the squat mud wall which surrounded the village.

Rikacheff duly discovered his friend, and, standing on a piece of ground littered with empty shell-cases, unexploded projectiles, and bits of twisted and tortured metal, they tried to talk. But, what with the rapid bang! bang! bang! of the shimose, the crash of falling masonry, and the ominous whistle of high-velocity projectiles passing overhead, it was almost as difficult to carry on a conversation as it would have been on board a ship during a typhoon.

This was the very front. It was one of the hottest points of the battle, and in order to get a good view of it I went into the village. What a desolation! There came into my mind biblical descriptions of cities wasted and empty and smitten by the hand of God. Soldiers whose faces were blanched with terror hid behind tottering walls. The grey-coated line in front fired steadily, steadily, as if they were automatic machines fixed to the ground. Meanwhile the Japanese outflanking army was sweeping round towards Pehling, the tombs of the Manchu Emperors.

CHAPTER XIII

THE RETREAT FROM MUKDEN

ON March 7 the Japanese outflanking army made a sudden sweep eastwards, which brought them close to the Imperial tombs and to the railroad. On the morning of March 8 I rode out to the north-west with my friend Rikacheff to see what was happening in that direction. We first came to Houta (or Howha, as the Russians call it), a village a little north of the Tsinmintun Road, and distinguished by a pagoda of much the same appearance as the famous pagoda at Liaoyang. Here we found the staff of the Second Army.

Then we pushed on towards Padyaza, a few miles to the north of Houta, but, long before we had reached that point, we learned from the dull rumbling and pounding and the continual flash of the shells that a terrible battle was raging there. Before us, a grey monotony of desolation, the level plain stretched away to the horizon under a pallid sky, which seemed to be the reflection of the wearied earth. O great, sad plains of Mukden, torn by shells and wheels and horses' hoofs, stained with blood and littered with shrapnel, ye seem a land that God has cursed and condemned to remain for ever sterile!

Scattered over this plain like islands were clumps

THE RETREAT FROM MUKDEN 281

of trees which marked the position of villages. Behind the villages which were close to us lay Russian batteries which went boom! boom! boom! steadily and exasperatingly. Their shells burst in clusters on the tree-fringed horizon, and at five or six points great sheets of flame and white smoke indicated where villages burned. A long column of Russians began to advance over the plain, in the midst of which shimose shells now began to explode in ominous black clouds. Half a dozen times in succession they burst in almost the same place. That place was in front of the column and on its line of march. The column turned at an acute angle and avoided the dangerous spot. It was evidently bound for Padyaza on the north-west. Everything seemed bound for Padyaza, where the smoke arose out of the earth as the smoke of a great furnace, and the sun and the air were darkened. Everybody watched Padyaza. Now and then batteries would rush past with all the clatter of fire-engines. Sometimes they stopped and unlimbered, but always they sent their shells towards Padyaza, beyond which there was something formidable massing. It is a vital point. It dominates the railway. If Nogi breaks through here, all is lost.

Rikacheff and I hurry forward. We join a line of soldiers lying on the open ground in front of Padyaza. The dusty officers receive us civilly, but no longer with their old cordiality. I, at least, am but a foreigner come with an opera-glass in my hand to watch, with a critical air, the last agony of the Russian army, to see the end of this formidable drama.

We are in an exposed position, and bullets are coming thick. A horse close by is hit. I feel somehow as if I were facing a gale of wind. A Japanese machine-gun spouts out a stream of lead which can be easily traced by the puffs of dust it raises from the clayey prominences in the field. It swings backward and forward in an acute angle, like a search-light. Rikacheff lends his horse to a soldier, who has been told to go back for more ammunition. A column of smoke bursts from Padyaza, and the broken remnant of a Russian regiment retreats from it. A few khaki-clad figures flit underneath the trees, and the captain, who has his binoculars to his eyes, tells his men to open fire on the village which, a moment before, was Russian.

As the Japanese fire now became very hot, Rikacheff and I retired, and were soon followed by the Russian firing-line. The number of wounded was very great, so great that many of them could not be attended to. In one case I saw two soldiers, not Red Cross men, carrying back in their arms a wounded comrade, to whom even first aid had not been rendered owing to want of bandages. I gave them the little packet of lint I always carried with me, and Rikacheff helped them to bind the wound, which was a shocking one. Afterwards, by means of their rifles and of a little *tente d'abri* which one of them carried, folded, athwart his shoulder, they managed to improvise a stretcher. There was a continual stream of slightly wounded men staggering or limping past unassisted, and I must say that few of them were bearing up well. They had the air of people that had got hurt in a row that didn't concern them. Most of them were moaning piteously. As they passed me, one of them drew his hand across his wounded forehead, and on finding the hand covered with blood, he said, as if grieved and astonished:

THE RETREAT FROM MUKDEN
THE FIGHT AT THE RAILWAY EMBANKMENT

"Kroff idyot" (It is bleeding). Another, wounded in the left hand, talked to himself and sighed. A pathetic figure was an untidy, bent, middle-aged man trudging towards the hospital, the butt of his gun sticking out underneath his coat.

Rikacheff and I now went further north. Behind many of the low mud walls that divided the fields we found lines of soldiers; and in one place there were no soldiers, but a great collection of boots, overcoats and blood-stained bandages, which probably indicated that a shell had wrought great havoc there. We sat down for a moment on this scarred, unlucky spot to eat some cheese we had brought with us, when suddenly a soldier rushed up and begged one of us to lend him a horse for a short time, as he wanted to order more ammunition. He got the horse and duly returned it, but no sooner had he done so than the Russian line in front of us—it consisted of a regiment belonging to the 1st Siberian Corps—began to fall back. Thus, on this day I saw our firing-line give way at two different points, and in neither case was the movement such as I had previously imagined a retreat to be. It was no *sauve qui peut*, for the men trudged back slowly and sullenly, covered by their own batteries.

They were too tired to go back quickly, and the Japanese were too tired to follow them up. On both sides the limit of human endurance had almost been reached, and, if finally the Japanese won, it was because their fanaticism had made them more than human.

We now entered the great forest that surrounds the Imperial Tombs of Pehling, where, in the deep shade beneath the murmuring pines, the ancient monarchs of Manchuria had wisely chosen their last resting-place. The peace that prevailed here was in startling contrast to the uproar outside.

Even a company of soldiers who passed at a distance through the forest aisles seemed, in that cathedral light, to be transformed, beatified. Standing in the shady path, with the gentle rustling of the trees in our ears, Rikacheff and I instinctively lowered our voices as if we had been in a basilica. We seemed to have stumbled by accident on an ark in which God had preserved a specimen of a beautiful world which had been wrecked, smashed and over-run by a deluge of armed men. It suddenly occurred to me that the Almighty could not, after all, be the pitiless Jehovah whom I had heard about.

There was not a soul in the great shady quadrangles, not a priest in the reposeful ancient temples. Nest-building sparrows and the long line of gigantic stone animals which flanked the avenue appeared to be the sole inhabitants of this sequestered ruin. The manes of dead Emperors seemed to guard the spot.

At length, however, a Chinese guide advanced cautiously towards us from a distant hut, but, in spite of his stolid appearance, he must have been very much upset, for he forgot to ask us, as usual, for money before unbarring the various iron-studded doors that led to the interior of the Mausoleum. Expecting to get a good view of the Japanese, I ascended the highest tower, but the huge trees and the white semi-circular earthen mound, beneath which lie the bones of Nurhachu, prevented me from seeing anything. Rikacheff and I wound up the day's proceedings by getting arrested as Japanese spies.

Thursday was a day on which no sensible person

would venture out of doors, for the dust-storm which raged was unparalleled even in the dusty annals of Mukden, and M. Naudeau, of the Paris *Journal*, and Mr. R. H. Little, of the Chicago *Daily News*, who returned from the front unrecognisable by their best friends, and looking as if they had rolled in dust all the way home, assured me that, even if I had gone out, I could have seen nothing owing to the storm. I employed myself therefore in the composition of a long telegram to the *Herald*, which I brought to the censor's office at the railway-station. Colonel Pestitch was not at home, being probably half-way to Tiehling by that time, but an English-speaking captain, who acted as his subordinate, took charge of my telegram and said he would translate it for the colonel. He assured me that the telegraph line was uninterrupted, and was so optimistic that I not only paid for this telegram in advance but made a small deposit with him to cover the expenses of future wires from Mukden. Of course he said absolutely nothing about it being necessary to leave the city that night, and nobody else gave me any warning.

On my way back to the town, I went astray owing to the fierceness of the dust-storm (which, by the way, proved so useful to Nodzu that very night), but at length I regained my house in safety.

Some six months earlier four correspondents—Mr. Charles Hands, of the *Daily Mail*; Mr. R. H. Little, of the Chicago *Daily News*; Mr. George Denny, of the Associated Press, and myself—had rented, for our use whenever we came to Mukden, a large Chinese house, which stood in a retired spot underneath the imposing south-east corner of Mukden's ancient battlements.

Late on the night of March 9 some of the correspondents—there were only six of us now left, and I was the only Britisher among them—were discussing in this house the position of affairs. With us were three American *attachés* and one British *attaché*. It was a serious and dramatic moment. We heard that Nogi had wrecked the railway to the north. We also heard that it had been repaired, but were not inclined to believe this. We heard that Oku had broken through the line to the south-west. It was now certain that the battle was lost. The gigantic army of Muscovy was going to pieces. The whole fabric might come down at any moment, and the disaster would be terrible.

We felt the responsibility of men on whom the eyes of the world are fixed. We were the sole representatives of England, Germany, France, and America —the only White Powers now left on the face of the earth—at a battle which would change the course of history; and as we stood there, with the Yellow Wave toppling over us, it almost seemed to us as if old Europe were undone. We talked gravely, like ambassadors burdened with a great mission.

"Can Kuropatkin make good his retreat?" was the question we all asked. The military men thought he could not. He was trapped at last. A terrible object lay across his path. That object was Nogi. Somebody muttered the word "Sedan."

We sat there discussing every possible aspect of the situation. We wondered if the Russians would try to escape by the west. If they did, it would be Napoleon's retreat from Moscow over again. The mere thought of that great army of nearly half a million of men flying across the frozen steppes of Mongolia with the Japanese army behind them, the Chinese army on their flanks, and the Mongol horsemen in front, made us shudder. It would be one of the most frightful disasters in history.

Probably the Russians would make a desperate resistance close around Mukden, and attempt to cut their way through the Japanese cordon at some point or other. This meant that Mukden would be shelled to-morrow morning. The *attachés* were so certain on this point that Captain Bill Judson, one of the American officers, proceeded to draw up plans for a bomb-proof to be constructed in our courtyard. Principally out of Irish "contrariness," but also with the object of lightening to some extent the gloom which had settled on our little party, I insisted that the Russians were not cut off at all that they would fight a successful rearguard action at Mukden as they had done at Liaoyang, and that they would not leave the city for three days yet. I made a bet on this subject with Mr. Little—principally because I felt certain that, if I lost, Mr. Little would have some difficulty in getting his money, as in that case we would be all scattered to the four winds of heaven—and I regret to say that when we met at Dalny, about a week later, this was one of the first things on which Little refreshed my memory.

Meanwhile I congratulated myself on having sent my baggage north with Philipoff and the Cossacks.

At Liaoyang I had missed some of the best fighting by leaving a day too soon, when, if it had not been for my baggage, I could have remained behind and fallen back with the Russian rear-guard; and I was determined not to repeat this mistake at Mukden. I would leave it with the very last Russian detachment. So I did, and I was captured with that detachment.

Meanwhile we solemnly used up our last tins of preserves and our last bottles of whisky, for it was a great occasion. It was the eve of the Deluge. There was bound to be a catastrophe next day, and God alone knew the form it would take.

In the next room, Little's Chinese boy "Ding" was cleaning up the supper things, as the occasional clatter of a spoon on the stone floor or the tinkle of cups and saucers indicated.

Outside there was perfect silence. The cries of the Chinese pedlars—various, mournful, persistent and mysterious as the cries of unknown animals in tropical forests—had now quite ceased. Nature was hushed in horror. With prophetic eye the earth was gazing, speechless, at a tragedy. She had already received into her bosom twenty-seven thousand Russian dead! She had seen the greatest defeat in Russian history. She had seen the bloodiest fight men had ever fought. And now she foresaw the retreat.

It is one o'clock. Hark! there suddenly bursts forth to the south-east a heavy sound of rifle-firing. We all jump to our feet and gaze at one another in silence.

For the last ten days we had been listening to rifle-firing day and night, but never had we heard anything so ominous, so menacing, so close as this. What gave an uncanny touch to it was the dominating, melancholy boom of a single great gun, which rang forth at regular intervals with surprising clearness, and was immediately followed by an echo almost as loud. No wonder that our faces paled with superstitious awe when we heard that funereal note, for it was the death-bell tolling for the loss of Mukden, for the passing away of Russia's empire in Manchuria, for the strangling in its cradle of a great Eurasian State whose arms might well, in manhood, have stretched to Bender Abbas and Cape Cormorin.

Nay, who knows but that it was the death-knell of the Russian Empire itself?

When that gun sounded, Nodzu had crossed the Hun River, and the ancient seat of the Manchus was for ever lost to Russia. Kuroki had crossed further east, and was advancing by forced marches in order to join hands with Nogi across Kuropatkin's line of retreat. Mukden was compassed with the armies of the Mikado.

With one accord we all rushed outside. A distant village was flaming redly in the south. Shells were bursting afar off. In the sky there were mysterious glows, like great signs from heaven. Ghostly searchlights were moving backwards and forwards like gigantic fingers. But we could not read that mysterious handwriting on the vast wall of night. We could not surmise what was happening. It was all a gigantic enigma. We did not know that the secret net of fate had already been thrown over Mukden, and that we were all of us caught in its enormous sweep. I went to sleep that night in a rather uneasy frame of mind, for in such topsy-turvy times there was scarcely any kind of development that would have surprised me. Early on Friday morning there was a stillness in the air which, combined with the absence of Russian soldiers, was decidedly disquieting, for it reminded me forcibly of the unearthly, unaccustomed calm which came over Liaoyang the day Shushan was evacuated, and which I had at first taken for conclusive proof of a Japanese retreat. It looked as if the Russians had withdrawn during the night, and, owing to the retired position of my house, they might easily have done so without my knowledge. Riding hastily forth, I found the gates of Mukden now guarded by Chinese instead of by Russian soldiers, the shops shut, and the streets swarming with a curious and excited populace. I felt rather nervous about riding through the city, now that it was no longer European, but there was no help for it, so I rode through. When I emerged at the west gate, I saw that the Russian railway station and all the buildings around it were in flames, while from various points on the outskirts of the city great columns of smoke and red tongues of fire indicated the whereabouts of Russian granaries.

Outside the west gate I called at a Lama temple, where I was well known, and found the old Daï-Lama greatly distressed about the burning of one of his houses, which had contained Russian stores. I felt vaguely refreshed by his irritation; for it proved that human nature had not, after all, been swamped and obliterated by the gigantic disasters that were happening. Incredible as it might appear, the old Lama evidently looked forward to a time when the world would regain its ancient calm. At that moment, however, he was very much afraid of the drunken stragglers who from time to time found their way into his courtyard, and he hailed my coming with great joy, for he seemed to think that I would prove a protector against these desperadoes, and,

THE RETREAT FROM MUKDEN

as ill-luck would have it, one of them came roaring into the temple just while we were talking. Telling me to tackle him, the Daï-Lama hastily retreated to his room and carefully barred the lath-and-paper door thereof; but in China a door is very often little more than a symbol of privacy, and the big soldier could have walked through this one with but little knowledge that there had been any obstacle in his way. In a very mild and subdued voice I asked the soldier in Russian what regiment he belonged to; and, taking me probably, in his drunken condition, for an officer, he soon went out again after some incoherent mutterings; whereupon the Daï-Lama and his shaven monks emerged from their hiding-places and hailed me with one voice as their benefactor and their deliverer, whom Buddha would reward. I went away, however, as soon as my horse was fed, for I was very doubtful of being equally successful with the next straggler.

At the railway-station the ground was covered with the usual litter of a flying army, and hordes of Chinese, looking like wreckers, were appropriating as much of it as they could, including some damaged rifles and bayonets. Many Russian soldiers were passing by in fairly good order, but dead tired. They frequently sat or lay on the ground to get a few moments' rest. Two or three of them had disinterred pathetic proofs of Russian aspirations in the shape of several ice blocks, of which the commissariat had buried a great quantity in the ground with a view to the coming summer, and were eating the ice greedily. I rode between the burning houses at the station until I found that, owing to the ammunition left behind in them, bullets were flying about as in a battle.

On one occasion I approached a soldier who was lying on the ground, evidently in a dying condition, and took a snapshot of him, feeling at the same time that I was a brute for doing so. To atone for my heartlessness, I afterwards approached the poor man in order to see if I could not help him in some way, but was disappointed when one of his comrades told me gruffly that he was only drunk.

At about three o'clock in the afternoon I began to suspect that the rearguard action which I was expecting would not come off after all, and that, in fact, *I* was the rearguard. At first I intended, despite the scriptural injunction, to turn back again to my house, to take up some things which I wanted to carry along with me; but on seeing the enormous crowds of Chinese through which I would have to pass, I changed my mind, and, riding as fast as I could, I soon overtook some tired and desperate-looking stragglers, one of whom shouted at me to stop, his object evidently being to deprive me of my horse. He continued bawling after me fiercely for about five minutes; but I rode on, preserving at the same time an appearance of imperturbable deafness and calm, although I expected a bullet to whizz past my ear at any moment, for unfortunately the man had forgotten to let go hold of his rifle. I was rather glad when I overtook a young officer on a white horse and a few mounted infantrymen, and I hastily presented my credentials to the former, but he only said cheerfully: "O chort! (devil!) *I* don't want to see your d——d papers," adding fiercely, "Have a cigarette!"

He belonged to the brave 1st Siberian Corps which had suffered so terribly during this battle, and he told me that he had not heard till that very day of the retreat having been decided on. "We, the under-officers, know nothing," he plaintively remarked, blowing a cloud of cigarette smoke through his nostrils; "the generals, you see, keep everything to themselves."

I reflected that it was very easy to understand why the generals had not told this poor fellow and his men that *they* were to be the scapegoats of the army. When travellers attacked by wolves in Siberia sacrifice a horse in order to gain time, they do not tell the animal why it is sacrificed. I took a liking to this young fellow, and decided I would stick to him as long as I could, so that I tried my best to interest him in myself. To convince him that I was above all suspicion, I began, first of all, to reel off the names of all the Russian officers belonging to his regiment that I knew; but I am afraid that I only made him sad, for after every single name I mentioned, including that of the colonel, he repeated the one dreadful dissyllable "umer" (dead). If was like the "Kyrie Eléison, Christi Eléison" in a Litany for the Dead.

As we went along, our party gradually grew larger, being joined by soldiers driving empty ammunition carts, by dismounted Cossacks, by slightly wounded men, by drunkards, by unarmed soldiers who seemed to be insane, and, generally speaking, by the flotsam and jetsam of war. We kept close to the railway on the eastern side, and, when we had reached a point a little north of the Imperial Mausolea at Pehling, we came suddenly on the traces of a big disaster. About a square mile of ground seemed to have been strewn thick with old mess-tins, over-turned carts, canteens, top-boots, socks, pelisses, dead horses, bags of flour, rifles, bayonets, cartridge-clips and cartridges. The bayonets and rifles seemed a new-cut crop of some kind. Alas! they were the only crop Manchuria yielded that year.

With large eyes, we stood contemplating this wreck, as one would contemplate a corpse, when suddenly our reverie was broken by a sudden shower of rifle bullets. Ping! ping! ping! ping! they savagely buried themselves in the railway embankment alongside us, raising little puffs of dust. Now, this embankment was ten feet above the level of the plain, but, about twenty yards ahead, a road crossed it, and for that road we all made an instant and simultaneous rush. I have a dim recollection of our party making immediate and generous contribution to the collection of curios that already strewed the ground, of frenzied soldiers flogging on cart-horses, of horsemen taking that ten-foot embankment at one bound, of infantry men running like hares, their accoutrements banging around them as if they were being whirled along by a typhoon.

The young Siberian officer with whom I had been riding pulled in his restive horse with a tug that threw it back upon its haunches and, without taking his cigarette from between his lips, cursed steadily. That was the last I ever saw of him.

When I got to the other side of the embankment (I was one of the first across) I found about five thousand soldiers there. Some of them were marching northwards. A long line of them were lying on the top of the embankment, firing as hard as they could on the Japanese, who were quite invisible. A good many were standing motionless. I went close to the base of the embankment so as to get the best shelter possible, but was horrified to find there the body of a soldier who had evidently been hit while he stood on that spot.

Let military men explain the phenomenon as they may, that embankment was no protection. Further on I found another dead man. Then I stopped. There was no safety anywhere.

Men now came rushing in out of the dust-storm to the north. They were in a hurry, as if pursued by cannibals. Among them was a young regimental surgeon, stylishly dressed, whom I ventured to question. For some time he could not speak, and his face worked as if he had taken poison. At last he waved his arms wildly and that seemed to relieve him, for he proceeded to tell a terrible tale. I expressed poignant sympathy, although I could only catch the words: "We were surrounded—shrapnelled—whole regiment wiped out." After a while, however, he was able to explain that the regiment with which he had been retreating had opened fire on some Buriat Cossacks whom they had mistaken for Japanese, and that, when the survivors were explaining matters to one another, the Japanese came upon the scene and were mistaken for Buriats until they had got very close. "It's the beginning of the tragedy," said I to myself, horror-stricken. "Like a wounded, blind, infuriated monster, the doomed army is beginning to devour its own children. God alone knows what's in store for us this coming night!"

On learning that I was a correspondent, the doctor implored me to go back to Mukden with him. I refused, whereupon he became hysterical and lost all self-respect. An officer who had seen us from a distance elbowed his way through the crowd, and asked what it was all about, whereupon the doctor told him that we were both going back to Mukden, to surrender.

"Well, you're your own masters, gentlemen," dryly remarked the newcomer, turning away, after having given both of us a look. That look was too much for me : my race and my profession seemed to be on their trial before all these foreigners ; and I told the doctor, once and for all, that I would *not* go back with him. Correspondents should not, I said, contract the habit of getting captured.

The officers with whom I decided to remain did not appear to care very much one way or the other. In fact, they seemed to regard me with distrust. So did the soldiers.

"What regiment do you belong to, golubchik (little pigeon) ? " I asked of one of them.

"We don't tell these things to the likes of you," he answered gruffly.

Softening somewhat, about half an hour later (probably because that, in the meantime, he had got wounded in the arm) he asked me what "goobernie " (Government division of the Russian Empire) I came from. He asked this in the tone of a kindly judge giving a criminal a chance to exculpate himself, and when I told him that I came from a part of Europe which was not Russian, he seemed very puzzled. It was like saying that I came from another planet. Shaking his head sadly and incredulously, he turned away from me and never opened his lips to me again.

Meanwhile the doctor continued to make a sad exhibition of himself.

THE RETREAT FROM MUKDEN

"Can any one give me a Red Cross brassard?" he cried, waving a bundle of rouble notes in the air, "for God's sake a Red Cross brassard!"

One youthful Feldsher hastily gave him one, but refused to take any money for it. Then the officer started for Mukden, without bidding any of us good-bye, and I have never seen him since.

Finding myself thus left alone among men who mistrusted me and who did not know me, I felt disheartened and desperate, and did my best to gain some sympathy from them, first by showing them my Russian credentials and then by climbing up the embankment and exposing myself to the dangers of the soldiers who lay there. This foolish performance seemed to touch them somewhat, and one of the officers then lent me a pair of binoculars, but I could see no Japanese. Coming down from the embankment I made the acquaintance of the other officers, who had now become friendly, and of the colonel, a brave old gentleman, who spoke to me in French.

As time passed, and I showed no signs of treason, by waving of flags or lighting of fires, or by any other suspicious performance, the private soldiers also began to relent and gather round me. One of them, called Soïkin, had been more than a year in New York, but could not speak one word of English. He had spent all that year in the house of a German whom he called Baris Enché, a rich man who had seven or eight horses and who spoke Russian. It was a corner house, he said, and situated on the main street. He seemed surprised that I did not identify it from that description.

My conversation with Soïkin was interrupted by the

order to march. The colonel devoutly crossed himself and said : " In God's name (S. Bogom) let us go."

Night was now coming on, and, as the dust storm hid everything, our leaders thought that it would be a good time to break away. Their plan was to cross the railway, march as far as possible east, and then swing round towards the north, so as to get round the Japanese obstacle in front, instead of going bang into it.

I then mounted the embankment and stood, probably for the last time in my life, between the metals of that fatal railway, that idol of wood and steel, for which tens of thousands of brave men had died—in vain. From Port Arthur to Telissu, from Telissu to Ta-shih-chiao, from Ta-shih-chiao to Liaoyang, from Liaoyang to Mukden, their bones were scattered on both sides of it, and, in the whirling dust, an army of gibbering ghosts seemed to rush northwards from a land over which the Russian eagles shall never wave again.

As I crossed the track I threw a glance at the plain behind. It was as desolate as the valley of dry bones. Its only occupants were two corpses. One, who wore the little iron cross of St. George which is given to soldiers, lay on his back, but as he was propped up behind, probably by his large canvas bag, he always seemed to be raising himself on his elbow. His mouth was wide open. His head hung far back, and he was glaring straight up at the sky with an awful expression in his frozen eyes. He seemed to be uttering a gigantic blasphemy against God.

The other lay on his face, his head resting on his bent arm, and he looked as if he were asleep. Beyond the dead men was a stunted tree with a single withered branch, which pointed ominously north. In the dust and mist it seemed to me like the gaunt figure of a prophet. In the background was a mass of dark, storm-driven clouds, behind which faded, like the hopes of Russia, the last faint light of day.

In the south, Mukden was now invisible, but, afar off, I could see the smoke of its burning. To the south-west, where there had been fierce fighting the day before, I could see a series of little fires. They were not burning villages, for all the villages had been already burned. No, they were the fires which the Japanese had lighted to consume their dead, and they twinkled in the distance like death-lights, like the ghostly flames which the Russian "mujik" sometimes sees glimmering above graves.

Once we got across the railway, our old colonel addressed his men in the usual sing-song style of the Russian leaders, calling them "molodtszi" (brave fellows), and telling them that they would win and crush the Japanese; but, instead of the long, measured shout with which the Russian soldiers are taught to reply to any speech of their commander, there was an absolute and ominous silence. The poor devils had heard that sort of talk too often.

Even the subordinate officers had no hope of success. "We are surrounded," said one young lieutenant to me, gloomily; "we shall be taken prisoners."

This was the refrain of every conversation. One continually heard the private soldier saying otryezalee ("cut off"), propalee ("lost"), and *nu bratszi shabash!* ("now, brothers, we're done for"). There was something poetical and at the same time disquieting in the way they always referred, vaguely, to the Japanese as "he" (on'), as if we were pursued, not by human beings, but by some monstrous beast.

For miles we seemed to be treading on nothing but rifles and cartridges, which some preceding column had thrown away. We also came across many of this column's wounded. One man, blinded in both eyes by a shot, rushed after us calling on us for God's sake (radee Boga) not to leave him. I halted till he came up, and spoke to him. He stumbled forwards with arms widely outspread so as not to miss me. At last one of his hands touched my holster, and he clutched it feverishly. "Thou art mounted, O brother, O little angel!" he said.

I did not know what to do with this poor fellow until a Chinese cart, driven by a soldier, came along and I tried to get him put inside; but as it was already choke-full of wounded, the soldier in charge of it suggested, with the gruffness of a man who is afraid that he is going to sob like a child, that my *protégé* had better walk behind this cart, holding on to the end of it; and, as this arrangement seemed to suit the blind man, it was adopted. A few minutes later, this vehicle with its load of wounded had disappeared as completely as if the earth had opened and swallowed it. It was the same with nearly everything else that I came in contact with throughout this evening and throughout the awful night which followed. I got acquainted with officers, baggage-carts, Cossacks, cannon, only to lose them again immediately, completely and for ever. A young lieutenant would come and speak to me in French. We would then walk side by side for a moment in silence, and when I would resume the conversation, lo! I would find that my youthful companion

THE RETREAT FROM MUKDEN

had suddenly become transformed into an elderly captain, sour and hirsute, speaking only Russian. The young lieutenant I would never meet again, It was a phantasmagoria, a wild jumble of transformation scenes, a feverish dream wherein all sorts of shapes and figures flit through the heated brain to disappear for ever. And, withal, it was a faithful epitome of life.

As I was riding along I nearly passed over another man, wounded in the leg, and unable to walk. Dismounting, I helped him into my saddle and got a soldier to lead the horse. I did this not so much from pity for the man as from the conviction that I myself would go to my Last Account that night. For some hours I had been vainly trying to recall any good that I had done since my birth, and, in a panic, I had resolved to lead a better life. Accordingly I gave the wounded men to drink from my water-bottle until the water was exhausted, and in every case they crossed themselves before tasting it, and thanked God and me. As Gogol say : " Pity for a fallen human creature is a strong Russian trait," and I think that if we had not spent so much time assisting the wounded, we might have escaped. I saw more acts of heroism that night than I had seen in twenty years of civil life. It was a mixture of the Millennium and Hell.

Soon afterwards I got separated from my horse, but at midnight, while we were resting for a moment near a burning village, I saw him again, and, with a sudden return of worldly prudence, determined to keep my eye on him, if only for the sake of the valuable collection of photographs which I carried in my saddle-bags. But, as soon as we started, he seemed to vanish, and I never afterwards laid eyes on him or on the wounded man whom he carried. They were not captured, they could not have escaped; it is impossible to say what became of them.

Other wounded men lying on the ground continued to make their presence known to us by cries calculated to wring the heart of a stone.

It was peculiarly affecting to notice the frequent use they made of the word "brother," and of the other affectionate terms of address in which the Russian language is as rich as the Japanese language is rich in honorifics. These affectionate terms of address strongly reminded me of the poetical expressions of the Gaelic-speaking Irish. So did the continual invocation of saints, and especially of the Holy Mother of God. One badly-wounded man prayed to the Holy Virgin of the Iversky Gate, another to Our Lady of Kazan, a third to the Smolensk Mátushka. One dying soldier called out with a loud voice, "O! Nicolaï Chudotvórets (Wonder-Worker), Saint of God!" and, immediately after, his life went out suddenly like the lamp before an ikon.

Many, who were delirious, called out the names of friends whom they thought they recognised in the crowd of men that flowed past like an invisible, gloomy river. Ivan Tikhonovitch! Andrei Petrovitch! One called out the name of a woman.

"Bratszi, Pomogeete mnye" ("Brothers, help me!"), wailed one poor fellow. An officer supported him till a cannon came rumbling along, and then managed, after a long argument with the artilleryman, to put him on the driver's seat, alongside a number of other wounded men who were clinging on, I don't know how.

We disposed in this way of many wounded who were almost insane with terror at the prospect of being mutilated by the Chinese. Several times I put myself to much inconvenience attending to men lying inert and speechless across the road, only to discover, when they turned their faces towards me, that they exhaled a smell of "vodka" strong enough to make me stagger backwards. They were not wounded at all. They were only drunk.

Yet, harassing as were these wails of the wounded, they were not so frightful as the silence of the dead, over whose stiffened corpses one or other of us sometimes fell. Squalid, unsightly corpses these; and yet at this moment, O poor soldiers! mothers in distant Russia are praying for ye before the shrines of the saints, are making long pilgrimages to monasteries containing miraculous ikons, are even, in the distraction of their grief, weaving spells as heathenish in tenor and as Oriental in expression as those which many a poor Japanese mother is making use of this bitter night.*

* Some of the spells are given by Sakharof in his "Pyesni Russkago Naroda." One runs as follows:—"From the red dawn have I wept all day long—I, his mother—alone in my upper chamber, looking out on the desolate plain. . . . There sat I in sorrow and in sadness, till the glow of the evening, till the heavy dews. But at last I grew weary of sobbing, so I pondered on what magic spells I should employ to charm away that bitter, deadly grief. . . . I charm my never-sufficiently-to-be-gazed-on child over my nuptial cup, over running water, over my marriage handkerchief, over my marriage candle. I wipe my child's pure face with my marriage handkerchief, I clean his red lips, his bright eyes, his thoughtful brow, his ruddy cheeks. With my marriage candle I light up his long 'kaftan,' his black bonnet, his

One corpse, that of a blonde-haired lad of eighteen or nineteen years of age, was quite naked, having been already stripped by the Chinese. It looked like a fallen statue of Hercules, and reminded me of the words which Nekrassov puts into the mouth of a Russian mother lamenting her dead soldier son, words which express with a pathos which goes to one's heart like a dagger the poor woman's pride in her big boy, whose magnificent proportions had, she said, so struck the General when he saw the lad stripped for the physical examination.*

figured belt, his stitched shoes, his fair curls, his young face, this swift step, . . . I avert from thee, O never-sufficiently-to-be-gazed-on child, the terrible devil. I avert the fierce whirlwind. I drive away the one-eyed wood-sprite. . . . And then, my child, at night and at midnight, throughout the hours and at the half-hours, on the highroad and in byways, sleeping and waking, be thou hidden and concealed by virtue of this, my powerful spell, from hostile influences and from unclean spirits, preserved from sudden death and from misfortune and from woe. . . . And should the hour of thy death come, remember, O my child! our great love for thee, our unsparing bread-and-salt, and, turning towards thy well-loved home, bend thy brow to the ground with seven times seven salutations, bid farewell to thy kith and kin and drop into a sweet and dreamless slumber."

Another spell says :—" Mayest thou never be hurt, O my child! by guns or by arquebuses, or by arrows or by wrestlers, or by boxers. May the champions not challenge thee nor strike thee with warlike weapons; may they not pierce thee with lance or spear, or cut thee with halbert or hatchet, or crush thee with battle-axe, or stab thee with knife. May the aged deceive thee not; may the young men do thee no injury; but mayst thou be to them as a hawk, and may they be unto thee as thrushes."

* " Podiveelsya sam eez Piter General na papnya etogo

We passed several other naked corpses, one of which was headless and still warm—for when I fell over it my face touched it. I had at first thought that it was the body of a living man, and it was only when I attempted to give it a drink that I discovered it to be headless. For a long time after this I feared that my nervous system had been permanently injured by the shock I received on this occasion. I could not bear to even think of this incident for, whenever I did, it gripped my brain like an insane obsession.

It was evident, then, that the Chinese were close by, and my heart sank like lead, for nothing so appalled me as the prospect of being beheaded and stripped stark naked, for I felt that, in that case, my own mother could not recognise me. I would lose my race, my individuality. I would lose that *cachet*, that special character which everybody imagines to mark *him* off from the common herd. I would simply become a lump of excrement dunged by War. Soul and body would, it seemed to me, be alike annihilated. Any one who has ever seen that monstrous spectacle, a headless corpse, can understand the horror which I felt, and the longing with which I longed at that moment for a consecrated grave on some green hillside in Ireland. I dare say that all of my companions had the same longing, for I heard a dismounted Cossack say that he would not mind getting killed if only he were buried near a great river.

kak v' rekrutskoe prisutstvie preevelee ego razdyetavo."
. . . ("Why, the General at Piter was surprised himself to see how strong my lad was, when they brought the boy naked into the Hall of Examination ").

Owing to a strange physical weakness that came over me at this time and also to the fear that I should be the first to fall in case an attack was made on us from the front, I tried to work my way into the centre of our column, but, as everybody else was trying to do exactly the same thing, I was unsuccessful.

Nobody knew where we were going or who commanded us or what troops we were composed of. " Ya nye magu znat " (" I don't know ") was the stereotyped answer of the soldiers to whom I addressed myself for information. We were marching through the valley of the Shadow. Between us and Tiehling lay a chasm like that which divides the living from the dead. I felt that I had ceased to be a human being, and had become a thing, a piece of wreckage, tossed hither and thither in the crowd.

I should soon have lost the party to which I had attached myself, and among which I had now made a few acquaintances, had it not been for the kindness of an officer who, seeing me fall repeatedly, told off a soldier specially to guide my wandering footsteps. I made the acquaintance of this soldier in deepest night, and I never saw him by daylight, so that I am to this day in ignorance of his appearance, but he seemed to be a bright, quick-witted young fellow. At first I used to lose him frequently, but then I noticed that the sharp top of his "bashleek," or the detachable hood of grey felt, which he wore over his head, pointed upwards at a slightly different angle to the others, and also that there was a peculiar glint in the tin can he wore at his belt, for it is extraordinary how expert one becomes in detecting these infinitesimal points of difference when it is almost a matter of life or death for him to notice them. The fraternally authoritative way in which he used to say to me : "Come along now, 'golúbcheek' (little pigeon)! come along, 'bràtetz' (comrade)!" when I had fallen behind or had continued to rest after the order to advance had been given, touched my heart like the embrace of a mother.

This mysterious soldier, whom I shall call " the Man in the Bashleek," was very quick at finding the way, at circumventing obstacles, at helping his officers ; and he was not, I am sure, told off to watch me as a prisoner, for he always walked in front, and I could easily have escaped him at any time. I was very glad to keep close to him, however, for had I fallen into the hands of some strange detachment I might have fared badly. He asked me once if I was a *barin* (gentleman), and expressed his amazement at my not having remained behind in Mukden. I was just as amazed myself.

I was carrying on my arm (for, though the night was cold, the walking had heated me) a very heavy fur-lined overcoat, under the weight of which I frequently stumbled ; and, perceiving this, a soldier kindly took the coat from me, saying, "Give it to me, O little brother (brateeshka)." For hours after, I was selfish enough to watch him staggering and tumbling under the weight of that unwieldy garment, but when dawn came, he and the ulster had both disappeared. Whether he had heroically fallen by the wayside still clutching that fatal coat or had wisely dropped it I cannot say ; but at such a time it was more than kind of him to carry it at all.

Of course we had thrown out no scouts and, at any moment, we might walk into the gates of death.

Before us was night, cruel night, inscrutable as the woman on whose forehead was mystery. Every tree, every shape was big with menace. A stray dog once caused a panic in which several of our soldiers shot each other.

There was some light from the stars, and more, for a short time, from a burning village far in front. Some miles in advance of us, rifle-fire continued at intervals until near dawn. We seemed to be continually knocking up against lost columns like ourselves, armed bands marching towards all points of the compass, moving like wandering comets in the abyss of night. Some of our men were always killed on these occasions, for each party mistook the other for the enemy and commenced firing. It was not till the wounded began to shriek in Russian that the mistake was discovered. A few of our men, who were most certainly insane, had to be forcibly made to cease firing, but their weapons were not taken from them. In one of these wandering columns Soïkin met his brother and went away with him, for none of these other lost battalions ever joined us. They had always some mysterious destination of their own. And yet, in the long run, we all reached the same sad goal.

Out of that impenetrable night there loomed up at intervals in front of us a mysterious figure on a white horse, but, though we called to it, it did not come closer, nor did it go away until we fired at it when it suddenly disappeared, the horse galloping wildly like a steed that is riderless. I reflected, with a sudden spasm of horror which made me sweat, that it might be the frozen equestrian corpse of the young Siberian officer who had given me a cigarette at the railway embank-

THE RETREAT FROM MUKDEN 309

ment some hours before. If this was so, our doomed column was being led on by Death itself.

Once, while we were all resting for a moment, I had just thrown myself down flat on my back when I caught sight in the zenith above me of a great star that fell from heaven, burning as it were a lamp. This grand celestial phenomenon at once recalled to my mind the obscure and terrible prophecies of the Apocalypse; and the soldiers seemed to be similarly affected, for they said it was the track of an angel flying to receive a departing spirit.

Once every hour or so we were allowed to lie down on the ground and rest for a few minutes. I used to appreciate this repose keenly, and became quite a connoisseur in earth-couches. I found that the best way to rest was to lie athwart the furrows, my hips in one hollow and my heels in another, the back of my head resting on one ridge and my legs bending at the knees over a second. I used to become so comfortable in this luxurious position that I always fell fast asleep the moment I assumed it, but, luckily, "the man in the 'bashleek'" always woke me up promptly, so that I never had time to get frozen. Despite their extreme fatigue, the soldiers did not like these pauses, for the intense silence horrified them. The men held their breath, so that I fancied I could hear my heart beating. Once, a dog howled dismally in a distant village.

I noticed that we passed through four different kinds of country, first flat country over which a gigantic steam-roller seemed to have just passed, levelling everything, and leaving behind it naught but wounded men, dead horses, and broken carts; then flat, cultivated land in which we had to cross the furrows; then flat cultivated land in which we walked along the furrows; and, lastly, grassy and slightly hilly country.

These furrows were frozen as hard as marble, and walking athwart them was worse than marching with peas in your boots, for they were not far enough apart for a single stride, and, as they were invisible in the darkness, one frequently came a "cropper." Every now and then a big soldier would come down with a thud, and a rattle of accoutrements that sounded like the fall of a harnessed dray-horse. It was like walking the treadmill, it was like tugging the oar in a Moroccan galley; but by-and-by I became used to it, just as I could, I suppose, become used to picking oakum, and plodded on stolidly and mechanically. It seemed as if I had been all my life engaged in this sort of work. I tried, but unsuccessfully, to imagine that at that very moment people were sitting down to *recherché* dinners in the Carlton, buying "extra specials" in the Strand, and laying down the law about the battle in the clubs. It was hard to realise that some parts of the world were bored by the whole proceedings, but whenever I brought my mind to bear on this problem I missed a furrow and went headlong to the earth. Walking down these furrows was also very tiresome, as they were just a shade too narrow. The hilly country in which we found ourselves before dawn next morning was not much better than that which we had traversed during the night, as it contained unexpected gullies and stumps of trees.

Towards morning we all became afflicted by a terrible thirst, and one of the officers earned my everlasting gratitude by allowing me on several occasions to drink from his water-bottle. At length this precious liquid gave out, and I keenly envied the soldiers who were able with their bayonets to cut lumps of ice from the frozen streams. At times, when the firing in front of us ceased, one might have thought that we had escaped, had it not been for a Japanese flash-light on the northern horizon. It was our constant aim all night long to hide from that flash-light, and, whenever we found its glassy, unpitying eye fixed upon us, a visible shudder ran down our whole line.

At first we marched like a mob, but finally, by dint of hard work, the officers succeeded in creating some sort of order. This was not easy, as we consisted of the fragments of seven regiments, and as officers and men had been thrown together haphazard.

I did not realise how demoralised the men were until once, when passing near a burning village, a Japanese patrol fired on us. Once again our whole force shuddered, but this time it was a shudder that might very easily have become a rout. The Japanese only fired a few shots at close quarters, but they probably hung upon our rear till morning, carefully shepherding us into the trap that had been prepared for us.

The soldiers are models of stoical resignation, and their conversation on the march seemed to consist of vague proverbs expressing fatalism. They trudged along with the humble resignation of beasts of burden, and, as I watched them, I could not help thinking of Tolstoï's Karatayef.

Several times throughout the night I tried to say my prayers, but, I am afraid, with ill success, for before I could concentrate my mind sufficiently, I had lost my place in the ranks, or stumbled over the trunk of a tree, or down a gully. Sometimes I was surprised to find myself mechanically saying my prayers in English, the language in which I had been taught them by my mother, but in which I had not said them for many years. I had none of those swift visions of my past life with which people about to die are supposed to be favoured. In fact, I had no time for visions. I was too tired and too much occupied in watching where I was putting my feet.

Dawn came almost suddenly while we were sitting down on a hill-side There were now about three thousand of us, but very few mounted men and no cannon or carts. What became of the guns and gun-carriages, the latter laden with wounded, I do not know; but as I saw some artillerymen riding artillery horses with the traces trailing on the ground, but no guns behind them, I surmised that cannons and cart-loads of wounded had all been alike abandoned during the night. My own horse I sought for long and anxiously, but in vain. Poor old "Sobersides," who carried me all through the war, what fate has befallen thee?

CHAPTER XIV

OUR CAPTURE

THE first thing I remember about March 11 was being awakened by a soldier, for I had unwittingly fallen asleep. I must have been dreaming, for, half awake, I thought that I had been washed up by the sea, and the roaring of the surges was still in my ears. I found the world, which I hardly hoped to see again, bathed in a faint, cold grey light, in which I strove to recognise some of the friends I had made during the hours of darkness.

It was a difficult task, for they seemed no more to correspond to the portraits which I had formed of them in my mind than mental portraits of authors formed by readers of their books correspond to the reality. I saw a soldier who might have been the "man in the bashleek," because he talked of our having been together throughout the night; but he was only an ordinary, stale-looking elderly private, who, when he stepped back among his comrades, became instantly undistinguishable from them. I shook hands with the officer who had given me water; but he, too, was quite different to what I had expected him to be.

The colonel, who was on horseback, bade me good morning in French, and thanked his men in Russian, calling them "Molodtsami, rebyata!" ("Brave fellows, children ") but there was no answering shout of "Radee starát'sya" ("Glad to do all we can") from the latter. They had heard these complimentary speeches too often.

Soon after, we entered a broad flat valley with some heights beyond, the character of the country being, as I have already pointed out, quite different from that of the level Mukden district.

To the south was a grove of pine-trees surrounding a little shrine and surrounded by a wall, and this grove some of our men went to beat, not for game, however, but for hunters—*we* were the game. And the hunters were there, as a volley from the grove and the whizz of bullets overhead clearly indicated. A lieutenant near me clapped his hand suddenly to his side and said "Chort vozmee!" ("The devil take me!") He had been wounded, and in ten seconds he was dead. Our Colonel shouted out directions; but, without listening to them, the men unanimously headed northward at a pace which very soon broke into a run. At the same time many of them shouted loudly that it was all a mistake, that the men concealed in the grove were Russians, and there were no Japanese there at all.

These optimists continued to run, however, as fast as the rest of us, and, as they ran, they raised a wild cry òf "Stoï! Stoï!" ("Stop! Stop!") evidently with the intention of getting those, whom they supposed to be their own men, to cease firing.

On reaching some rising ground to the north, we caught sight, in a plain far away to the west, of some squadrons of unmistakably Japanese cavalry; but though they were as different, of course, from the Cossacks as chalk is from cheese, some of our men joyfully cried out, "Slava Bogu! Nashe! Nashe!" ("Glory be to God! Ours! Ours!"), and clapped their hands with delight.

They were not long clapping their hands, for a volley from some concealed infantry to the northward soon drove us back like a flock of sheep, and showers of bullets from the east and the west completed our demoralisation. One man who fell wounded, cried: "Wait for me, my brothers, dear" ("Brátsui moï mílenkiye"), but we left him lying there.

The cry of "Stoï! Stoï!" was now taken up by almost everybody—including, I think, myself—and the effect was inexpressibly weird. It was varied by a wild, uncanny, lugubrious, inarticulate wail, which rose and fell at intervals like a funeral cry. When a child in Ireland I heard one night the unearthly cry of a banshee; and on this Manchurian hillside, mingled with the despairing shrieks of those unhappy soldiers, rushing wildly backwards and forwards, lashed by bullets, maddened by fear, I heard again the blood curdling warning of that messenger of death.

On getting into the broad, flat valley that I have already alluded to, the men all lay down instinctively along two shallow furrows, about a hundred yards apart, and, as I stepped over one of these lines in order to get inside, a man discharged his rifle close to my leg. It may have been an accident, but if I had been hit at such close range the wound would have been a bad one.

The Russians now began firing, although they could see nothing, while the Japanese increased their fire because they could see us perfectly. Our furrow was no protection whatever, even if the Japanese had not occupied higher ground. All our men had not yet taken their places on the ground with their companions, and many of them were still wandering aimlessly at large in the space between the two furrows, when suddenly there was a loud report, and a shrapnel shell exploded a little way off. At the same instant about a hundred men simultaneously bit the dust, falling down as suddenly as if each of them had been shot through the heart. A few moments later a good many of the corpses got up again and raced swiftly, with head bent, towards one or other of the absolutely unsheltered furrows. Of those that remained lying on the ground, it was easy to distinguish between the quick and the dead, for the latter lay in a position of absolute *abandon*, while the former crouched and looked watchful.

The bullets had frightened us, but the shrapnel drove the fear of God into our souls, and after several shells had exploded right in our midst, there were to be seen between the two furrows many men standing up waving their hats in sign of submission. Some mounted their busbies on the points of their bayonets and agitated them furiously; but evidently the Japanese wanted more unequivocal tokens of surrender than this, for, after a moment's pause, they commenced shelling us harder than ever. The Russians now became panic-stricken. Those who had been lying down threw away their arms and sat up in such a way that the Japanese could not fail to hit them. Some, who must have lost their senses, stood up, gazing stupidly and listlessly at the bursting shrapnel, while the bullets whizzed around them and struck the ground at their feet.

Somebody shouted to the bugler to blow the "Cease fire," and, lying on the ground, he blew for all he was worth. No officer ordered the blowing of the "Cease fire" or the hoisting of the white flag. The men did these things of their own accord, while the officers stood by, listlessly expecting death. We could see that at the other furrow conditions were much the same as with us. The soldiers had all thrown away their arms and were exposing themselves carelessly. Between the two lines many soldiers, who still thoughtlessly retained their rifles, were walking about at random over the ridges from which the stumps of last year's "kiaoliang" crop still projected. One of them waved a large white flag, but still the Japanese made no sign, and their fire continued unabated.

There now arose a fierce cry of "Throw away your arms!" and some soldiers, not content with having got rid of their rifles, began to throw away their cartridges and their belts.

Even at this stage there were still men foolish enough or crazed enough to shout: "That's not the Japanese at all. That's *our* artillery. It's all a mistake! Stoï! Stoï!"

And again the wild wail of "Stoï! Stoï!" would rise and fall like the waves of the sea, the melancholy bugles blowing all the while a useless "Cease fire!"

I am convinced that the men who led this cry of "Stoï! Stoï!" were insane. They ran around like wild-eyed prophets who see a whole world rushing to perdition; and I feared that they would undo us all.

In battle the Siberian soldier is apt to become unhinged. At Tah-shih-chiao I had seen nearly a dozen insane foot-soldiers brought to Mishchenko's battery, and one of them, in a sudden access of fury, nearly routed the whole staff at a time when we were hard pressed by the Japanese. In his book on the war, M. Recouly tells a horrible story of a staff officer who went mad at the battle of the Shaho ; and a German correspondent who was captured with another detachment during this retreat from Mukden, and who was my fellow prisoner in Japan, where he showed symptoms of great nervous excitement, afterwards shot himself.

Close by was lying a thin, cold-faced man with his face wrapped up in his overcoat. He was nursing a minor wound, and kept ejaculating to himself at intervals the word "Smert! Smert!" (Death). Suddenly he rolled over like a person turning uneasily in his sleep, but nobody suspected that anything had happened to him until the Japanese came up, when we found that he was dead. A burly man, standing in the open field about fifty yards off, collapsed without a word, like a heap of old clothes. The colonel fell from his horse, shot through the brain, whereupon the frightened animal bolted.

A short time before, some of his officers had warned him to get off his horse ; but he had answered, almost in the words of the heroic Grand Duke Svatoslav Sgorevich, that there was no disgrace in dying,

Not perceiving at first that he had been shot through the head, we tore open the breast of his coat. Around his neck and inside his shirt were six or seven most beautiful religious medals and miniature "ikoni" of silver and gold suspended by fine chains of pure gold.

The officers were not in the least intimidated by the colonel's fate, for they continued to expose themselves recklessly, and were killed or wounded one after another. Good sharpshooters were evidently picking them off.

These happenings froze every one of us with fear, and there were continual cries of " Gospodee Bozhe!" ("O Lord God!")

A private soldier, evidently the spokesman of several others, now approached me on his hands and knees. His face was streaming with tears which made clean channels down his dusty cheeks, and he implored me to go out to the Japanese and beg them to cease firing.

"You are English, Batyùshka (little father)," said he, "and the Japanese will do whatever you ask them."

I refused, and told him to ask one of his officers, but he said, "We have no officers. These officers don't belong to our regiment at all;" and continued to entreat me until I told him that the fire would cease directly.

But it seemed hours before it ceased, and slowly the awful conviction began to dawn on me that the Japanese did not intend to give quarter. They were, after all, the bloodthirsty pagans they had been represented to be. The tales which the Russians had told of their savagery were true. They had got too many prisoners on their hands already. Our crowd would only be an incumbrance to them, so they had determined to shoot all they could and then finish off the rest of us with the bayonet. I was going to have convincing proof of Japanese barbarity, but I would never live to tell the tale.

Just as I had given up all hope, the fire suddenly ceased, and at a distant point on our right a long line of men rose out of the ground and advanced rapidly towards us. The order in which they marched and the sunlight shimmering on their broad sword-bayonets showed that they were soldiers, and, when they came nearer, their uniforms and their small size proved that they were Japanese.

Onward they came, just as I had often seen them years before on the Aoyama parade-ground. At that time, I must say, I was no more impressed by their gorgeous French uniforms than if they had been Orange bandsmen parading the streets of Belfast on July 12; for what were they but copyists, birds in borrowed plumage, men who would, like all Asiatics, fade away before a White army like sinners before the wrath of God?

But now it was all different. Fifty thousand dead had made that uniform historic. A year's fighting had placed them among Cæsar's legions and the Old Guard of Napoleon.

I had seen them, in mimic fight at Kumamoto, performing, under the eyes of the Mikado, feats which every foreign military *attaché* present declared to be impossible in real warfare. In Manchuria I had seen them prove these foreign critics wrong a dozen times over.

I was now to get a closer view of them than ever I had had in my life. On they came, all the same size, all wonderfully alike, as if they had been turned out of the same mould. On they came, with quick, elastic step, until I could distinguish each boyish beardless face, until I could see a long line of gleaming white teeth and glittering jet-black eyes.

It was a dangerous moment, for they had heard as much of Russian treachery as the Russians had heard

RUSSIAN PRIESTS BLESSING RENNENKAMPF'S COSSACKS BEFORE THE RUSSIAN ADVANCE ON PEN-SHI-HU, OCT. 1904

of Japanese treachery, and some imprudent act on the part of a crazy Russian soldier might have cost us all our lives. From the ugly gleam in their slanting eyes, from the angle at which they held their rifles clutched, I knew that they were prepared for anything. But they had nothing to fear from the poor Russkies, who stood all the time as calm as a herd of cows.

On seeing the enemy approach to disarm them, a great weight seemed to be taken off their minds, and they even joked. One of them asked me if I was a Japanese officer, and, without waiting for an answer, expressed his candid admiration for the way in which I had done it. He even scowled on a companion on whose face he fancied he could detect a slight shade of disapprobation. An officer consulted me about the best manner of surrendering his sword.

" Shall I throw it away," he asked genially, "or give it up?"

A second officer rushed forward to ask if he should continue or not blowing the bugle to announce the *cessez feu;* but on this last point my expression of opinion was not waited for, as everybody roared simultaneously at the bugler to blow with all his might. Also, everybody roared at everybody else to continue waving white handkerchiefs. There seemed to be an impression abroad that if anybody ceased for a moment to wave something white, all was lost.

The Japanese were now within forty yards of us. They were preceded by a breathless little non-commissioned officer. The language difficulty remained, but it was an obstacle which was easily brushed aside.

The Russians genially shouted " Hodya ! " a friendly

term they apply to Chinamen when they want the latter to come to them. The Japanese cried out in more unexceptionable Chinese "Li! Li!" ("Come! come!") At the same time several soldiers rushed towards us, breathing hard, devouring us with their almond eyes, still uncertain that there would not be treachery.

One of them came near me, evidently taking me for an officer, but went away, puzzled, on seeing no sword and no epaulettes. Another, more fortunate, rushed up to a real officer, who stood close by, and laid his hand on the hilt of the latter's sword. This officer (who, by the way, had received a contusion on his head) smiled, and cheerfully allowed the Japanese to take the weapon. The next thing I was aware of was that the enemy had closed in on us all along the line, and that a tremendous amount of enthusiastic handshaking was going on between them and their captors. The Russians were laughing with joy, as if they had met long-lost brothers, and were trying to express their feelings by the frequent repetition of such "pijin" Russian phrases as " Shibka Znakom " ("Very good friends "), etc. The Japanese did not evidently understand these phrases, but their genial smile was worth a bookful of polite protestations.

They seemed as pleased as children who have got new toys, and made no objection when, with eloquent gestures expressive of extreme thirst, the Russians went down on their knees and emptied the water-bottles that hung at the waists of their captors. Meanwhile several mounted officers rode in among us, giving directions to the men, some of whom thereupon made signs for us to come along with them, while others picked up our guns and began discharging them in the

OUR CAPTURE

air. A number of Chinese coolies afterward appeared on the scene and followed us, dispassionately, with numerous bundles of surrendered firearms.

All this time I was allowed to rush about, taking snapshots with my two cameras. Even the Japanese privates understood perfectly what I was about, and merely said to one another "Shashin-kikai desu" ("It's a kodak"). Judging from past experience, I am afraid that it would not have been so safe to take photographs had I been with the Japanese and my captors been Russians.

A long train of disarmed captives, we now wended our way slowly between two rows of armed Japanese, who accompanied us toward the hill from which the shrapnel had been launched and on which a great crowd of Japanese now stood revealed. Our captors took advantage of this opportunity to deprive the Russian officers of their binoculars and of some other objects which, under the rules of war, they were hardly entitled to seize. Spying a pair of fine fur-lined gloves in my pocket, a young private briskly snatched them from me, checking my remonstrances by threatening gestures. I afterwards heard the Russian officers complain to the Japanese commander of these petty thefts; but as the Russian officers could not identify the culprits—for the Japs looked as alike as ducks' eggs—and as the Japanese commander sorrowfully lamented his own inability to do so, the matter went no further.

At the foot of the hill we came to a frozen brook, from which the Japanese cut chunks of ice with their bayonets for the now bayonetless Russians, who, still tortured by thirst, proceeded to eat this ice greedily.

Then we moved on again toward a gully from which the frozen stream proceeded, and while *en route* I casually remarked to a Japanese soldier who was walking alongside me : "Anoné! Anoné! Watakushi-wa Igirisu-jin desu" ("I say! I say! I'm an Englishman"). On hearing this remark the soldier jumped as if he had been shot (he was the party that had "swiped" my fur-lined gloves), and regarded me with bulging eyes. He could not have been more astounded had it been his horse which had spoken.

"Sayo de gozaimasu," I continued affably, in Japanese, which, if not faultless, was at least intelligible. "Watakushi-wa shimbun kisha desu." ("Yes, I'm a newspaper man.") Whereupon the soldier, after exchanging a few hasty words with his sergeant, rapidly disappeared.

I felt as pleased and gratified at the outcome of this little incursion of mine into the Japanese language as a magician who has just tested a new and mighty spell with very satisfactory results. It seemed that, in spite of his colour, the tiny Jap had more respect for the Press than his European antagonist ; for on several occasions when I had told Russian privates in their own language that I was a correspondent, their faces remained as blank and expressionless as if I had informed them that I was a herbivorous dinosaur.

We now entered a long narrow gully along both lips of which, Japanese soldiers were ranged. The Russian privates were told to accommodate themselves as best they could in the flat bottom of the gully, while their superiors were requested to sit down on an upward break in the side of the glen, at the top of which stood a group of Japanese officers, one of whose horses was held by a Chinese soldier in uniform. I seated myself on the ground and began to write up my notes, when suddenly a youthful Japanese lieutenant appeared before me, and said winningly in English:

"You are an English newspaper man, I understand. May I ask if you represent the London *Times*?"

I had at first a wild idea of saying that I did represent the *Times*, judging that a correspondent of that paper would be more favourably received in Japanese circles than a correspondent of the *New York Herald*. But I sternly repressed this inclination and told the truth. It made no difference, however. The young officer professed to be delighted.

"Perhaps you are an officer in your own country?" he asked. "Ah, no! But no matter. Come here and sit with the Russian officers. We shall treat you as an officer." And the young man scurried up to the top of the hill to report.

Next came the leader of the detachment, Captain Takashima, adjutant of the Imperial Guard. He introduced himself to me gracefully, and began filling a large beer glass for me.

"Oh, thank you!" said I; "but you are giving me too much. It's white wine, I suppose?"

"No," said he, "brandy. You'll need it all after your fatigues in Manchuria."

The Russian officers also got plenty of brandy, and they did immediate justice to it. I am certain that, just then, they would have preferred cold water or tea, but the Japanese is firmly convinced that at no hour of the day or night will a Russian object to brandy neat, and plenty of it.

Then came Lieutenant Shibouya, also an adjutant

of the Imperial Guard—a young man who speaks French, and who inquired very particularly after a Russian officer called Ecke, an acquaintance of mine—in fact, we had been together on the *Novi Kraï* in Port Arthur—whom he had met under a flag of truce just before the battle, and with whom he had, soldier-like, exchanged vows of eternal friendship on that occasion. Several of these meetings occurred just before the battle of Mukden. One took place in the centre of the line, and General Zarubaieff's son was one of the Russian delegates. The other took place on the right flank on February 20, and most of the Russian representatives—there were three officers and three soldiers on each side—were Cossacks. Both parties had brought white wine, cooked chicken, and champagne with them, and, as the Japanese spoke Russian very well, a most enjoyable hour was spent, and everybody on both sides got impartially drunk and was photographed in that condition.

It was the Japanese who had suggested these social meetings, and I think that they had no ulterior object in view. They simply wanted to show that they, too, could glory and drink deep even with the men whom they were going in a few days to attack with unparalleled fierceness. They wanted to demonstrate that, despite the disgraceful stories that had been circulated anent their prudishness and their Sunday-school sobriety, they, too, were human and could sin as heinously as anybody.*

* Since the above was written I find that, writing in a military periodical published in the United States, an American military *attaché* takes a diametrically opposite view. He regards these meetings as instances of supreme Japanese craft.

Next came to me a number of Japanese war correspondents. Mr. Ota, of the *Jiji;* Mr. Konishi, of the *Asahi;* Mr. Saito, of the *Nippon*, and others. Several of them I had known in Japan, and one I had met at the annual manœuvres there. He explained to me how much Japan had profited by the observations she had made of European troops and their arrangements during the Boxer troubles, and was, as usual with Japanese, almost apologetic in speaking of his country's successes. A Japanese who boasts of his country's warlike prowess is to me inconceivable.

Finally I met Colonel Hume, the British *attaché,* with Kuroki's army; Colonel Crowder, the American *attaché;* Major von Etzel, the German *attaché* (whom I had formerly known very well in Tokio), and two other continental *attachés*. All these gentlemen were very kind to me, and so, I must say, were the Japanese, who pressed on me a limitless amount of hard biscuits. On learning that I was English, every private soldier seemed to consider it his duty to give me a box of cigarettes, until finally I had got a collection which it would require a small cart to remove. I appreciated this kindness all the more when I discovered how extremely little this Japanese column had brought with them in the shape of provisions or tobacco.

One of the Japanese officers spoke Chinese. Another spoke Russian, and was in great demand as an interpreter. The Russian officers made much use of him, addressing him in loud and genial tones, such as they would use toward an equal. The Russian soldiers were also quite at home, being ordered about by a Japanese private who had been in Vladivostock, I suppose, and who spoke Russian; but I could see from the first that, despite the courtesy of the Japanese officers, there was a fundamental difference between the Russian estimate of a prisoner's status and the Japanese. The Russian seemed to think that a prisoner who has done his best has nothing to be ashamed of and can hold his head as high as anybody; while on the inscrutable Japanese countenance I could detect a shade of contempt for men who had allowed themselves to be taken alive. In the Russian view a prisoner of war is a brave man, deserving not only to be treated but even to be spoken of and thought of as such; in the view of the Japanese soldiery in general a prisoner is a disgraced person whom the rules of war save from the indignity of discourteous treatment, but who cannot be spoken of or thought of save with contempt.

Holding this view, the Japanese could not sometimes conceal their astonishment at the free-and-easy way in which the Russians bore themselves, at the loud manner in which they talked and laughed. In their opinion a prisoner ought to hang his head, to speak in a low and broken voice, and, if he had any spunk left in him at all, to avail himself of the first favourable opportunity to commit suicide.

I took an early opportunity of hinting that, though awfully sorry to leave them so quickly, I did not mind if they sent me as soon as possible to Newchwang, the residence of the nearest consul; but they entreated me to consider that I needed a rest "after my fatigues in Manchuria," and said that, in any case, politeness required me to call on General Kuroki. A prisoner! Oh! no! of course not!

CHAPTER XV

FACE TO FACE WITH KUROKI

FOR a long time we waited in that valley, and I took advantage of the delay to get the senior surviving Russian officer to write a short statement in my notebook describing my part in the affair, that is, saying that I had tried my best to join the retreating army and that I had acted with correctitude all the time I had been with the party. I had judged it well to do this, as the Russians are extraordinary people for inventing and believing stories about spies and traitors; but when the Japanese saw me thus closeted, so to speak, with the Russian leader they sent a messenger to tell me most politely that, not being a military man, I was not to sit with the Russian officers, but was to come up and favour the Japanese staff with the light of my countenance. I obeyed these instructions, and, having done so, promptly fell asleep, and slept for several hours.

Meanwhile the wounded were carried in and attended to. Then the Russian officers and men were led away. Some of the men were fast asleep and refused to get up. I saw a little Jap spend about half an hour gently trying to rouse one big giant who lay snoring on the ground, and who, even when aroused and set upright on his huge legs, became abusive and threatened to fight. The man seemed to have had liquor, but, in spite of his disorderly conduct, the Japanese, in accordance with their invariable custom, did not resort to force. They simply smiled, and seemed to regard the proceedings as funny. It was exactly as if the big grey-coated giant was a naughty child.

In contrast with the loud and burly Russians, the Japanese officers seemed peculiarly slight, slim and effeminate, and their subdued and gentle manner greatly heightened this impression of fragility. After having been for a long time accustomed to the large Russian grasp I thought their hands remarkably small and thin, and everything else about them seemed to me to be in proportion. They did not take much interest in the spoils that were captured, the maps, bottles, horses, etc., but I saw one of them holding for a long time in his slender hand a large crucifix and gazing at it long and curiously. One of our officers turned out to be a lady. She was a rather hard-featured woman of about twenty-five or twenty-six, dressed in the complete uniform of a sub-lieutenant of infantry and with her hair cut short. There was not the slightest fear or embarrassment about her; she seemed to be perfectly unconcerned, and whenever she wanted anything she asked for it in a voice which, although a woman's voice, had that clear decisive timbre in it which bespeaks the habitude of command.

The Japanese showed great tact in dealing with this unusual capture. There was no crowding around her, and neither by look nor by sign did any one betray the fact that he knew her secret. Some privates gazed at her curiously from afar off; but though really very much interested in her, the Japanese officers seemed to regard her just as an ordinary sub-lieutenant. At Kuroki's headquarters, however, she was allowed as much privacy as possible.

Not being a very strait-laced people themselves, the Japanese were rather tickled than otherwise at this discovery, but it is remarkable how well they managed on their side to eliminate the lady peril from the field of military operations—far better than the English succeeded in doing in South Africa or the Americans in Cuba. Even lady nurses were not allowed to mix among the wounded as freely as on the Russian side, and I hope I am not reflecting in any way on the Russian Red Cross Sisterhood as a whole when I say that there were to be found among them women who were unworthy of the robe which they wore. These women were seldom professional nurses—they generally obtained the sacred robe of a Sister of Charity in order to be able to follow some influential lover in the field.

I suppose there were, on the Russian side, cases of pure women dressing as men, in order to follow their husbands and lovers, for such a course would strongly recommend itself to the romantic-minded Russian damsel. I dare say that the Japanese will, with their usual care, collect all the facts bearing on this subject, and the collection ought to be very interesting. In some cases the girls passed for some time as youthful soldiers, until the fear of the public and compulsory bath at the Japanese quarantine station forced them to disclose their secret. In other cases ladies whose lovers had been captured rode into the Japanese lines and surrendered, so as to be able to rejoin their beloved ones in Matsuyama.

Each of the Russian privates had now fixed to his shoulder-strap a tag, such as the express companies in America fix to your luggage, and the whole batch was sent off to Kuroki's headquarters some eight or nine miles distant. I was told that I would be sent with the next batch. "We expect to capture another small force," said Captain Takashima, "and you'll be sent on to headquarters with them."

I took advantage of this opportunity to speak with the captain on a confidential matter. With bated breath, I confessed that I had on my person a loaded revolver and ammunition. I was willing to surrender it, but the captain laughingly declined to insist on my disarmament.

"Keep everything you have got," said he cheerfully, "You are a correspondent, and we don't want to take anything from you."

And as a matter of fact that loaded revolver was never taken from me. I also kept a Russian map, and, more important still, a list which I had compiled in my notebook of the Russian forces in the field, for I was never searched even in the most cursory manner, and never questioned as to what documents I had in my possession.

The other "small force" of which Captain Takashima spoke was duly captured, but, nevertheless, I was eventually sent on alone in charge of a little Imperial guardsman with red riding breeches and a horse which he and I rode by turns. He was so polite that, every time I dismounted, he protested that I had not remained in the saddle long enough, and he was hardly a moment astride the horse's back before he wanted to get off in order to make place for me.

FACE TO FACE WITH KUROKI

In fact, we spent so much time trying to persuade one another to mount that there was serious danger of our never reaching our destination at all. He allowed me to fall behind or to gallop on in advance just as I liked, so that I was in mortal fear that I would accidentally escape and get the poor fellow into trouble. As a matter of fact, I would probably have tried to utilise my knowledge of the country in order to escape here or afterward on the way to Dalny, had it not been that my guards were invariably such kind, confiding fellows that I had not the heart to abuse their confidence. Several other things cooled my ardour for escape. Firstly, I might fall into the hands of the Chinese and be tortured to death. Secondly, I might, if captured by individual Japanese or Russian scouts, be killed by them for the sake of the large sum of money which I carried. Thirdly, I stood a fairly good chance, even if I reached the Russian lines, of being shot at by some of the outposts before I could explain myself.

The country through which we passed was hilly, and near the end of our journey we crossed a river. Little Red Riding Breeches asked me the name of that river, and I replied, "the Liao-ho," at which answer he seemed mightily pleased, for he had evidently got instructions to lead me backward and forward in such a way that I would quite lose all sense of direction. Of course it was not the Liao-ho at all.

Sifontai, or Kuroki's village, as I had better call it, for I believe that the Japanese purposely gave us the wrong name, was a very small and a very much overcrowded hamlet, in which there was not enough accommodation for troops, much less prisoners. It was surrounded by a cordon of guards, one of whom challenged us, but allowed us to proceed on my guide giving the password. I was at once brought to the principal house in the village, the residence of General Kuroki's staff.

In the outer room some clerks were working. In the inner room General Fuji, the chief of staff, received me very affably and offered me tea. He said that as the Japanese had derived much moral support from England and America he could not but regard me—at one and the same time British subject and American newspaper man—as doubly a friend. I so shocked General Fuji by bluntly asking him if I were a prisoner that, for a moment, he was unable to speak. "Why, didn't I tell you that you're our guest?" he cried, as soon as he had recovered his voice; "but," he added benignantly, "you need to have a rest, a long rest, in Japan."

And in these words I read my fate.

I was then sent to a Chinese house, in which I found the Russian officers who had been captured with me. The house had previously been occupied by soldiers of the Imperial Guard, and we slept among them that night, packed together like herrings in a barrel. They were clean lads, however, far cleaner than any Russian privates, cleaner, even, than the average Englishman, and they were very accommodating, too, for one of them gave me a blanket to cover myself with.

The next morning I woke up late, to find everything in an awful muddle. The orderlies of the Russian officers, who had slept three deep on top of one another out in the porch, were continually rushing in with the object of making tea for their masters at a fire which burned on the floor, and the Japanese soldiers were continually putting them out again. The Russian officers could do nothing without the assistance of their "vestavoï," while the Japanese guard had had orders to admit no privates to that room, and were determined to enforce those orders.

Some orderlies solved the difficulty by making the tea outside and handing it through the window, but the bawling out of orders, which were not obeyed, and the wails of hapless "vestavoï" seized at the doorway with steaming teapots were heartrending and ludicrous. A young soldier of the Guards who slept beside me, and who turned out to be a Greek Christian, greatly amused his comrades, on awakening, by reading them extracts from a Russo-Japanese phrase book which he had captured. The humour of the situation can readily be imagined on the discovery that some of the questions asked were:—"Where is the road to Kobe?" "Who is the Governor of Osaka fortress?" "What is the strength of the enemy in Matsuyama?" "Has the Mikado fled to Nikko or to Aomori?" The Japanese Greek Christian laughed so long and so heartily at these unconscious witticisms that I thought his little looped-up eyes would never open again. Evidently he had no great belief in the political infallibility of his co-religionists.

Meanwhile we were very much cramped for room, and I decided to go out into the yard, where I found a considerable number of Japanese guardsmen and a sprinkling of Russian officers.

Thanks to the kindness of one of the guardsmen I again enjoyed the luxury of a wash, after which I returned to the house and had some tea and hard biscuit, on which spare diet I lived for fully a week afterward, practically, in fact, until I reached Dalny.

Next day more officers and soldiers came in, and the difficulty for the Japanese was to know where to put them. Some were taken in hand by a rough-looking Japanese private, who spoke Russian and had evidently been a coolie of some kind in Siberia. He ordered them into an empty outhouse, and told them they could sleep on the floor. The poor, long-bearded greycoats followed him meekly and made no remark. The main body was turned loose in a field behind General Kuroki's house. Then the Japanese soldiers were all removed from our cabin and the place given over to us entirely. A few "vestavoï" were allowed to attend us, and it was touching to see the affectionate way in which these poor lads waited on their masters, although the common disaster which had overwhelmed them might have led them to assert their independence. The Japanese privates seemed, by the way, greatly amused at the zeal with which the Russian privates discharged all sorts of menial duties for their officers. To them it seemed that their big Russian antagonists were more like nurses than anything else, for in the Japanese army all menial work is discharged by "styohé,"or military coolies.

The Japanese officers often bring their own servants with them, and in any case the simplicity of their life and of their food is such that their orderlies do not have to spend more than half an hour every day in what I may call personal menial attendance on them. The Russian officer, on the other hand, is always shouting for his "vestavoï,"and his "vestavoï" spends all the day and often a considerable part of the night, cooking for him, opening bottles for him, cleaning his clothes, etc. In Russia men are cheap, in Japan the soldier is a precious object. Japan emerged in thirty years from the intensely pleasant, intensely impracticable, old clan system, in which every "daïmyo" and "samuraï" was attended by crowds of retainers. Russia is still in the patriarchal stage. The soldiers are little children, the officers are their "fathers." Despite the "emancipation of the serfs," the agreeable, old Biblical slave system still really survives in Russia, and it will require a whole series of military disasters, and perhaps a great national upheaval, to do away with it completely. But why should you pity Russia for the pain this revolution will cause her? Do you think that it cost the "daïmyo" of Japan no pain to leave their moated "yashki," to disband their faithful "samuraï," to sink from gods to common men?

On this day (Sunday) I was allowed to have an interview with Kuroki, the leader whose death by dysentery I announced in October 1904 in the *New York Herald* on the authority of a Japanese prisoner. Dressed in a plain black uniform, this great Asiatic captain lived in a small bare room at the back of the building occupied by his staff, and when I entered he was seated cross-legged on the "kang," just as if he were sitting on the "tatami" of his little white lath-and-paper dwelling at home. One or two small rectangular trunks, evidently containing clothing and personal effects, lay beside him on the "kang," while his sword, overcoat, and hat hung on the wall. On a small Chinese table beside him lay a Japanese map, which he had been apparently studying.

The general's appearance was strictly in keeping

with the severity of his surroundings. He was a medium-sized unpretentious gentleman, with a greyish moustache and thick greyish hair. He greeted me very naturally and pleasantly, and, after the Japanese custom, continued smiling all the time I remained with him. He asked me to excuse him for being seated, as he was in his stockinged feet; and he talked only in Japanese through an interpreter, Captain T. Okada, I think. As his back was to the window, I could not get a very good view of his face, but I carried away with me the impression of a plain, firm, grey-toned, friendly physiognomy, that could, however, be terrible if it liked. It was unmistakably military, but in the crowds at Shimbashi Station or Uyeno Park it would have attracted no special attention. You could only say, "That's some officer," but it might be a major, a captain in the navy, or somebody connected with the transport service. Yet this unimposing man dwarfs all the ancient heroes of Japan—Nobunaga, Hideyoshi, Ieyasu, Kato Kiyemasu, Konishi, and all the rest of them. If Japan's religious customs do not alter he will yet be a god like Ieyasu, like the Soga brothers. Other countries look back through the mists of years for their greatest captain. In the person of General Kuroki, Daï-Nippon has got hers in the flesh to-day. He may not be Japan's greatest general, but Europe will never forget his name, for he is the first Yellow leader who has beaten white men with modern weapons.

The general did not ask me any leading questions regarding the Russians (he seemed to leave all this sort of thing to the astute Fuji, to whom, however, I refused to give any information that could do harm to Kuropatkin), but he wanted to know how long I had been with them. "Since the outbreak of the war," I replied.

"Then," said he, casting a keen glance at my Russian coat, hat, and top-boots, "you have been so long with them that you have almost become a Russian yourself—so far at least as your dress is concerned."

I explained that there had been no other kind of warm clothing to be had in Mukden, and that, besides, it was better for me to wear Russian garments, since if I looked too foreign, I might have had frequent difficulties with sentinels and patrols.

He laughingly admitted the truth of this. When I asked him what he thought of the Russian generals he first turned the question by a compliment. "If they were as brave as the correspondents," he said, "they might do better."

I thanked him on the part of the correspondents, but remarked that I thought the Russian generals were often too brave and exposed themselves too recklessly. I mentioned the case of Count Keller, who had been killed, and of Generals Mishchenko, Rennenkampf, Tserpitsky and others who had been wounded.

General Kuroki did not seem impressed, however. He thought that the Russian generals were none of them capable men.

"But hasn't some one of them given you more trouble than the others?" I asked.

"No," he replied, laughing. "They're all on the same level."

He admitted, however, that the Russian soldiers were good fighters. Like General Fuji, he seemed anxious to know if the Russians were aware of the domestic troubles in their own country, and laughed pleasantly when he heard that they were. As a matter of fact, the Japanese had taken particular pains to keep the Russians well informed on this point. For some time they used to send soldiers with a flag of truce and a bundle of literature regarding the trouble in Russia to places near the Russian outposts; but, as after a while the Russians threatened to fire on any one who came on such an errand, other means for the propagation of information were resorted to.

When I asked General Kuroki if the Japanese would be satisfied with the capture of Mukden and if there was any chance of the war ever coming to an end, he paused for a moment, like a man in deep thought, and then answered impressively: "The war must go on." In fact, the impression made on me at that time by all the Japanese officers and men was that they would mutiny almost if the war were brought to a termination before the capture of Harbin and Vladivostock. Instead of being tired, they seemed to be only warming to their work.

It is a Japanese custom to give presents of trifling value to visitors, and, on my leaving his room, General Kuroki presented me with a box of Turkish cigarettes. I then returned to my prison, where I was visited during the rest of the day by a number of very sympathetic Japanese correspondents and English-speaking Japanese civilians employed at Kuroki's headquarters as censors and so forth.

As I have already intimated, there was very little to eat or drink, for the Japanese carry few luxuries with them, so that they can never display anything approaching the lavish hospitality of the Russians, but they seemed to do all they could to entertain us.

CHAPTER XVI

BACK TO LIAOYANG

ON Monday, March 13, I was told to get ready to start in an hour for Dalny. I did not take five minutes to get ready, for I had no packing to do, and at daybreak I set out with—or, rather, "in custody of"—a young soldier called T. Hara. Hara San, who speaks English well, was a delightful travelling companion, and possessed in an exceptional degree the Japanese qualities of tact, good humour and physical endurance. He said to me: "Sir, you will be much civilised when you reach Dalny," meaning that I would have an opportunity of getting a good wash, and I thanked him for this piercing, but well-intentioned, comment on my personal appearance.

During our little trip to Dalny Private Hara taught me some Japanese, and discussed all sorts of subjects with me, from the merest trifles to the most abstruse problems of philosophy, and his smile, his "aliveness" and his fine teeth were my entertainment all the way. In sooth, he was a very engaging little fellow, and if Japanese privates are all like him I am afraid that there will soon be no chance for us poor whites on the face of this planet.

Like all Japanese, Hara was entirely under the Anglo-American influence, save in the matter of religion.

"None of us, Japanese, believe in religion," he said, proudly; "we believe neither in a God nor in a hereafter. In our funeral services, it is true, we address the spirits of the dead as if they were present, but that is only our politeness. Besides," he added cheerfully, a question twinkling in his eye, "no educated European or American now believes in Christianity."

I quote him because, from a four years' experience of Japan, I am convinced that he speaks not only for himself, but for the more advanced portion of his nation. Of few things is intellectual Japan so perfectly certain as that religion is merely an old wife's tale; and if an earnest man from Oxford or Maynooth thinks he makes a good impression on a Japanese philosopher by confessing that he believes in Christianity he errs grievously; in fact, he might as well seek to make an impression on his Japanese friend by assuring him that he is one of an ancient band of believers who hold that the earth is flat. In short, the Japanese think that what they regard as the extraordinary delusion about Christianity is, perhaps, the one weak point in the European intellect.

Hara said that the Japanese generals had no religion, and, so far as he was concerned, that settled it. He told me that there were Buddhist and Shinto priests in the army, some attached to the forces in the capacity of chaplains, some wearing the uniforms of private soldiers which they temporarily discarded for the sacerdotal robes whenever the necessity arose, but that, though the officers attended their services, they "did not believe in them."

This did not, however, prevent these officers from encouraging the simpler soldiers to wear Buddhist amulets and phylacteries, so that in no way, even in the faith in supernatural assistance, would the Russians have the advantage of them. The Japanese have already adopted the Russian "bashleek," and in the Russian Prisoners' Quarters, where I was afterwards incarcerated, at Shizuoka I heard squads of soldiers engaged in a cheering drill *à la Russe*. If Christianity is found to increase the fanaticism of the soldier and to lessen his fear of death the Japanese will also adopt it.

A long residence in the Far East is calculated to shake one's faith in Christianity. You find non-Christian tribes and nations contain about the average number of respectable citizens. If you bring forward the good points of Christianity, the educated heathen will promptly dig up something of the same kind out of Buddhist or Confucian theology. The sight of the Russian prisoners saying their prayers three times a day amid a circle of their polite but incredulous conquerors tempts you to believe that Christianity is, after all, a superstition, and that the agnostic Japanese are right.

Soon after leaving Kuroki's village we passed a long train of transport carts driven by Chinamen, who grinned at me and shouted sarcastically, " Ta ta de kapitan ! " (" Great captain ! "), and " Cush cush mayo ! " (" No food ! "), whereupon little Hara got angry and threatened them with his rifle, shouting at the same time as loud as he could, " Yingwa-Rin ! Yingwa-Rin ! " (" He's an Englishman ! He's an Englishman ! ") We also passed long trains of Japanese pack-horses led by "styohé," or military coolies, from whom, sometimes, but seldom, a single abrupt, dispassionate shout of "Russky!" proceeded. At first Hara used to stop to explain to these good people that they had made a great mistake in calling me "Russky," but after he had done so for the two hundredth time or so, he got tired and even assented, if silence meant assent, to the people who asked him if I was not a Russian "shoko" (officer).

The first *étape*, or, as the Japanese call it, communication station, was at a place called Tudyatun, where we had dinner. The commandant of this *étape* asked me if it was true that, just before the battle, a number of wounded Japanese had been bound with ropes and dragged through the streets of Mukden, in order to make the Chinese believe that the Russians were winning. I said that I only knew of some unwounded Japanese having been marched through Mukden, and that they were not bound and not ill-treated along the route; but I am astonished that, with tales like these, told them by constitutionally inaccurate Chinamen and accepted as gospel by the General Staff, the Japanese, who took me for a Russian, did not indulge in any hostile demonstration. I am afraid that things would have been different in any other country, but it is not impossible that the Japanese themselves would behave differently in case they were losing. It is to the credit of the Russians, on the other hand, that, despite their uninterrupted succession of defeats, they treated Japanese prisoners with unvarying kindness.

All the way down the Liaotung peninsula and all the way from Hiroshima to Shizuoka I was taken for a Russian, but not even once was an angry remark addressed to me or an angry glance cast at me, either

BACK TO LIAOYANG

by the Chinese, who have suffered so much at the hands of the Russians, or by the Japanese. Sometimes Japanese soldiers, taking me for an officer, saluted me respectfully; and once, while standing at the gate of my Japanese prison, a little girl of about three years of age was induced by some companions a year or two older to toddle forward and present me with a bough of cherry-blossoms.

After leaving Tudyatun I passed further trains of Chinese transport carts, the Celestial drivers of which grinned at me with one accord, and shouted, "Poo ko bin!" a Chinese term which really means "cannot sell," but which seems to be used by the Japanese and the Chinese in their employ as the equivalent of "You are powerless. You cannot do anything."

Some of them shouted "Kupetz!" the Russian word for "merchant," whereupon, sooner than be taken for a camp follower, I resumed the brass-buttoned, double-breasted Russian coat which had previously caused me to be mistaken for an officer.

Midway between Tudyatun and Kandalusan I came across a little village occupied by military coolies, who invited me into their best house, offered me such simple food as they had got, and were very inquisitive, friendly, and sympathetic. Most of them introduced themselves to me in a state of nature, for they had just been having a bath in a new bath-house which they had erected; but as they themselves did not seem to realise that there was anything improper in their lack of attire I for my part did not manifest any surprise.

All morning we passed long strings of pack animals led by "styohé," alternating with longer strings of Chinese carts driven by Chinamen; and at noon a faint sound of cannonading, away to the northward, showed us that Kuroki was again fighting, as I had fully expected, for, on the morning on which I left him, his headquarters had been in a state of feverish activity.

Passing on this day a collection of dug-outs, Hara began calculating the force of Russians it had contained. He also used every opportunity of enlarging his vocabulary of English military terms, taking care to jot down in his notebook every unfamiliar word that he heard me use. As I was equally keen, however, on enlarging my Japanese vocabulary, there was a fair exchange on both sides. He had got three books in his knapsack, one Colonel Churchill's " Japanese Military Terms," the second a little Anglo-Japanese dictionary, and the third a Sino-Japanese gazetteer of Manchurian geographical names. When with the Russian army, I had sometimes heard privates reading novels aloud for the delectation of comrades who could not read, but I never knew any of them to possess even as much as a map.

But in the Japanese army the First Soldiers, as they are called, had always maps, and so had even ordinary privates sometimes.

A Chinese countryman joined us in the evening and enlarged for a long time, in his own language, on the oneness of the Japanese and Chinese peoples. According to him they were "yeega yang" (all the same)— same eyes, same black hair, same absence of beard, same rice, chopsticks and character writing. I realised that the occasion was a solemn one. I was watching the birth of the Yellow Peril. But Hara tactfully discouraged this conversation.

In regard to the treatment of Chinese, I think the

BACK TO LIAOYANG

Japanese are ahead of the Russians, but there is in general as little fraternisation between the Celestials and the Japanese soldiers as if the latter were the troops of some civilised Malay empire which had adopted Chinese character writing. Contrary to my expectations, the Japanese do not speak Chinese any better than the Russians, but they have the advantage of being able to communicate with the Chinese in writing.

In the evening I reached Kandalusan, about a day's journey to the south-east of Mukden, and formerly the headquarters of General Zassulitch, commanding the First Siberian Army Corps. As my next day's journey was to take me to the Yentai coal mines it will be seen that I was sent around in a semicircular sweep, so as not to be able to see anything of what was going on in the vicinity of Mukden.

I found Kandalusan so little changed that I almost expected to hear the merry music and the sound of dancing which had proceeded from it when I had last visited it, several months before. But, alas for worldly grandeur, it had fallen from its high estate, and, instead of being the headquarters of a General, was now a mere communications station. Never again shall the voice of Muscovite harpers and musicians be heard in Kandalusan.

The very house in which General Zassulitch had given me a frosty welcome and a frostier dinner was desecrated by the presence of a commissariat officer of low degree. This functionary received me almost as coldly as if he had been an English postmistress and I a customer coming to buy a stamp. He gave me good quarters, however, and got the servants to make several attempts to light a fire in the "kang," but these attempts were all failures, and I woke up very cold at a quarter past 2 A.M. to find one soldier sleeping on the "kang" alongside me and another sitting at my feet with his rifle between his knees and his bayonet fixed to the rifle, watching me intently by the uncertain flicker of a new candle which he had just lighted, the first one having burned out. The guard over me was relieved every half-hour, the relieved always saying "Yoroshii!" ("All's well!") to the relievee, in the bated breath of a man guarding incalculable treasures.

Next morning I asked Hara for an explanation of this singular watchfulness.

"Oh, sir!" said he, "that guard is simply there to do you honour as correspondent."

I thereupon thanked God that I was not a general, for in that case they would probably have taken it into their heads to have a brass band playing all night in my bedroom.

Early on the morning of Tuesday, March 14, we started for Tanko, near the Yentaï mines.

An instinctive fear that the Japanese batteries would fire on us seized me as soon as we left Kandalusan, for, the last time I had been there, it was dangerous to wander to any considerable distance south of the Russian lines. But at length we passed what had long been the Land Debatable and reached what had long been the Japanese outposts. On one side of the Shaho (which was then, like the Hunho, almost free from ice and difficult to cross) the outermost Russian posts, with their palisades, their barbed wire fences and their pitfalls ; on the other side, the simpler Japanese dug-outs and trenches. The Russians seem to have been everlastingly preparing against attack; the Japanese to have been ever getting ready for an advance.

All the way from the Shaho to Yentai ran a trolley line of far simpler and cheaper construction than the fine narrow-gauge railways which the Russians had constructed to the east and west of Mukden and which afterward fell entirely into the hands of the conquerors.

On this day I met the usual endless stream of military coolies and Chinese carts. A Japanese soldier, asleep in one of the latter, was roused by the excited driver thereof, who shouted to him: "Quick! quick! Look! look! A white man! A hairy barbarian caught!" But, greatly to my disgust —for up to that time I had attracted as much attention as a cow with two heads—the little Jap only cursed the Chinaman and went to sleep again, without hardly condescending to favour me with a glance. In the old days our fondness for having a whole bedroom to ourselves in Japanese hotels, our dislike of the publicity which obtains in the Japanese bath, and our unaccountable repugnance to going about like them *in puris naturalibus*, led the Japanese to suspect that there was about our mode of existence and our bodily form something mysterious, something of which we felt ashamed and which we wished to hide; but now that they have captured tens of thousands of us—men, women and children, including sick, wounded, naked and insane, now that they have buried our mangled dead, all the way from Port Arthur to Kaiyuan; that they have watched all sorts of specimens of us day and night with the care of a naturalist studying a new variety of beetle; that they have superintended us taking our compulsory bath, scores at a time in the quarantine stations at Ninoshima and Nagasaki, the edge must surely be for ever taken off their keen curiosity.

I dined this day at a place south of the Shaho, called Sudyaze, where there was an enormous depot of Japanese stores of rice and barley packed in gunny bags covered by closely woven straw mats, and ready to be carted or carried off at a moment's notice. The officer in charge of the *étape* was hospitable and communicative. He said that he had expected one hundred thousand prisoners, and was disappointed at getting word to prepare accommodation for only ten thousand. The total number of captives was higher than ten thousand, but the balance was going southward by another route. Personally he did not dote on Russian prisoners, whose clothing was, he said, dirty. He complained that a Russian regimental doctor who had been captured three days before and whom he had treated very well, had stolen a Japanese soldier's overcoat and vamoosed in the night-time. The soldier on guard had been deceived by the colour of the coat, but this did not save him from punishment next day at the hands of his incensed superior.

While sympathising to some extent with the latter, I could not help feeling some sympathy for the unfortunate Russian also, because I had been often thinking of doing as he did. At the same time this problem of escaping from watchful guardians is one of the hardest that ever confronted any ordinary man; for, apart from the great difficulty of getting past sleeping men and armed sentinels, there is the equally great difficulty of getting across a flat, bare, wasted country traversed everywhere by the enemy. The more I pondered on this problem the more profound became my admiration for Jack Sheppard. In some ways Jack was a greater man than Napoleon Bonaparte.

Here and elsewhere in Manchuria, more especially in Dalny, I found in the hands of the Japanese fine Russian dogs, which, seeing that I was a white man, used to rush towards me with sorrowful whines. Although they were well treated by the Japanese, it was rather sad to see them forced to lick the hands that had perhaps shed their masters' blood.

Near Tanko we called on a friend of Hara's who had something to do with the canteen business, and in his house, strange to say, I found two Japanese servants who had been in Siberia and could speak Russian.

The Chinese inhabitants seemed to be getting on fairly well under the Japanese sway in this part of the country. They had not begun to till their rice-fields yet, but this was, I suppose, because the ground was still frozen. A handsome young Chinese woman with a baby in her arms regarded me, as I passed, with curiosity, but not with hatred; while the usual stream of Chinese carters indulged sometimes in the usual good-natured chaff, but generally confined themselves to a blank stare of wonderment.

The Japanese had made themselves at home in such of the Chinese houses as they occupied hereabouts. They squatted with stockinged feet on the "kang," they had improvised "hibachi" out of old oil tins, and they generally had a fire burning in a hollow in the centre of the room, as in Hokkaido and other cold parts of their own islands.

After having had a fine Japanese dinner with Hara's friends we crossed a ridge of hills at sunset, and, lo! beneath us lay a lost Russian town! a fine collection of European houses like those at Dalny or Tsingtau, with well-gravelled walks and with long lines of stone steps before the doors. Chinese lions carved in granite guarded the approaches to these steps, potted plants of many varieties adorned them all the way up. Lights twinkled from windows. Blinds were drawn. I could almost believe that I was in a prosperous Russian settlement had it not been for the flag of the Rising Sun, which was hauled down at sunset from half a dozen lofty flag-poles.

Descending the hill we climbed one of the biggest flights of steps and entered a large room, all around which Japanese sat at desks. Some were in European civil dress, some were in semi-military dress, some were in "kimonos," and all were working hard at big ledgers and account books.

Leaving me standing severely alone in the middle of the room, Hara went forward to the manager, with the air of a man who is going to spring a good joke. He saluted, but for about five minutes the manager was oblivious of his presence, and in the meantime the clerks stared at me coldly, tittered slightly, and exchanged comments on my appearance. One of them hit the right nail on the head with the remark, which he made in Japanese to a companion, that, judging from my camera, I must be a newspaper man. When Hara told his story, however, and he always told it, whatever it was, with great gusto, a sudden change came over the scene. The manager shook hands with me heartily and asked me to pray be seated, while the glances directed at me by his satellites became all at once sympathetic.

Nevertheless, I could not help thinking how unenviable must be the feelings of a Russian prisoner, coldly received and coldly stared at, in a house which his money had built and in defence of which his blood had perhaps been shed. This must, however, have been the fate of many unfortunate Russians, for the manager told me that a colonel and one hundred and fifty prisoners had passed through to Liaoyang the day before, while about five thousand were expected next day. He also informed me with a laugh that formerly the Russian military governor of the place lived in that very house.

I had so long identified myself with the Russians, I had so often eaten their khleb-sol (bread and salt), that this laugh of triumph somewhat jarred on me; but, after all, I cannot say that I felt out of place among the Japanese. Although their ways are not always our ways, the Japanese are human; and it does not take very long for a white man to forget that their skin is not quite the same colour as his. If there is ever a "yellow peril," it will be an educated peril, and not the wild, barbaric, mysterious and inhuman monster with visions of which some people have tortured their brains.

Fortunately there was a train leaving at once for Liaoyang, and Hara and I secured an empty goods waggon, in which we made ourselves comfortable with numerous red army rugs which the Tanko manager kindly lent us.

About half-past ten at night we were in Liaoyang station. Liaoyang? I could hardly believe my eyes. When last I had seen Liaoyang, the station platform was crowded with Russian officers and the crowd in the buffet was dense. Angry cries of "Boyka!" ("Waiter"); "Chelovek!" "Peevo!" ("Beer"); " Itte syuda!" ("Come here"); and deprecatory responses of "Sichas!" (" Immediately") filled the air. Here and there was a Red Cross sister, or a Korean boy, who looked very much like a Japanese, and who did not seem to push the sale of his basketful of cigarettes with all the zeal that you would expect of a *bonâ fide* pedlar. Away down at the dark end of the platform a crowd of big, patient, clumsy privates were bargaining hoarsely with a Greek sutler, who kept a store there. A stone's throw from the station the lights of sundry Greek stores gleamed through innumerable rows of bottles and were reflected in an intervening lake of watery mud which was, in places, almost deep enough to drown one.

Liaoyang had now the sober and settled tranquillity of a prosperous little market-town in England. Five pairs of rails glistened in the lamp-light, the buffet had become a traffic manager's office, and the station was divided into compartments wherein prosaic, sedentary little men worked patiently and noiselessly. There was no crowd on the platform. Several people crossed it hurriedly with luggage. A few porters walked along it swinging their lanterns. Like one in a dream I issued from the train and passed through the wicket. Outside was no crowd of loud, abusive "jinriksha" men wanting three or four roubles to bring you a few hundred yards, no long line of pure-breds held by patient orderlies, no crowd of privates competing with Chinamen for the few kopecks the holding of a horse would bring them.

The lofty tower of Liaoyang rose above me; the houses of the Russian settlement twinkled with lights; afar off the triple summit of Shushan looked as calm as if it had never known shrapnel. I passed over a road hard as iron, and after visiting several offices wherein pale, studious, polite young men, in semi-military costume and with spectacles and hollow cheeks were still writing patiently, sadly and silently, I was finally led into the gendarmerie quarter, a quadrangular block of buildings situated at the base of the old pagoda. Here also, despite the lateness of the hour, sallow, sartorial-looking clerks were still at work. But there were others. At a sign from the chief clerk, to whom Hara had, with his usual swing and vim, told the whole story and handed his documents, two sturdy little soldiers, with rifles and fixed bayonets, came from somewhere or other and quietly but firmly attached themselves to me.

CHAPTER XVII

FROM LIAOYANG TO DALNY

WHEN I got up at 7.30 A.M. on Wednesday, March 15, I found everybody had already breakfasted and gone out to work, that the kitchen fire was cold, and had to be lighted again in order to prepare my breakfast, that the commandant of the gendarmerie had already been twice to see me. When I found this out and thought of the old Liaoyang, which regarded ten o'clock in the morning as scandalously early, I began to realise that there is something, after all, in that saying about the early bird.

The commandant was very polite. He said that it would have been a dreadful thing if an English or American correspondent on the Russian side had fallen by a Japanese bullet, that it was an honour for me to have been captured as I was, and that it was an honour for him to be my host. But on learning that I had been in Liaoyang before and knew the lie of the ground perfectly, his jaw fell, and, immediately after, my guards began watching me intently, evidently under the impression that I was a kind of Irish leprecaun that was liable to disappear the instant its captor took his eyes off it. I was also refused permission to visit the city, to take a walk, to send a note to my old friend, Dr. Westwater of Liaoyang, or to do

FROM LIAOYANG TO DALNY 357

anything save remain all day in my room. I was treated, however, with much courtesy, and supplied with enough food and drink for two men.

Despite his suspicious nature, the commandant of Liaoyang pleased me by the paternal interest he took in his involuntary charges. He consulted with me anxiously as to what the Russians got to eat when at home, and seemed surprised when I told him that, even in their worst times in Manchuria, they had always got plenty of black bread, thick soup, meat, "kasha" (porridge), and tea. He had evidently imagined that in their own country they lived exclusively on dog biscuits. He was a minute, conscientious, scrupulous man, however, and begged anxiously to know if four pieces of a hard cabin-biscuit kind of production per meal were not sufficient for each man. He was visibly disappointed and distressed when I told him that I hardly thought this sufficient. The Russian soldiers themselves were decidedly of opinion that it was insufficient, and in conversation with me they contrasted the warm "zeemlyankee," abundant "borsh," and huge chunks of fresh black bread supplied to the Japanese prisoners by the Russians with the treatment meted out them by the Japs.

Finally I rather put my foot in it by telling the old commandant that, when the next Russo-Japanese wa broke out, I would again join the Russians. "Then," said he sharply, "next time you are my guest it will be in St. Petersburg."

In the afternoon I was brought to the station, and on the way I saw a sight that moved me more than anything I had seen during the whole war. In front of the Liaoyang railway depot there is a large fenced-in space, and this space I found to be crammed with Russian prisoners who had passed the whole night there on the bare ground without any kind of covering. They were cold, hungry, dirty and miserable, to such an extent that their worst enemy might have wept for pity; and, all round, Japanese and Chinese pressed against the railings and grinned at the unhappy captives inside.

There were eight tents for officers—for a time I occupied one of them myself—but, as far as I could see, there were no latrines, no decent privacy, and the natives watched the white men discharging the offices of nature with a critical and disgusted air. The unfortunate Russkies were exactly on the level of a collection of gorillas that had just been captured and rendered harmless. Poor devils! they had hardly room to turn round in, and as they had not washed for weeks, and as no soap or water was now given them, it is not surprising that the neat little Japanese soldiers, spruce as if they had just stepped out of a band-box, with shining cheeks and glistening white teeth, sometimes held their noses, and that even the dirtiest Chinese coolies seemed to regard this Russky nuisance as something too great to be borne in silence. It was a fall indeed; a fall so tremendous that words fail to convey a just idea of it. To be captured and driven into a cage by the yellow soldiers whom, at the beginning of the war, they had only one designation for— "makaka" (monkeys)—was a come-down in the world for the haughty Muscovites. To be driven into an enclosure like cattle, and allowed to stand or lie there, on a night when a considerate man would scarcely like to let his horse or his dog sleep out in the open, was bad enough ; but what made it worse was the fact that in the neat houses which the Russians had built for themselves years ago all around the station, the Japanese were now very snug and comfortable.

Some of the Russians tried to converse with the Chinese whom they had formerly known in Liaoyang, while others accepted cigarettes which good-natured Japanese soldiers passed to them through the bars of the fence, the same as you would pass biscuits to a caged monkey at the Zoo. It was pathetic to watch the vain attempts of one or two to light a fire with a handful of twigs and dried grass they had collected in order to boil water in the few sooty and dented old mess-tins that still remained to them, for the purpose of making their beloved "chaï" (tea). Some prayed, with faces turned towards the sun and with the frequent crossings which the Orthodox Catholic employs. Japanese soldiers occasionally imitated them out of a spirit of fun, but the Russians did not take this unconscious irreverence in bad part. They only smiled, and taught the Japs how to cross themselves properly.

I cannot say that the Russians were dignified in their misfortunes. They "bummed" around the limits of their cage, fraternising quite affably with the few Japanese who allowed them to become familiar, and begging piteously for food, for tobacco, for anything their keepers would condescend to give them. None of them seemed by his conduct to feel that he represented Europe and must behave accordingly. It cannot be said that any of them stood gloomily apart like a Byronic hero in the hands of his enemies. On one occasion, however, when a young Russian private began to tell me how his party had been surrounded, an elderly comrade interrupted him with the angry exclamation: "What's the use of talking about these things now? Can't you wait till we get back to Russia?"

Late in the afternoon the Russians were led from their cage to the railway-station, where they were driven like cattle into open trucks. This long line of tall, patriarchal-looking, bearded men marched between two grinning rows of Chinamen and Japanese. As they did not march fast enough to please their masters, the latter made them run, and then laughed the silent, Asiatic laugh—at the "bashleeks" and the "papakhas" bobbing up and down as the big, docile men raced obediently towards the railway.

There were about twenty trucks in the train and fifty men in each truck. For every fifty prisoners there was one armed Japanese, who sat stiff and upright on the side of the vehicle, his black eyes shining brightly above the high, fur-lined collar of his pepper-coloured overcoat, his rifle between his knees, the sinking sun glinting red on his broad naked bayonet, whose point and edge were as sharp as a razor. The Russians were all littered in the bottom of the trucks, only their heads and shoulders projecting. Personally, I felt like one of the conquered in a Roman triumph. I had touched the lowest deep of abasement. Chains would not have added materially to my humiliation.

After having passed one night, without covering, in an open field, the Russians were now to pass the next night without covering in open trucks. The Japanese evidently meant to test the boasted ability of the Muscovites to withstand cold. There was a moderate-sized crowd of Japanese and Chinese at the station, but they did not cheer or make any demonstration. The Japanese never cheers even when the "Tenno Haiku" (whom foreigners call the Mikado) passes by, and now he looked on with a grave smile at the loud undignified uproar of the Russians, among whom tins of hard biscuits were being divided. The Japanese guard in each truck had the task of distribution, and he threw the stuff among his prisoners as a man throws bread to dogs. Like dogs, too, the Russians scrambled for the food, with shouts of "Vozmee syuda!" and "Dai khleb!" that were not unlike barks. The decorous station precincts echoed to the roars of one big fellow who had got nothing, but the sentinel's only reply was gravely to raise the empty tin to show that there was no more. Some wounded Japanese officers in white "kimono" with a red cross on the shoulder, stood on the platform and looked on in contempt. They knew that had they been in the position of the Russians they would have starved to death sooner than raise such an unseemly clamour.

To appreciate the significance of this historic scene, one should have lived for a long time in the Far East, and fully entered into the spirit with which the white settlers there regard the yellow inhabitants. When, seven years ago, I first travelled from Tientsin to Peking, a Chinese attendant on the train ceremoniously ushered me into a car in which only white men were allowed to travel. Mandarins, coolies, Chinese princes and Chinese prostitutes were all piled together in dirty third-class carriages. They were all yellow; why make any distinctions between them?

No Chinese guest ever desecrated the sacred precincts of the Shanghai Club (which, up till a couple of years ago, would not allow a Japanese to cross its threshold—no, not even if that Japanese bore the name of Togo or Kuroki), and no European, unless he were mad or drunk, would ever dream of asking a Chinese gentleman to dinner.

The Japanese were tarred with the same brush, and the language anent " yellow monkeys " in which Port Arthur used to indulge was tame in comparison with what one heard in the bar-rooms of the Yokohama hotels even after the outbreak of the recent war.

I could hardly therefore realise that I was awake when I found myself at Liaoyang station surrounded by examples of Russian architecture, in a train drawn by an American engine ; but, nevertheless, one of a crowd of broken white men whom the despised little slant-eye had compelled, by the keen logic of the bayonet point, to travel in trucks which might have been useful for carrying coal or ballast, but in which, at that season of the year, no cattle-dealer would care to send cattle any considerable distance. Although the events of a year might have prepared my mind for it, this turning of the tables was so sudden and so complete that I looked on dazed and thunderstruck. It was like going into Calcutta and finding all the white men of that city acting as street-sweepers, coolies, syces, shoe-blacks and in other menial capacities, while the obese Bengalee lolled back in the best places on the trains and in the hotels. In making this comparison, I do not wish to offend the Japanese. My only object is to give the reader an accurate idea of the impression made on the mind of one who has lived half his life among the conquering whites of Asia.

Nor do I wish to accuse the Japanese of having deliberately selected open trucks for the Russians in order that all Liaoyang and all the country between Liaoyang and Dalny could see their shame, for perhaps they had not got a sufficient supply of closed carriages ; but a more efficient way for destroying the prestige of the white race and dragging the renown of Russia in the dust could hardly be conceived.

At dawn next day we reached the station of Vangaleen, and it was strange to see the Russian letters on the station and the Russian buildings all around. The Russians now looked so wretched, dirty, red-nosed, and blear-eyed that, in comparison with them, Kentish hop-pickers would be regarded as models of fashion. We had only a few moments to stop at Vangaleen, but the Russians hastened to avail themselves of those few moments, some for the purpose of discharging the offices of nature in the open space near the train, and others of lighting a fire with lightning rapidity for the sake of boiling tea. "Much civilised!" said Hara, when he saw several of them using soap to wash themselves with. He had evidently thought that the Russians only used soap as an article of food.

Some of the prisoners stand stupidly around an ex-Russian interpreter, really a low Chinese coolie, who happened to pick up a few words of Russian somehow or other, while he prods them familiarly with a walking-stick, at the same time impressing on them the fact that "all this would not have befallen you if you had not come to 'our' country," indicating, with a wave of the walking-stick, the Japanese and himself. As regards their treatment in Japan, he explains to them authoritatively, but in execrable Russian, that they will get bread and rice, but no "vodka." A Russian remarks humbly that the Japanese prisoners are well-treated in Russia. "Oh, yes," says the "perevodcheek" loftily, "but the Japanese prisoners are very few — 'ochen malo' — whereas the Russky prisoners are very numerous—one million!"

The bell announcing the forthcoming departure of the train now rang, and this coolie-"perevodcheek" made himself officious by driving the soldiers into the trucks with his cane, at the same time airing his knowledge of Russian expletives. Some, poor devils, suffering, perhaps, from bowel complaint, brought on by sleeping on the bare ground, were hardly in a position to re-enter their trucks just then; but the Russian-speaking Chinaman had no mercy on them, and the Chinese and Japanese, who had been watching their performances with the critical air of vulgar-minded children watching strange brutes evacuating, were delighted at the uncouth stampede of these grey, bearded animals, adjusting their tattered clothing as they ran. The men who had been making tea were driven off mercilessly just before their water had reached the boil. O Russky! Russky! Thy ill-trained "perevodcheek" has turned and rent thee!

It was an uninterrupted yellow grin all the way to Dalny. I have never before had such an opportunity of observing the mirthless Asiatic smile. It was a kind of noiseless laugh, and conveyed, not only an appreciation of humour, but amazement, keen satisfaction and scorn sharp enough to pierce the hide of a rhinoceros. It was like the smile you might see on the faces of London street arabs gazing at the corpulent form of a pompous but unpopular police-sergeant who had got beastly drunk and was being solemnly carried frog's-march to the police station, only that the street arabs would dissipate a lot of their venom in jocular and abusing shouts, while the Chinese concentrated all theirs in that characteristic smile. There was no tribute to bravery, no pity for suffering in that cruel grin. The Chinese can see nothing honourable in captivity; most of them were probably convinced that the Japanese would hereafter make slaves, draught-cattle, of these white-skinned prizes of war. Being Orientals and belonging to a nation as old as Assyria, they probably thought that the natural thing to do with us was to treat us in the shameful way that prisoners of war were treated in the days of Assur-Nusir-Pal.

It seemed impossible to sate the curiosity of these Celestials. They drank in the tremendous significance of the scene with their eyes as thirsty men drink water, and their curiosity seemed unappeasable. Many Chinamen, who had probably supposed the Great White Tsar to be God in Heaven, were suddenly petrified when they saw us, and remained in that condition until the train had passed. Chinese boys in padded winter dress that gave them the appearance of corpulent little elephants, ran wildly across fields to see the show, intimating meanwhile by shouts and gestures that they fully grasped the enormous significance of this great haul. Parents, with an historical prescience that did them credit, brought out their little children to gaze on the train-load of fallen white men passing by.

And how shall I describe the way in which the Chinese regarded the Japanese? To borrow M.

Bérard's fine comparison, they seemed to look on this victorious, kindred people, whom the infallible Occident had declared to be smitten by the same inferiority as themselves, as Homeric soldiers might be supposed to look upon comrades who had all at once and without effort assumed the mighty casques and armour of those vast gods whose weight made the axle-trees of their chariots creak.

Meanwhile the Russians talked of their capture just as if they had been captured by the Germans or the English or any other race of kindred. They failed to grasp the fact that the Germans and the English are their brethren, while, to all Europeans, the Japanese are as mysterious and incomprehensible as the inhabitants of Mars. They failed to see that they were prisoners of this strange and monstrous Asia, which, since the time ot Herodotus, Europe has constantly regarded with distrust and hatred, not unmixed with fear. They were captives to the vague, legendary Cipango. They failed to see the fact, clear as the sun in the heavens, that history had opened a new account, that the axis of the earth had shifted, that the Universe had entered on an entirely new phase. They were as little alive to the tremendous nature of the occasion as was Columbus's cabin-boy when the New World was first sighted. Not since the days of the Golden Horde, since the days when Russian princes had to kneel in person before the Khan of Seraï, has Russia endured such a gigantic humiliation. No such disaster has befallen the White Race since the time of the Mongols. Adowa was nothing in comparison with it. No such disaster befell the Russians in the recent war. There were not many Chinese to see the shame of

Port Arthur, while Ta-shih-chiao and Liaoyang were practically barren of captives. But the publicity of this dishonour may be gauged by the fact that for two months, according to the jubilant Japanese calculation, it would take a train like the one in which I travelled, running daily, to convey all the Russian captives through Manchuria to Dalny. By the end of that time the Manchurian peasant might well be excused for believing that the entire White Race was tilling the soil of Japan under the whip of the Japanese slave-driver.

The shame was so flagrant, so glaring, that one felt reluctant to regard it, just as he would feel reluctant to regard the shame of a man dragged naked to prison in broad daylight through howling streets. One longed to shut his eyes. One wished for the darkness to come and hide the horror, for some natural catastrophe to take place and distract the universal attention. One wished to be small and beardless like a Japanese. One felt ashamed of being white, inasmuch as his white skin exposed him to some of the unspeakable reproach.

It were nothing if the disgrace had been fictitious, temporary, but it was real and eternal. Some sixteen months before, General Wogack had told the statesmen of Peking that, if Japan dared to attack Russia, she would be crushed like a fly on the wheel of a war-chariot. During their sullen retirement from Liaotung and the Yalu, the Russians had declared that they were only enticing the Japanese to their doom, and that very soon they would roll down like a tidal wave, not only on Port Arthur, but on Tokio. Yes, the Russians were now rolling swiftly towards Port Arthur and Tokio, but not exactly in the manner of a tidal wave.

The man who had borne the White Man's burden, to the easternmost limits of the Asiatic Continent, the lineal successors of Alexander, Crassus, and Heraclius in their revenge—Greek, Roman and Byzantine—on Asia, was now being borne along himself by some of the fluttered folk and wild whom he had come to civilise, while I, much to my astonishment, found myself guarded by Japanese soldiers and figuring prominently as one of the new-caught, sullen peoples.

We were an army of long-bearded patriarchs escorted by a handful of smiling, chubby-cheeked school-boys. Truly the Russians are a docile folk. If we had been all English or American captives, I am inclined to think that we should have made short work of the handful of Japs who were guarding us, and immediately afterwards have made tracks westward for the Liao river, only a day's march distant. But what did these poor Russians know of the Liao river or of Chinese neutrality? As little as a sheep being led to the slaughter knows of the Habeas Corpus Act.

We could now see of what enormous value to Japan were her three lines of communication, the line from the Yalu which Kuroki had opened up and in which Kawamura had worthily trod, the line from Dalny, and the line from Yinkow. Over the two last lines came an enormous quantity of supplies, not only by train but by road. This advantage alone would have been almost enough to secure the victory for Japan.

It was war—or at least the memory of war and the preparations for war—all the way down to Dalny. Enormous stores of supplies at Liaoyang, Ta-shih-chiao and elsewhere along the line. Japanese soldiers at every station, Japanese soldiers convoying transports, the Chinese seeming to exist only for the purpose of working on the railway or of driving waggons.

What, I wonder, will these lads from Niigata and Kagoshima and Aomori think of the boasted white man when this war is over? Forty years ago the white man was a mysterious being in Japan, an objectionable being perhaps, but one possessed of diabolical powers and therefore to be cultivated. The Japanese have pretty well analysed him now. Half a century ago the "black demon-ships" of the American Admiral Perry excited awe and terror as, spouting smoke, they steamed into Yedo Bay. Some Japanese who—like Admiral Togo—were boys of ten years old then, know a thing or two about these "black demon-ships" now.

Later still, we find England bombarding Shimonoseki simply because Shimonoseki had not behaved with proper respect to white men, although these particular white men were not Britishers. In those days England believed in making common cause with her white brethren against the yellow race, and that feeling has scarcely died out yet among the English in Japan. Many of these people used, after the Japan-China War, to complain of the overbearing, I'm-as-good-as-you-are style of the Japanese officers, meaning that the white race was treated as if it were not superior to the yellow. What reputation is now left to the white race in Japan?

On went the train with its load of captives. Station after station it passed. As the names of some stations were cried out, the Russians raised their heads with the air of men who, in a foreign land, hear familiar

2 A

words. They had heard the names of Russian defeats—Haicheng, Ta-shih-chiao, Telissu, Kinchow.

It was midnight when we passed Ta-shih-chiao, with its long line of provision stores which Mishchenko's Cossacks might so easily have destroyed on the previous January. It was morning when we came to Telissu, with its broken bridges and overturned locomotives—the only relics of the great battle that remained.

At Kinchow the Russian barracks still stood, also some huge, damaged Russian guns. Many of the prisoners left the train, but not to weep over these reminders of their lost dominion. It was only to get, for the purpose of making tea, some of the hot water which a Chinese coolie was distributing. But the Chinese coolie ordered them away with a threatening wave of a stick and insisted on serving the Japanese first. The Japanese looked on, laughing in the good-natured, self-complacent way in which one laughs at an imbecile. They laughed until their eyes looked like two oblique slits, at the big, uncouth, bearded babies waddling after them, meek, docile, dirty, utterly humiliated.

At some distance apart, a well-groomed group of Japanese officers, station functionaries and doctors had collected, and were smiling in an affable and patronising way at the awful specimens of humanity that disfigured the landscape. Beside them orderlies held magnificent Russian horses, some of the wide-strewn spoils of Port Arthur.

Dalny! the name brought vividly to my mind the first visit which I paid to Liaotung, in September 1903. I recalled the profound impression of Russian might the place made on me then. I recalled my first sight of that fine European town, the easternmost limits of a White Empire, of Europe, my first glimpse of the harbour fit to shelter navies, of the enormous piers built not for an age but for all time.

This monument of Russian might was now an eternal monument of Japanese bravery. This fine European town was Japanese. This frontier post of Europe had ceased to be European. This harbour sheltered only Japanese ships. These piers echoed only to the triumphant clink of Japanese "geta."

At Dairen I met three other correspondents who had been captured at other parts of the battle-field— M. Ludovic Naudeau, of the *Journal* (Paris), Mr. Richard Little, of the Chicago *Daily News*, and Baron Bilder von Kriegelstein, of the Berlin *Lokalanzeiger*.

CHAPTER XVIII

FROM DALNY TO JAPAN AS A PRISONER OF WAR

THE most interesting sea trip I ever made in my life was the trip from Dalny to Ujina, Japan, in the middle of last March. I went as a Japanese prisoner of war in a hospital ship, the *Awa Maru*, a fine little vessel, formerly on the Nippon Yusen Kaisha's European run, with a German captain in command of her, and, down in the engine-room, two canny Scotch engineers, who were making big pay but were mortally afraid that if they went hame to their ain countrie they would be promptly run into gaol under the " Foreign Enlistments Act."

The number of wounded Japanese on board that boat was considerable, and the way in which the privates were accommodated in tier upon tier of shelves in the hold was marvellous and economical. Japan did wonderful things in the late war, but nothing more wonderful than the way in which she cut down expenses without sacrificing efficiency, presenting in this respect a great contrast to Russia, which, although comparatively a poor country, spent money with a lavishness which would make even wealthy nations like America or Great Britain stand aghast.

FROM DALNY TO JAPAN

Without paying anything for it, however, Japan derives from her geographical situation advantages which all the gold in the Russian treasury could not buy. The Russians brought their wounded by jolting carts to the railway, and such of them as survived that preliminary trial were brought by jolting trains to Chita, Verkhnyudinsk and Irkutsk, where they ran a good chance of dying from *ennui* in the monotonous Siberian plains, while the Japanese wounded could in a few days be transported from the battle-field to the loveliest islands in the world.

The change from dusty Manchuria to the clean sea, the bright sky, the green islands, the snowy seagulls, the glad vinous air, the sunshine sparkling on the polished brasswork of *Awa Maru*, the snowy billows dancing before the prow, the white foaming water spouting continually from the condenser at the side, the sea churned into foam underneath the propeller, the deck as white and spotless as the snowy quarter-deck of a British warship, the clear-cut horizon,—this change was so great that I felt—well, I felt as if I had just drunk a deep draught of some rare wine.

A narrow white fringe of crumpled water leaped before the bows and formed on each side an ample band of tossing creamy surf, running back, swift as a mill-race. Behind the screw the carded, torn water rushed away like the stream below a cataract. On every side stretched a glassy sea, glassy save where we cut through it, and there it effervesced, and one could see myriads of white air-bubbles dancing below the surface and showing distinctly against the deep blue. I spent hours listening in the intervals between the rhythmic beats of the calm, pulsating engine, to the delicious fizz of the water, and watching the creamy foam that mantled on its surface, and the little, joyous, crested wavelets rushing back gracefully, like sea-nymphs, in feigned alarm from the rude touch of the keel.

The first astounding thing we noticed once we got out of sight of land was that there was no dust! Air —real air—without a solitary speck of dust! Was it possible?

The four correspondents, who had passed a year in Central Manchuria, looked in one another's eyes amazed, and all asked the same question simultaneously: "No dust?" It was almost disquieting. It was as if some ever-present phenomenon, absolutely necessary in the economy of nature, were by some strange chance missing; as if we had suddenly found ourselves in a sinless world.

How came it that we could at last see the blue sky above us, the white fleecy clouds? We seemed to be regarding nature through some wonderful optical instrument which heightened the colours, cleared the air, made all things marvellously and exuberantly distinct. For my own part, I felt as if I were looking again on the world of my childhood, that world which had all the glory and the unexpectedness of a new, brilliantly painted wooden horse, but which had, alas! for such a long time past been common, grey, and stale.

It is on occasions like this that one realises how much we owe to the sea. It makes nations clean, great, and adventurous. A single turn on the clean wind-swept deck of the *Awa Maru*, "fierce with the flavour of illimitable seas," is enough to show how this war was won, is better calculated than a cart-load of learned treatises to explain the predominance of the Anglo-Saxon.

And to imagine that few of these Russian soldiers have ever before gazed upon the sea! To-day ought to be a red-letter day in their lives, but, as a matter of fact, it isn't. Their minds have been too cramped by a long, vegetable-like existence in Siberia to be capable of solving at a glance the riddle of the Deep. As well expect a man who has never listened to music to appreciate Wagner at the first hearing.

In their attitude toward the sea these soldiers belong to the ancient world, to the school of Horace and Dr. Samuel Johnson. The only things in the ship that seem to interest them are the mysterious orifices from which they can get hot water to make tea.

There are on this ship two cabins superior to the others, and the Japanese have given both of them to the captured correspondents. The material comforts are beyond praise, and the consideration shown us makes us feel like princes. Really, it is not good for a war correspondent to get captured by the Japanese! He is liable to imagine that he is a minister plenipotentiary. He runs the risk of degenerating into a sybarite.

When Nippon next draws the sword I should not, however, advise any newspaper correspondent to get captured by the Japanese if he can help it; for Japan is on her good behaviour this time, and next time she can permit herself to indulge in the usual barbarities of Christian nations.

When, in the red rays of the sinking sun, the binnacle flamed like a pillar of gold, a sudden revulsion of feeling seized me. Would I never more live with the free wandering people of the Transbaïkal? Was I back again in this artificial life from whose trammels I thought that I had for ever emancipated myself? Would I never again press the hand of Serge Ivanovitch or Nicolaï Mikhaïlavitch, or give orders to my faithful Philipoff, or listen to the entrancing old Malorussky melodies in the "Sobranie," or see the Cossacks dance the gay "Kazatchok"? With a desire that was almost pain, I longed for the society of the rude friendly Cossacks, in whose sad superstitions and songs and mysticism there was so much to remind me of my own folk, the merry, melancholy Gael. I longed for old Mukden. I hated these snug berths with their immaculate linen. I pined for the sleep in the open air with the solemn moon overhead, the free wind of heaven blowing on my face, the large vague sounds of the night coming wafted gently like fairies' whispers o'er the dim swaying harvest fields, the tethered horses nosing around in the vicinity, sometimes tumbling awkwardly to the ground asleep, sometimes kicking and whinnying and raising an uproar fit to wake the whole "sotnia." I heard again the reassuring sound of the sentry's footsteps, I heard him calm the frightened horses with soft musical Slavonic sounds such as a mother might use to soothe a fretful babe. Again was I lulled to sleep by the gentle, continuous munching of my faithful pony "Sobersides."

Neither the deep philosophy of M. Naudeau nor the sparkling wit of Dick Little sufficed to reconcile me to my sumptuous imprisonment, and, as late that night I sat on the deck of the *Awa Maru* while the foam-flecked sea rushed past like a flood in the calm radiance of the electric lights on board, I thought, with a heart full of unutterable sadness, of the bivouac, the night alarm, the joyous ride with the Transbaïkalians in the red of the morning, the creak of leather, the tinkle of steel, the clickety-clack of the horses' hoofs, and sorrowfully reflected that in all probability I would never see those days again, that never again would I gaze so close on the glorious face of danger. I felt that the leaden hand of peace had descended on me, that the most interesting chapter in my life had come to an end, that, like all picturesque and interesting things, the Cossacks were coming to an end too.

After having tasted of the horror and the sublimity of war I was to return to the contemplation of—nay, more, unfortunately, to an active part in—that sordid, eternal squabble for pence which they call peace—a squabble in which there is no red cross, no quarter, no regard for age or sex, no truth, no dignity, not a single redeeming feature.

Farewell, O Cossacks of the Transbaïkal! I shall always hear your melancholy songs resounding in the infinite immensities of Russia. I shall always hear the hoof-beats of your little ponies ringing in boundless waste places. But yourselves I shall never see again.

It may seem a humiliating and unmanly confession to make, but I must confess that my anguish was such that, instead of going to bed like the good *bourgeois* I now was, I sat for half the night on that cold deserted deck, weeping in secret, like a child.

Our companions in the first-class are all wounded Japanese officers going home to places whose names sound like music—Omori, Arima, Oiso, Hanada, Nara, Tosa, Mito, Orio. They wear spotless white "kimonos," with a small red cross on the shoulder, and they look far better in them than they would in foreign dress; while, on the other hand, the Russian wounded look in their "kimonos" like men in their night-shirts. Small, slender, beardless, gentle, young, moving noiselessly about in their "waraji" or straw sandals, they remind one of Franciscan nuns. Two years ago I would have laughed with contempt if you had told me that these men would hurl headlong from the city of Mukden an army of three hundred and fifty thousand Russians.

To me, fresh from the Russian camp, everything about these Japanese officers is as striking as if they came from another planet, but two things especially strike me: one is their youth, the other is their gentleness. Accustomed for over a year to married, middle-aged Russian lieutenants and captains, I feel it odd to find myself among a shipful of officers most of them not over twenty-three years of age, and not one of whom is married. It is like being in a boys' school or in the warrant officers' mess on board a British gunboat, say the *Espiègle*. Russia sent to this war her old, grey-bearded, grandfatherly reservists. Japan sent the cream of her manhood. The result is clear for all men to read. It is also, like everything else in the topsy-turvy world, paradoxical. The enthusiastic youth, with strong limbs and with a long life before him, throws that life away with a laugh; the fretful, pessimistic grey head, with only a few sordid years to live, hugs his life as if it were valuable.

The gentleness of the Japanese officers is hard to describe. In no other country is there such an officer. America, England, France, Germany, Russia, have all in their armies men of much the same type—but it is a type which is not found in Japan. Some drink more than others, but all of them drink. Some are gayer than others, but all of them are gay. It is only a question of degree.

A timid, girlish youth who enters the British or American army soon changes his character or leaves the army. An ocean of tradition, old as Julius Cæsar, sweeps away either him or else his little sand-heap of principle or prejudice. Missionaries and strict parents may deplore this state of things, but men of the world recognise that ample allowance must be made for the overflowing vitality required in one who embraces the military profession. Gordon may be enshrined in the British Nonconformist heart, and even military men may like him, now that he is dead; but the language British officers use about living comrades of the Gordon type is not fit for publication.

You cannot both eat your cake and have it. If you want an army you must nerve yourself to stand a lot. You cannot expect it to be a Sunday-school. Old-fashioned parents sometimes imagine that they can find for their little Francis Xavier a holy regiment. They can never find it. They could not have found it among the Crusaders or in the Papal Guards. It does not exist. It never existed. It is a contradiction in terms.

In the Japanese army, however, there seems to be no tradition of boisterousness. I noticed this during my residence in Japan; I noticed it in Manchuria; and now again I noticed it on the *Awa Maru*. It would almost seem as if the Japanese army borrowed asceticism from their enemies the Jesuits, even as the Jesuits borrowed some points in their organisation from the army.

If the *Awa Maru* had been a Russian boat you could not have heard yourself speaking for the noise in the dining saloon. Orderlies in top boots would be tumbling over one another in their haste to execute the orders of their respective masters. Cold ham, novels by Danchenko, spilt beer, the *Novoe Vremya*, smashed match-boxes, somebody's revolver (loaded), a number of cigar ends, a half empty box of cigarettes, and a bottle of vodka, would be inextricably mixed together on the table.

But the dining-room of the *Awa Maru* is like a Trappist refectory. White-robed figures glide in, eat sparingly of the simplest Japanese food, converse in subdued tones and then glide out again. It is not that they are in a low state of health, for all belong to the "slightly wounded" class, the greater number of them suffering from simple bullet wounds in the arms or legs. It is the Japanese custom.

After dinner some of them play the game of "go," while one, with some musical pretensions, gently murders various simple European melodies on the piano, always winding up with the "Kee Mee Gai' Yo," the national hymn of Japan.

They are extraordinarily clean. As they go barefooted, save for their sandals, one can see that their toe nails have evidently been washed and polished and pared as thoroughly as a fashionable lady's finger nails.

Their teeth are so white and their mouths so well washed that one is inclined to believe that their saliva consists exclusively of soap suds. Their only drawback is their high Mongolian cheek-bones and their wide nostrils. It is a trifling drawback, but Japan must still spill oceans of blood before Europe consents to overlook it completely.

Some of them are, however, of almost perfect European type, straight eyes, unobtrusive cheekbones and small nostrils. I told a young lieutenant, answering to this description, that he was descended from the Portuguese who settled in Kyushu in the sixteenth and seventeenth centuries, but he did not appear to be flattered. No Japanese is complimented by being told that he has foreign blood in his veins. Nevertheless, in the case of this young man, I was probably right in my surmise, for he came from Kumamoto, a great missionary centre of the Portuguese, and he looked more like an Iberian than a Japanese.

During this trip I was brought into closer relations with the Japanese officers than ever I was before, and I must say that I found them very pleasant companions. Their courtesy and their clear pronunciation of their own beautiful language were delightful, while their English was quaint, with an unspeakable charm. Nor were they suspicious. They told me everything they knew about the disposition of their forces; but the Japanese War Office need not be alarmed, as, in the first place, they did not know much, and in the second, I have not communicated what they told me to anybody.

And here I may remark that, as a rule, the young Japanese officer is as civil and unsuspicious as any young English middy. During this war he was, however, under the influence of the stern men who were born under the rule of the Shogun and fed in their early days on the iron traditions of the Samaraï; but it is, in the nature of things, impossible that this stoicism can last much longer. I could, if I liked, give many instances of its breakdown.

In these days of commercialism, when many of us have become cosmopolitans and few of us are disinterested patriots, the little Jap officer can teach us a good lesson. He gets at first only thirty-three yen fifty sen (or about £3 10s.) a month, and his salary, even when he has attained high rank in the army, would be scornfully laughed at by the average foreign clerk in Yokohama. With him, therefore, money is as little an object as it is with a Carthusian novice.

He devotes his life to an ideal—the glory of Dai-Nippon—and if, philosophically considered, it is not a very high ideal, it is surely better than none at all. It is a great privilege in these decadent days to be able to die for something.

The conversation of these young men was as original and piquant as the first taste of an excellent strange wine or the first perusal of an interesting foreign author. I shall select some examples of their small talk:

" Russky no Heitai-wa wari-wari no teketoshite-wa amari yohaee."

"The Russian soldier is not worthy to be our enemy, because he is too timid."

* * * * *

"When come Russky prisoner, then I feed poor man (awaré-nashto); I give whisky, b(u)randy, cake and milk. Prisoner not enemy. . . . Yes, I catch Russky prisoner, many I catch" ("watakshi-wa horio wo takusan toriimashta ").

The above, by the way, from a young fellow of

FROM DALNY TO JAPAN

twenty-one, with a face so mild that you would think butter would not melt in his mouth.

* * * * *

A phrase, often repeated during the latter end of this trip, was "Nippon-wa chikaï desu" ("Japan is near").

* * * * *

A youth, whom I congratulated on his luck in getting home, responded seriously :—"I am not glad to return to my native country because the war is not finished, and, when my wound is healed, I shall again return to Manchuria."

* * * * *

It was surprising the unanimity of opinion they showed with regard to their enemies. The Russian soldiers were good, the officers not good, the generals bad.

It was also surprising how unanimous they were in thinking that Kuropatkin ought to commit suicide sooner than accept a subordinate command.

* * * * *

"I have a bottle of whisky for when my courage is gone; severe attack of enemy, long, long march down the hills, along the valley, then whisky very grateful."

* * * * *

"Watashi-wa Tokio-no Rikogun daï gakko ko ni haïrimaï sosh'te sambo shoko ni narimasho."

("I will re-enter military college, Tokio, and from that school will become staff officer.")

* * * * *

One officer admitted that the Russians were braver than the Chinese—an admission which reminded me that, just before the outbreak of the war, Russian privates at Port Arthur used to admit that the little Jap would give them more trouble, perhaps, than the Chinaman.

* * * * *

It is significant of the very different spirit with which the Japanese and the Russians entered on this war that an intensely poetic, imaginative and musical people like the latter have no songs about the conflict save one very long and very dull ballad written by an Orenburg Cossack ; while the Japanese, a materialistic people without music, have produced a considerable number of rousing war songs. Many of these songs are written to European and American airs, but the style is typically Japanese—that is, the hearer is generally left to guess at the meaning, for even Kipling himself is not as cryptic sometimes as a Japanese ballad-maker. One song, a great favourite among the soldiers, goes to the air of " Marching through Georgia." The chorus runs like this :—

> Heerah ! heerah ! to goon kan kee !
> Heerah ! heerah ! to nisho kee !
> Itsu tzu no chayenju fu setsu ritzu shee
> Kai beewo genishay you ya !

A rough and ready translation of the above would be :

> Hurrah ! hurrah ! for our sun-burst flag !
> Hurrah ! hurrah ! for our rising sun flag !
> Five naval camps have been formed !
> Five impregnable war-ports are ready.

Another, beginning "Ana uray-shee yoriko-bashi," may be translated as follows :

> O ! gladly, gladly, I welcome the battle !
> We are victorious !
> Many foemen fell before us !

All the enemy are gone.
Glorious, glorious, this victory for my country, for my Emperor!
Happy any of us whom death awaits!

CHORUS.

Fight for country! Fight for Emperor!
Mother said to me, "Be patriotic!"
Joyful will my father be to hear of this great day.
Homeward, full of honours, shall we finally return.
The happy day of meeting with our parents is not far.

These songs indicate that the Japanese are coming into line with the rest of the nations. In fact, they are now introducing regimental singing and shouting after the Russian fashion. The officers are even beginning to drink Scotch whisky. Like all novices, they dislike it, but the time will come when they cannot do without it. I have, therefore, said a good deal about them as they now are, because in their next war they will have lost all the charm of originality which they now possess.

As we watched the sea one day we saw a whale spouting, and the Japanese officers described to me with great vivacity the way the fishermen capture whales at a certain island called Oshima, not far from Kobé. The animal is first lured into shallow water, and made fast. Then follows a scene the description of which reminded me of gory Bacchanalian rites. All the people of the village swarm round the great helpless beast, and, while it is still alive, make huge wounds in it, into which bloody openings naked men plunge bodily, emerging again covered from head to foot with blood, and evidently intoxicated by the experience, for they shout and dance like madmen and slash the still quivering body with their knives. The Japanese seemed to revel in these horrible details; but I, on the contrary, rather sympathised with the poor whale, just as I had sympathised with Russia while that gigantic and unwieldy Empire was receiving stab after stab from these fanatical little islanders. To make the parallel more exact, the Japanese had often during the great heats of the previous summer charged the Russian positions in a state of total nudity. At Haicheng, hundreds of them had fallen before a strong Russian position on which they had rushed with no clothing save rifles, bayonets, a belt for carrying cartridges, and a cap to protect their eyes from the sun. The pile of naked corpses which lay in front of that Russian trench reminded me of a mediæval battle-field after the corpse-strippers had done their work.

Japan! Japan! Seventh Great Power! *Enfant mystérieux* of the world! The keel of the *Awa Maru* cuts at last through the deep narrow seas which intervene between the innumerable, green, tumbled, rocky islands, amid the gnarled pines on whose slopes and summits is bred this extraordinary race of soldiers. We are now in the lion's mouth. We have entered the one country in the world where the white man has not prevailed.

We are now among those ultimate, mysterious islands wherein the forlorn hope of Asia is fashioning its thunderbolts. And what a beautiful land it has chosen for that deadly work! How lovely are these volcanic peaks emerging from the most profound abysses of Ocean! The Japanese do not believe in Adam's sin, and I do not blame them for their disbelief, for theirs is the world before the Fall. I can well believe their legends which say that these beauteous isles were born of the gods, and grew up, little by little, like children.

After the cataclysmal happenings I had seen during the preceding year I expected to find Japan unrecognisable; but, in sooth, nothing had changed outwardly. The little fishers' huts were there still, and the broad semicircle of lights on our lee showed that the fisherman was still pursuing his toilsome occupation in the night.

And when we went inland we thought, at first sight, that everything was much the same as usual. The despatch of half a million men to Manchuria did not seem to have caused any sensible decrease in the male population.

It was a novel sensation to be taken through Japan at this juncture as a prisoner of war, but it was not altogether a disagreeable sensation, as one was compensated for his loss of liberty and for the undesirable attention which he excited by the conviction that he was assisting at the birth of great events. There was an electric feeling in the air around him, for though outwardly all was the same, a new soul had entered into Kami-no-kuni, the Land of the Gods. It was like passing through England at the time of the Spanish Armada, during the breathless pause before Trafalgar. Verily those were spacious days in Daï-Nippon!

The destruction of the Russian power in Eastern Asia has had the same effect on the yellow races as the fall of Napoleon had on the white, as the collapse of the Roman Empire had on the Europe of the time. It is the overthrow of invincibility.

The conveyance of the Russian troops through

China as prisoners of war is only comparable to the carrying into captivity by the northern barbarians of the generals and senators of Imperial Rome. All along the China coast Russia's disgrace was advertised by smashed ships, broken soldiers, and penniless refugees.

Hitherto the white man has been, in Japan, the Sensei, the master, at whose feet the little Jap sat for thirty years, and whose very shadow must be respected. But, while the war with Russia lasted, Young Japan regarded with a rather irreverent smile the spectacle of the white master being carted through the country wholesale, and with no more respect than a trainful of returned empties.

When foreigners first came under Japanese jurisdiction, Europeans in treaty ports used sometimes to write indignant letters to the local papers, pointing out that they had seen with their own eyes drunken British or American men-o'-war's men marched through the street by "native" policemen, their arms screwed behind their backs, and on their faces a consequent expression of anguish calculated to lower the prestige of the white race in the eyes of the Japanese.

I noticed that in 1905 these indignant scribes were dumb. Some of them had, I suppose, died of apoplexy, induced by the sights they saw that year.

To one who could recognise the greatness of the recent crisis in Japanese history there sometimes seemed to be lacking in the Japanese people a proper appreciation of that crisis. There was a certain amount of phlegmaticism; there was an absence of appropriate external display. It was as if you gave a cabman a tip of twenty pounds and he pocketed it with an expressionless face. But perhaps the same might be said of all the great events (with the possible exception of the Deluge) that have taken place since the world began—of the passage of the Rubicon, of the miracles of Christ, of the fall of Rome.

Many Japanese gathered at the railway-stations to see us pass, but a greater number preferred to continue at their ordinary avocations in field or shop.

Those who came to see us were silent, but on their faces I fancied I could detect a strange, half-amused, half-pitying expression, such as one might expect to see on the faces of good-natured gentlefolk watching the gyrations of a lord mayor in liquor, a man on his honeymoon, or a person guilty of any other pardonable weakness.

This journey through Japan made Japan's victory seem to us all the more wonderful. Our train load of hairy giants, with voices like thunder, gazed with bulging eyes at those frail, delicate, fairy-like people, and asked themselves, "Are these the folk who gave us that awful beating?"

Slender women passed with little black-eyed dolls of children clad in rainbow-coloured garments. On the platforms variegated infants tottered towards happy chubby-cheeked mothers not much older apparently than themselves. In ten years more some of these children will be Japanese officers.

A youth in a "kimono" and with a startling extent of bare leg sauntered home from the village bath, singing like a lark. In a month's time, I said to myself, that youth may be one of the iron legionaries of Nogi. Gentle girls with eyes turned up towards the temples, looked at us with infinite sadness. A young man passed by, carrying in his arms, without the slightest trace of self-consciousness, his own tiny baby; and the Russians did not know whether to wonder most at so boyish a person being a father or at so small a baby being capable of independent existence.

Often we passed southward-bound trains of soldiers, trains of ammunition, trains full of horses. The soldiers were young, hardy, filled with youthful enthusiasm; the stations were gaily decorated in their honour with Rising Sun flags and lanterns, and crowded with friends come to see them off.

Afar, on the hillsides, we could see new troops drilling, advancing cautiously against an imaginary enemy, carrying off "wounded," going through all sorts of military evolutions with the zest of born soldiers, and at the same time with the solemnity of priests engaged in some solemn rite. Imperial Guardsmen pranced about like fierce dolls on horseback. Formerly I used to laugh at them when they came a cropper. On this occasion I didn't. Groups of demure "nesan," groups of bare-legged boys with children on their backs watched them seriously.

A very young soldier with a very new uniform, made of fine cloth and evidently by a good tailor, also with a painfully new sword attached to his person by straps and buckles that seemed to have come out of the harness-maker's hands only the day before, came into our carriage, followed at a respectful distance by his old father, who had probably come to see his son off to the wars, and who, after the lapse of an hour or two, offered him rice, lighted his cigarette and attended on him generally as if he were a god. So might the father of Marcus Curtius have treated his son before his departure for that yawning chasm in the forum;

and such a reversal of the relations usually existing between parents and their children would be no less remarkable in ancient Rome than it is in modern Japan.

All the officers who from time to time accompanied us as ordinary passengers had been wounded, most of them in that Place of Death, Port Arthur. Every one of the young soldiers who mounted guard over us in the little Japanese house wherein we were confined at Shizuoka had been wounded in Manchuria, some of them repeatedly wounded; but all were intensely anxious to start again for the front.

One brisk young fellow, who had got permission to go, was as envied by his comrades as a schoolboy who gets home before the holidays. He came to me in my picturesque little lath-and-paper prison to bid me goodbye, and I remember that he was accompanied by a bright-eyed companion somewhat older than himself, with whom he was on such terms of joyful intimacy that I thought they were merely "pals."

But the companion turned out to be his father! "Isn't he young?" said the son to me later on, looking after the retiring form of his parent, his eyes glistening with filial pride and affection.

In this extraordinarily strong desire of the private to get to the front lay the secret of Japan's success. The meanest soldiers and coolies in her army were mad to win, while the Russians were generally indifferent. But it would, of course, be a mistake to suppose that in this respect the Japanese are unequalled in the history of the world. The conscripts of Montmirail, the Americans who fought at Bunker Hill, the British tars of Nelson, the Germans of 1870, were all quite as fanatic and probably more capable than the Japanese soldier of to-day. But it is too much to expect that the French, British, Americans or Germans will display, in defence of their respective possessions in the Far East, the same fanaticism as they displayed in fighting for their national existence and their homes. So far as I can see, therefore, the Japanese are bound to have it all their own way in the Far East for a long time to come. But I question whether, at the apex of their prosperity, they will enjoy anything like the national happiness which is theirs to-day. Success will bring satiety. Knowledge will bring disillusionment. They will learn, alas! that Matsuhito is the last Mikado who is divine. Time and wealth and factory servitude, the great corroders of all martial virtue, will gradually take the fine edge from off their valour.